THE 7 PILLARS
OF VISIONARY LEADERSHIP

THE 7 PILLARS
OF VISIONARY LEADERSHIP

ALIGNING YOUR ORGANIZATION FOR ENDURING SUCCESS

MICHAEL COX, Ph.D.

MICHAEL E. ROCK, Ed.D.

DRYDEN

Harcourt Brace & Company, Canada

Toronto Montreal Fort Worth New York Orlando
Philadelphia San Diego London Sydney Tokyo

Copyright © 1997
Harcourt Brace & Company Canada, Ltd.
All rights reserved.

No part of this publication may be reproduced or transmitted in any form or by any means, electronic or mechanical, including photocopy, recording or any information storage and retrieval system, without permission in writing from the publisher.

Requests for permission to make copies of any part of the work should be mailed to: Permissions, College Division, Harcourt Brace & Company, Canada, 55 Horner Avenue, Toronto, Ontario M8Z 4X6.

Every reasonable effort has been made to acquire permission for copyright material used in this text, and to acknowledge all such indebtedness accurately. Any errors and omissions called to the publisher's attention will be corrected in future printings.

Canadian Cataloguing in Publication Data

Cox, Michael, 1947-
    The 7 pillars of visionary leadership

Includes bibliographical references.
ISBN 0-03-923117-8

1. Leadership. I. Rock, Michael, 1942-
II. Title. III. Title: The seven pillars of visionary leadership.

HD57.7.C695 1996   658.4'092   C96-931056-X

Director of Product Development: *Heather McWhinney*
Acquisitions Editor: *Ken Nauss*
Projects Manager: *Liz Radojkovic*
Director of Publishing Services: *Jean Davies*
Editorial Manager: *Marcel Chiera*
Supervising Editor: *Semareh Al-Hillal*
Production Manager: *Sue-Ann Becker*
Production Co-ordinator: *Sheila Barry*
Interior Design: *Irving Perkins Associates*
Cover Design: *Sonya V. Thursby/Opus House*
Printing and Binding: *Webcom Limited*

This book was printed in Canada.

1 2 3 4 5   01 00 99 98 97

With gratitude to . . .

Diane, Sarah, and Stephanie
and
Janice and Julianna

𝔇.𝔒.𝔐.

Wisdom hath builded her house,
she hath hewn out her seven pillars:

Proverbs 9:1

CONTENTS

INTRODUCTION xi

Global Economy, Globalized Mind	xi
Emotional Intelligence	xii
The Ability to Learn	xiii
Dead Reckoning: Stop or Go?	xiii
The Leadership Value Path	xvi
The Seven Pillars	xvii

PILLAR I: VISIONING 1

The 20/20 Leadership Path	5
Dead Reckoning	5
New Directions	6
Adding Valuing: Putting People First	9
The Path of the Ancients	13
20/20 Vision: Danger Ahead	13
Sensus Fidelium	18
Valuing the Spirit	20

PILLAR II: MAPPING 23

The 20/20 Leadership Path	24
Parting of the Mindsets	24
Breaking Mental Maps	28
Valuing Net Worth	30
The Path of the Ancients	34
People of the Way	34
Wilderness Journey	36
Preparing for the Journey	40

PILLAR III: JOURNEYING 42

The 20/20 Leadership Path	47
Revolution of Imagination	49
Seeing the Vision	50
Value Path to 20/20 Vision	51
The Path of the Ancients	53
The Inward Journey	55
Stages of the Journey	58
A Pilgrim's Progress	62
Tribal Tensions	64

PILLAR IV: LEARNING 73

The Art of Archetypal Learning	74
The 20/20 Leadership Path	77
Assessment of Opportunity	77
Measuring the Costs	81
Harvesting the Benefits	86
The Path of the Ancients	88
"Know Thyself"	88
Mens Sana in Corpore Sano	93
Inward Bound	99

PILLAR V: MENTORING 102

The 20/20 Leadership Path	106
Reformation of Learning	106
Content with Learning	108
Learning with Content	110
The Path of the Ancients	113
Spirit of Enterprise	113
Reformation of Work	120
The Work of Reformation	121

PILLAR VI: LEADING 125

The 20/20 Leadership Path	128
The Leadership Value Path	128
Steering, Not Rowing	134
Principles of Duty	136
The Path of the Ancients	138
Idol Worship	138
The Learning Circle	143
Revaluing the Future	146

PILLAR VII: VALUING 150

The 20/20 Leadership Path	152
The Value of Insight	153
The Value of Courage	155
The Value of Action	156
The Path of the Ancients	157
An Ancient Perspective: The Value of The Seven Pillars of Visionary Leadership	158

APPENDIX 170

Personal Assessment Profile	170
Organization Assessment Profile	173
Mindscape Value Assessment Profile	176
Discussion Questions	181

NOTES 183

INDEX 196

INTRODUCTION

We live in extraordinary times. Indeed, we are at a social, economic, philosophical, emotional, and spiritual crossroads. Ours is a time of new genesis, as we come out of the ashes and rusty thinking of the declining industrial mindset.

This genesis requires a new vision, one that enables us to see the future clearly, while it reunites us with the classical roots of wisdom that we have left behind. It requires that we put behind us once and for all the attitudes and behavior that have split us off from this wisdom.

Global Economy, Globalized Mind

Today we are citizens of the world. We have nowhere to hide. The Internet has us cornered. So have the competitive nations and products and services and convergent thinking patterns of the world—unless we move out of our ethnocentric backyard and see ourselves as members of a world community. We must work together or wither together. According to Harvard's Rosabeth Moss Kanter, we are caught between two choices: staying myopically local in our thinking and practices—a sort of psychological and physical protectionism—or seeing ourselves as a community of communities.

To flourish in a globalized, borderless economy, we *must* develop our minds because ironically, at the same time that our wired world is bringing us all together, we are lacking the skills, the insight, and the moral will to build relationships. We need to build bridges, not borders. We must stop thinking in terms of self-sufficiency and begin to see ourselves as dependent, independent, and interdependent.

Springing up all around us today are partnerships, alliances, joint ventures. True, the motivations of various human and corporate relationships may not be the most sublime. But the fact that partnering is happening speaks volumes about the economic necessity, at least, of relationship.

Emotional Intelligence

Thriving in our new world will require us to overcome the loneliness and isolation of *head* thinking and open ourselves to a new kind of thinking that joins head and heart. What Yale psychologist Peter Salovey and the University of New Hampshire's John Mayer call "emotional intelligence"—the awareness and mature disciplined inclusion of emotion in our personal and working lives—will become paramount for the global traveler. Being "smart," according to Daniel Goleman, a Harvard psychology Ph.D. who is a *New York Times* science writer and the author of *Emotional Intelligence,* includes not only the traditional measure of success—your IQ, or intelligence quotient—but, more important, your "EQ"—or emotional intelligence, your character set and quality of thinking and responding in life. You could say that IQ gets you hired, but EQ—or lack of it—gets you fired!

Studies from the Center for Creative Leadership (CCL) in Greensboro, North Carolina, show that success eludes many senior executives not for lack of technical skills but because they lack interpersonal skills—such as sensitivity, listening, empathy, integrity (EQ factors)—and instead display arrogance, poor social manners, and betrayal of trust.

New organizational charts and technology make these relational skills more important than ever. In the traditional hierarchy orders didn't have to be delivered with tact or empathy. But today's flatter organizations are inspired by teamwork and collegial relationships instead of power and prestige. Emotional intelligence and highly polished relational skills spell the difference between success and failure in these organizations.

Emotional intelligence is also surging in importance as managers and economists begin to recognize the critical importance of learning *and* people to organizational success. The World Bank, in its "Priorities and Strategies for Education: A World Bank Review," reaffirms the need to harness human capital, an essential component in the formula for higher incomes and sustained economic growth. The twenty-first century will hold out success only to those organizations that include people issues in their strategic contexts and decision making, to those that expand return on investment (ROI) to include return on integrity in relationships (ROIR), and to those that focus not merely on plans and policies but on people.

The Ability to Learn

When the beliefs and attitudes that help us navigate through life become meaningless, they need to be revalued. Learning new ways to think, feel, and act can be painful because our predispositions or attitudes were learned and shaped by our families and our society in our early years. What has been grasped for such a long time is often hard to let go.

Organizations are the centers of transformation in society today. It is where people find their meaning. Organizations must value the new beliefs and attitudes in order to stay healthy. For many of us this relearning will be our first conscious appreciation and application of new mindsets and mental maps. It will indeed be a revolution of our imaginations. We will forever be changed. If we did all this, we would have a vision of a future.

This learning challenge is not just a new management theory or a new approach to employee training and development. It is *the core task of today's organization.*

Dead Reckoning: Stop or Go?

We are at a dead reckoning in our history. Sailors used dead reckoning to chart the position of their ship when overcast skies prevented the navigator from seeing sun, moon, or stars. By starting with the last observed position of the ship, and considering courses steered and distances run, they were able to calculate their present position without instruments or observation. The term *dead* is thought to come from the era in which unknown seas were considered "dead," not shown by geographers on their world maps.

A night sea is a journey of personal transformation. Every historical leader has at one time gone through it. It is the testing ground for the development of character. We, too, have been on a night sea journey, one that has taken three hundred years. But what have we achieved on this journey and what has it cost us? Our night sea journey started with a vision that said we had the power to control our universe. Unfortunately the dead seas we encountered had not been anticipated. At this time of dead reckoning we should review our mental charts, learn our lessons, and then start out again on a voyage of discovery to become all we can be.

Many in our society today are struggling for a sense of meaning in the midst of a culture that has elevated the standard of living to heights unimagined by earlier generations. Material wealth is evident, and technological know-how has exploded. The Internet and the World Wide Web are connecting us in a way and with a speed unimaginable ten years ago. We have created a technological paradise, but what has it left in its wake?

Today many of our organizations are like the crew at the end of a long voyage, filled with exhaustion and lacking energy to continue the journey. We have a new crew on board: "techno-peasants" doing the rowing, who are disposable, and "techno-elites," often steering in another direction. At the same time we see on the horizon the global crew who have the intelligence and skill from ancient wisdom to stay the course. It really is a dead reckoning! Technology has compressed time and place and shifted the axis of economic production. Institutions that gave nations and families a sense of self-worth, well-being, and belonging are deconstructing. It is not unlike the collapse of a beloved community or the death of a trusted old friend. If we have won the technological war, we may have lost ourselves as a community in the process.

We let this happen because we lost our compass. We went off course when our organization cultures raced from management theory to management theory in a dizzying attempt to ride the waves of change to find the fastest road to profits and productivity.

Leadership has been on a search for the Holy Grail of efficiency. This has taken organizations down many roads to try out "new, improved solutions" to the problems of their rapidly changing workplaces. The learning journey has included advice on how to beat the Japanese (William Ouchi's *Theory Z: How American Business Can Meet the Japanese Challenge*), and how to thrive in an interconnected and interdependent economy (Japan's Kenichi Ohmae and Harvard's Michael Porter). Just as companies were bloating themselves by swallowing competitors, Michael Hammer and James Champy's *Reengineering the Corporation* inspired a devoted cadre of "reengineers" to solve the challenge of economic efficiency baselines using the practice of Business Process Reengineering (BPR). Around the same time Total Quality Management (TQM) began telling us to focus on quality as part of the new prescription to cure efficiency problems.

These foggy theories have blurred our vision and gutted many organizations. The result has often been corporate anorexia. The body looks good, but the energy to deliver has gone. What does the corporate report card say now that the "lean and mean" look has become commonplace? The American Management Association's survey of companies downsized between 1989 and 1994 shows that while profits increased 51 percent and productivity jumped 34 percent, employee morale decreased 86 percent! Only in 43.5 percent of the companies, moreover, did operating profits improve.

As James M. Stanford, president of Petro-Canada, says, "You can't shrink to greatness." Anorexia is a disease. Many corporations are quite ill. How can we make ourselves, our organizations, and our communities healthy? We believe it starts with a vision of what we can become. We believe it requires a personal transformation, an inward journey. It needs a leadership value path and a corporate compass so that we can get back on track to rebuild our future.

Thanks to the rational paradigm of Newton and Descartes, we built an industrial civilization that provided the heart and muscle of community living and helped us develop the infrastructure and wealth we have today.

Many of the challenges we face today are unlike anything we

have faced in the past, yet ironically it is the past to which we must turn to find pathways to contemporary solutions. As management theorist Edward E. Lawler says, we're looking for a new model or paradigm of how things should work, but the new paradigm has a lot of the old values within it.

The Leadership Value Path

Good leadership is *valuing leadership.* It has its roots in the good mentoring we received as children, parenting that served us on our path to maturity. Our parents validated us as human beings; provided feedback that built us up instead of knocking us down; affirmed our importance, presence, and role in the family system; took joy in the value of our contributions, however small; and acknowledged the importance of others and treated them with due respect and honor. It was a time of process and valuing. This is an image of what visionary leadership is about.

But something happened. We ended up in workplaces and in a society that saw us as just additional cogs in the machine, as disposable, of little value. We let the quantification experts take over; we were seduced by things because that was our mindset. We were attitudinally focused only on *what* we did and ignored, repressed, or, even more sadly, were ignorant of *who* we were. We brought in outside experts instead of listening to the wisdom of the corporate family.

John A. Byrne's *The Whiz Kids* tells how the management theology espoused by early industrial managers worshiped efficiency at the expense of responsiveness, elevated numbers over people, and sacrificed product quality and customer satisfaction to managerial hubris and arrogance. Sadly, it was this theology that was passed on to a whole generation of American managers. The human being was simply a factor of production to be manipulated on the altar of the bottom line.

But it needs to be replaced—by an archetypal vision of leadership and learning that is at the heart of this book. *The Seven Pillars of Visionary Leadership* will take you from your place of dead reckoning—the place where our ancient and contemporary wisdom meet—to start your own leadership journey.

Our personal journey requires repentance (what we will be calling metanoia), humility, courage, and perseverance (what we will be calling temenos). It will require that we know that our true place in the world: to be both open-minded and inquisitive (head) and attentive to the inner pulse of timing and purpose (heart).

We must become modern Prometheans, willing to steal the fire of consciousness (awareness) and relationship. The Promethean task—to risk all in choosing return on integrity in relationships (ROIR)—will take us away from a safe myopic map but ironically open us to a new leadership value path. The human journey is our only journey. It is one of trust, relationship, competence, and fulfillment. It is also a one-way journey. We irrevocably choose as we go along.

The Seven Pillars

A 20/20 vision is at the heart of this book. If you're ready for a new way of seeing things—a new way of leading, a new path to self-discovery and regeneration—*The Seven Pillars of Visionary Leadership* will act as your value compass and mind map. It aligns the issues of transformation that take you beyond the mental borders that constrain us to the emerging galaxy of workplace communities that share a common lifestyle and desire to reach for the stars.

The Seven Pillars outlines a leadership value path that embraces ancient values and modern practices in order to develop a 20/20 vision that lets individuals anticipate, align, and achieve self-worth. Our seven-pillar archetypal path combines the thinking of the ancients with a pragmatic business bridge to 20/20 vision. It offers decision-making navigators like you a mind map you can use to ride the crest of the next wave of our economic evolution. It offers an organizational compass that directs you along learning paths that harness mind, body, and spirit and return meaning to your life and your workplace.

Along the way it explains the core competencies that will be required of all of us in the future, the seven pillars, if you will, that will support and sustain us, our organizations, and our communities for generations to come.

The seven pillars that we have developed are a synthesis of the rational and the intuitive. They provide a "book of changes" to enable people and firms to develop their own recipes for success as well as to integrate the continuous flow of management ideas. They outline a path to visionary leadership that will see us safely into the future.

Pillar I: Visioning

Visionary leadership begins with vision. We need to acknowledge the blindness of focusing on short-term goals of return on investment (ROI) and learn to see the abundance and common sense of working together toward a shared objective of return on integrity in relationships (ROIR) so that we are committed to rebuilding healthy organizations through work, wealth, and well-being.

Pillar II: Mapping

Visionary leadership requires a new mental map. Globalization of our economy requires globalization of our minds. Open borders need open thinking. With a new mental map we can understand and chart our future and shift our management paradigm from a nineteenth-century mindset to a twenty-first-century mindset.

Pillar III: Journeying

Visionary leadership is a shared path on a new corporate journey. It asks us to keep one eye on our past and one eye on our future in order to value and protect our inheritance.

Pillar IV: Learning

Visionary leadership will create new organizations. Archetypal learning is the new architecture for those new organizations. It uses passionate, transformational images to inspire and liberate hearts and minds on the new corporate journey.

Pillar V: Mentoring

Visionary leadership requires mentoring. People who can clearly see a higher vision and are trying to live it themselves have the insight, courage, and action to inspire others to embrace that vision. Their example will inspire learning across the organization.

Pillar VI: Leading

Visionary leadership is servant leadership. It means leading *and* following. It asks us to open our minds and harness both hemispheres to align our thinking and our organizations for enduring success.

Pillar VII: Valuing

Visionary leadership requires veneration and values. We need to value our venerable traditions from the past in order to focus on a common purpose. By reflecting on our ancient valued path—the historical value roots that have sustained us throughout the centuries—we can better understand and anticipate our collective global future reality.

Today we urgently need leaders with vision, integrity, hope, promise, and inspiration, leaders who will commit themselves to the challenge of learning to live. Out of the new global vision of the individual, organization, and community can emerge a profound spirit of human endeavor. We have the potential to achieve greater things, to return to the human journey of becoming all that we can become, as if for the first time.

PILLAR I

VISIONING

> "Where there is no vision,
> the people perish:
> but he that keepeth the law,
> happy is he."
>
> PROVERBS 29:18

IMAGINE AN OPEN WINDOW of new clear thinking as you begin your leadership journey. This window opens and expands your mental universe; it lets you reframe and reinvent your own future to become all you can be to achieve wealth and well-being at work and in the community.

Change begins in the imagination. To transform ourselves, our organizations, and our communities, we need nothing less than a revolution of the imagination. We need to focus our individual decision windows on a 20/20 vision of all that we can be in order to create the power to unleash our full human capabilities.

Throughout history our dreams have inspired us, our visions have guided us, and our values have sustained us. Indeed, our visions have motivated our journeys. But for three hundred years we have shared a vision that we now realize has been narrow indeed. Instead of seeing the abundance of alternatives and the richness of human imagination, we have looked only at what we can measure. Instead of harnessing the abundance of *both-and* thinking—an ability to look at many dimensions, including our intuitive side—we have confined ourselves to the kind of dualistic *either-or* thinking that weighs alternatives almost exclusively in terms of return on investment. Downsizing is a classic example of this dualistic approach: "Either you increase profits by the third quarter, or you lay off a third of your people!"

This kind of linear either/or solution tends to be simplistic and is often wrong. It separates instead of uniting, and it creates adversarial relationships and costs that we can no longer afford. Our downsizing may be creating efficiencies for profit, but as we cut the value of people out of the equation, not only do we create a permanent underclass that severely taxes the quality of life of all, but we also communicate our belief that people are disposable. If we continue to follow either/or thinking, we will be cornered by our choices.

Consider the impact that vision has on a company's future where a CEO's "binary mind" traps the organization in either/or thinking. History now shows that NorTel—formerly Northern Telecom—paid a big price when a short-term CEO replaced its long-term focus with a short-term vision. An arrogant leadership style and an emphasis on the bottom line resulted in furious customers, lost business, poor morale, a talent exodus, and a surprise loss that shook investors. "The old, Neanderthal methods don't produce industry leaders," says Anna VerSteeg, a former deputy manager at Northern's repair facility in Morrisville, North Carolina, and now the president of Competitive Solutions Inc. of Cary, North Carolina.

NorTel was a high-tech star, but an either/or vision seriously undermined its people, pride, and profits. NorTel has learned from this costly experience the importance of having the right visionary at the top. In public the CEO declared that "our people are our strength," but in private he said that people perform better when they have to live in fear of their jobs. This either/or short-term visioning crippled NorTel's future, killed the spirit—and lowered the share price almost 30 percent, shaving $3.3 billion off the company's stock value.

Either/or thinking follows the fixed-pie approach, in which business leaders and organizations believe that there is only so much to go around and it is incumbent on each party to get the biggest slice possible. This attitude sets up an illusory competitive game, a survival-of-the-fittest instinctual business path in which it is "every man for himself." Fixed pie thinking triggers a "we versus them" mentality all too common in today's labor relations.

However, a 20/20 foresight shifts us to the expanding-pot approach, in which all parties realize that there is enough for all. USX Corporation, the largest U.S. steel company, has worked to shift away from the fixed-pie approach. CEO Thomas J. Usher's philosophy? "Whether you are a manager or a member of a union, everyone wants to do a good job, and they want to provide for their families."

This kind of connection is part of 20/20 vision. 20/20 vision "loops the loops" to connect and align thinking with three connecting circles in life: individual, organization, and community. The decisions we make and the strategies we pursue need to unite these three circles and acknowledge their interdependence. By seeing our blindness and then recognizing our abundance in each of these connected circles of life, we can begin to develop a sense of our own true north—a known compass point we can rely on to develop our own leadership path. This personal compass can be used for dead reckoning to reroute our thinking and our lives to true north when all seems foggy and we feel lost.

Our new global map demands a new vision. In an age of open borders that require open minds, our self-worth can no longer depend on the hierarchy and the security of the predictable for the attainment of work, wealth, and well-being. We need to reframe prosperity in the context of both self-worth and community worth. Both the individual and the community need to be the focus of learning and decision making.

We need to stop relying on the stranglehold of strategic planning, and try a new kind of thinking process called discovery planning, which takes in and anticipates the unknowns as the venture unfolds. Discovery planning recognizes that transformation is a human journey. It treats assumptions not as facts but as intelligent estimates. This kind of thinking process acknowledges the possibility of the future.

We need to embrace learning that respects both the value of teams and their congruence and leaps of faith, hunches, and relationship matters as important to the recipe for success.

We desperately need a vision of who we are and where we are going. Such a vision can give hope for the future. Sadly many of us receive our visions through the prism of a commercial worldview without validating them through personal discovery. Our university and college students often interpret and measure their self-images through this limited commercial mirror, yet they yearn for a vision that will prepare them for the human and corporate journey.

This same quest for meaning is also necessary for our organizations. A new vision can free up their thinking and breathe a new spirit of enterprise into the organization. Reimagining the workplace of the future begins today. Tom Peters is correct in saying that spunk, innovation, and imagination are the spirit of enterprise and the oxygen that frees up corporate energy for long-term well-being.

In the new workplace what is critical is the creative and innovative spirit of enterprise. We need to free up our most important resource, people. We need to give them the spirit to voice and value their valued judgments. We need to embrace and believe in the path of people, pride, and profits.

In this chapter we will begin to develop a new vision, one that can guide us along our personal pathway through the uncertain storms of change. This new 20/20 vision is one of interdependence and connection, not isolation and separation. It is one that reconnects us with our trusted founding values and lets us develop the foresight to invest in ourselves and rebuild the crucible of community. It lets us connect the scientific with the spiritual and value both in our lives.

Before we can begin the journey to visionary leadership, we need a vision. The great testing moments in each of our lives tell us that we often grow most when personally challenged with adversity. Blood, sweat, and tears can indeed be shed if we have a personal and corporate vision worthy of our humanity.

THE 20/20 LEADERSHIP PATH

DEAD RECKONING

The "good ol' days are gone"—if they ever existed. Much of the thinking and primitive images that we carry around in our heads are remnants of the old thinking and simply have no relevance. It is as though we have become mental beachcombers trying to make sense of the debris of our lives in the old organization washed up by waves of unprecedented change that, like great tsunami waves, first pound a shoreline and then suck out to sea almost everything they touch. In many ways this is archetypally what has happened to the thinking we have trusted.

Waves of globalization, rationalization, the wired organization, and the dejobbed world have flooded over our organizations. These waves challenge us all to reassess the validity of old mental maps, attitudes, and patterns of decision making, so we can respond to changing work and relationships.

When we look at history, we can see that in times of great change people have always had to pick themselves up, dust themselves off, and build a better future. Our ancient tribal wanderings show that a new spirit has always supplanted the old mental map when societal values have begun to disintegrate and a new order has dictated a new path. Henry David Thoreau, for instance, tells us that in the Middle Ages people roamed the country and asked for charity under the pretense of going *à la sainte terre*. Children exclaimed, "There goes a Saint-Terrer!" a saunterer, a holy Lander.

Today many individuals are also saunterers: They are looking for direction; they are looking for values; they are looking for hope. These are the new wanderers. Perhaps you are one of them, in search of a personal Holy Grail, a 20/20 vision of hope centered on a future of work, wealth, and well-being.

Today our tribal economic evolution demands a transformation of individuals and institutions. As a local and global community we are at a mental crossroads, a dead reckoning. To paraphrase Einstein, everything has changed except our thinking. It is time we became people of value. It is time to reassess and see where we are going.

New Directions

Open borders require open minds. As in the Renaissance, a new technology with no respect for borders is disseminating an explosion of ideas and innovations. It stands to reason that people will no longer assent to be bound by bordered thinking.

In response, we need to transform ourselves, our organizations, and our paradigm. The Western obsession with "bottom-line thinking" is shortchanging our future. A dose of "top-line thinking" is critical. To achieve it, we need to look through the other end of the telescope and put people first.

The telescope is a good example of how we conduct our present thinking. Through our telescope, we see only our limited perceptual vision maps and talk in terms of "doing more with less." What a limiting way to build a future! We believe that we should be doing "more with more"—that is, using *both* sides of the brain, both the left, or linear, portion and the right, or intuitive, side.

We need to see the abundance around us—especially the abundance of intellectual capital around us. Intellectual capital is the lifeblood of the new organization. We have successfully mined beneath our feet to build our communities and our organizations. Now we need to mine between our ears and develop a new paradigm of the learning organization.

Success will result from connecting both the right and left side of our brains, both the intuitive and the rational, both the unconscious and the conscious. It will come from recognizing that we are interdependent, that the three circles of individual, organization, and community simply must be connected. It's time we had a Declaration of Interdependence to acknowledge this connectedness and break away from the slavery of the Newtonian world.

To thrive locally in an interdependent world, we need a strong cultural, social, intellectual, and psychological infrastructure. We need to have not only pride of self but pride of place. Place is the spiritual home, physically and symbolically "the circle of life," that gives energy to the integrity of work, wealth, and well-being. It is the container, or temenos, of all that we value; it is the spirit at work; it is the place where creativity is given life. When we look at communities with high standards of living—what we call places of high energy—we can see that they have nurtured social and intellectual capital in their learning processes. They have become knowledge communities and symbiotic nodes of learning connected to other communities for their growth and well-being.

Harvard's Rosabeth Moss Kanter undertook a civic action research project in five regions of the United States. Each of these regional communities—surrounding Boston, Cleveland, Miami, Seattle, and Columbia, South Carolina—connected with the global economy in different ways. She discovered that in an interdependent economy, comparative advantage comes from the location's ability to leverage the place's social and intellectual capital. Today a community has added value if it has a well-diversified mix of companies that have a common drive for innovation and learning. Kanter maps out intellectual capital as *concepts* (thinkers), *competence* (makers), and *connections* (traders). In our experiences in community economic development, these three elements build the new community home founded on economic vitality, sustainable development, and healthy community.

We propose a Declaration of Interdependence for the individual, the organization, and the community. In order to develop their work, wealth, and well-being for the twenty-first century, all three will require a shared mantra of investing in *people, pride,* and *profits*. In this knowledge economy, *people* are the conceptual thinkers, the intellectual capital; *organizations* are the competence makers; and our connections in the global *community* are our trading alliances, which demand return on integrity in relationships (ROIR), an understanding that our personal success is dependent on a web of interdependent relationships and decision making, not just on our individual efforts to climb a now-disintegrating corporate ladder.

Like the ancient tribal peoples of the old covenant, we need an epiphany to "show forth" the wisdom of new principles of learning. One way to develop this is to honor the oral tradition—the spirit of the corporate voice—in our own companies and use it as a learning path to wisdom.

In our first organization—the tribe—we valued the storyteller, keeper of the corporate memory. The corporate memory contained the myths, the legends, the heroes, the deeds that spoke of the tribe's worth. That sense of worth in turn fueled the tribe's willingness to change, make sacrifices. This shared memory gave the tribespeople a mental map that connected them to one another and created a spiritual center for them in their lives. To lose that center of vision of a shared map was to self-destruct.

Today's corporate visionaries and their storymaking are the new oral tradition for the organizational tribe. A people with vision makes good sense; it bonds people to achieve great things. Stanford business professors James C. Collins and Jerry I. Porras have demonstrable evidence to prove that vision-driven companies perform fifty-five times better than the general market and eight times better than their competitors.

But in many companies there is no vision. Thanks to "*right* sizing," many of us have let our corporate memories walk out the door. We have devalued these trusted messages, replacing them with manufactured theories based on abstract case studies that have no connection to our individual and unique needs as a people. Our management theories have lost their connection to putting people first.

ADDED VALUING: PUTTING PEOPLE FIRST

We've come this far with a vision whose genesis lies in the seventeenth century. The vision it presented changed the nature of learning, which in turn changed the face of the world. Now we need to move to a new paradigm. But we simply can't jump from one paradigm to another; we simply can't walk away from the problems. We need to recognize that the challenges we face will not be solved by technology alone and that adding value in the organization will be achieved only by added valuing: putting people first.

Our new vision needs to include value, a sense of what people bring to their jobs. Organizations are organisms. They are born, live, and die. What keeps them alive is the added valuing of people—the spirit and oxygen of the organization. This higher vision achieves the new "top line" or ROIR by focusing on people. It creates an abundance so that the organization and its members can do "more with more" with their intellectual and intuitive resources.

Value-added is a very common expression today. It suggests that people make choices about a product or service because of the perceived additional value that they experience. According to this theory, what makes someone choose product a over similar product b is the value that is added by company x versus company y.

We think the idea of added value needs to be taken one step further: to added valuing. To us this means valuing the customer or the knowledge worker, not just adding value to a product or service. When was the last time you as a person were truly valued by an organization? When was the last time you were valued in addition to the excellent product or service you developed?

The critical point here is: As inside, so outside. In a world dependent on relationships, strategic empathy happens only when organizations have the vision to see both employee and customer in the same ethical framework. Karen Boylston, director of the team leadership group at the Center for Creative Leadership, says that customers are telling businesses, "I don't care if every member of your staff graduated with honors from Harvard, Stanford and Wharton. I will take my business and go where I am understood and treated with respect."

If you are a leader, you may wonder how to get your team to take that extra step into added valuing. There is only one answer that we can give: Valuing has to be one of the key emotional and intellectual pillars that are "bought in to and lived" in your department or company. It is the seventh pillar in our visionary leadership path, but it cannot exist without vision. You must build the seven pillars of the new architecture so that the spirit of enterprise can take root.

When you and your organization begin to put all the pillars in place to rebuild your institution, everyone will have ownership of the leadership value code that gives you the fresh oxygen and new clear thinking so necessary to create a spirit of enterprise.

In our consulting work we have helped senior management and leadership teams see that demonstrating added valuing with both internal and external customers immeasurably bonds the customer to the service or product being offered and builds a community partnership to succeed. Added valuing also pays off in productivity. Researchers from Michigan State University and the Department of Management and Organizations at the University of Iowa compared the top 1 percent of high performers with average employees (Figure 1.1) and with the bottom 1 percent or low performers (Figure 1.2). After separating jobs into three categories—low complexity (frontline workers in a fast-food restaurant), medium complexity (production workers in a high-tech factory), and high complexity (an associate in an investment bank)—they found that the top 1 percent of performers outperformed average performers in the same category (low, medium, high) by 52, 85, even 127 percent! Comparing the top 1 percent with the bottom 1 percent ("the slackers" or, as one senior vice-president told us, people who have quit but haven't left the company) indicated 300 percent more productivity on the part of those at the top in low-complexity jobs,

1,200 percent more productivity in medium-complexity work, and the-sky's-the-limit-productivity with your top 1 percent who have high-complexity jobs.

These figures clearly show the extraordinary effort, commitment, and results obtained from the top 1 percent employees, the very people you need to value. Too often managers take for granted the high-producing employees since much of their attention is spent propping up the efforts of employees not per-

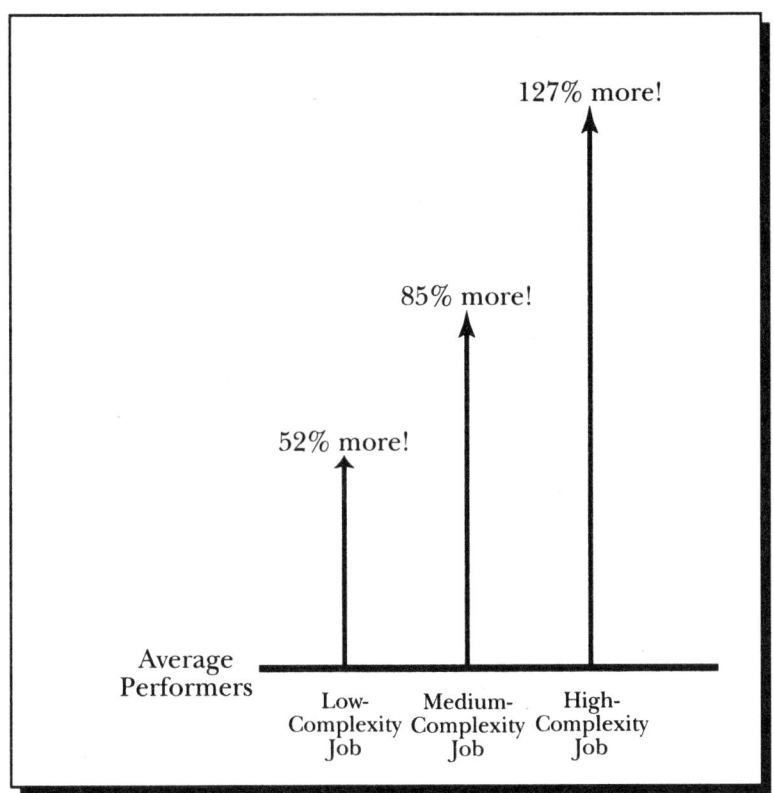

FIGURE 1.1

Productivity of Top 1% of Performers Compared to Average Performers

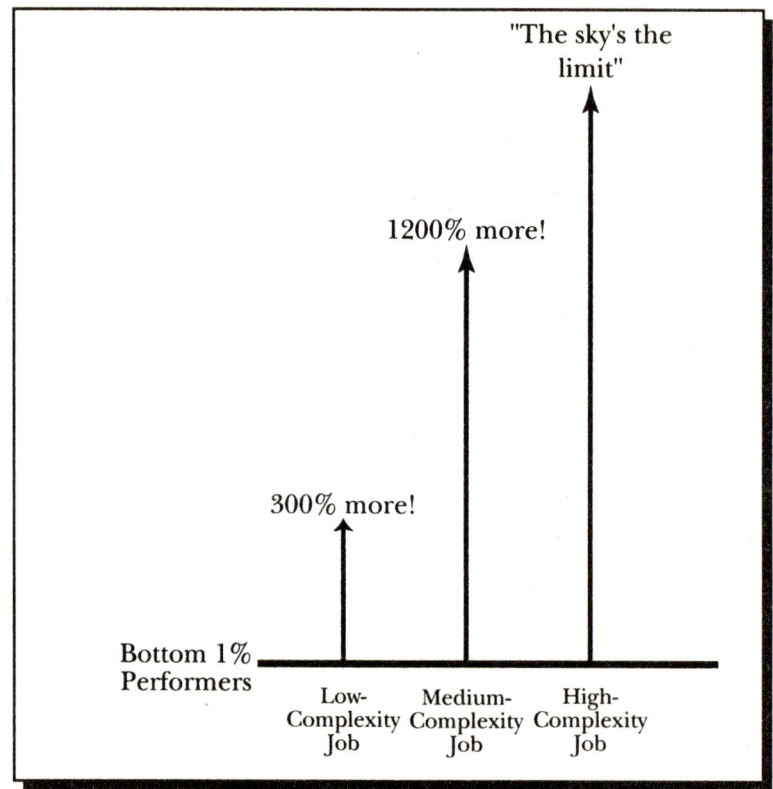

FIGURE 1.2

**Productivity of Top 1% of Performers
Compared to Bottom 1% of Performers**

forming up to par. But alienating top performers by ignoring them can be a mistake.

Why is it that the 1 percent produce so much? Does it have more to do with the way we treat people than with the expectations spelled out in corporate objectives? The key is to foster and maximize the added valuing of your employees, so it may be transferred to your products and/or services and into the hands, hearts, and minds of your customers or clients.

We believe that visioning is the leadership edge. Without the visioning we won't see the real potential of added valuing. We are still seeking solutions to profitability by focusing on the potential of the customer. There is an added value in 20/20 visioning: the full potential of the organization. That means putting people first.

People are the most important asset of any organization today. By putting people first, we can build the trust to liberate hearts and minds and leverage intellectual capital. Your visioning process should include learning valuing. Ask yourself: How do you value yourself, your organization, your community? Do you value celebrating their success?

THE PATH OF THE ANCIENTS

20/20 Vision: Danger Ahead

Our tribal ancestors often found themselves at learning crossroads. Like us, they had choices to make. Ironically what often brought them to this state of affairs was a collision between their inflated sense of themselves—their hubris—and the dictates of their heart—called faithfulness to the covenant established between them and their higher vision. Then, as now, the crossroads involves not just a choice of head *over* heart, but the more difficult choice of head *and* heart as leadership principles. It takes wisdom to connect the head and the heart. For the heart is the full personality—body, soul, and spirit. We do not live by head alone, though our three-hundred-year-long Newtonian-Cartesian thinking would have us believe so. Head alone leads to too much ego; heart alone leads to too little ego. Wisdom is the balanced path.

If you think for a moment about the peak experiences in your life—those that were good and those that were painful—wouldn't you say that your whole person was involved in the experience? If you have been "dehired," laid off, "released," the experience is usually such a shock—even if you were expecting it—that your first reaction is one of denial: How could this happen to me after all I've given? In her work with dying patients, Dr. Elisabeth Kübler-Ross found that people going through a death or dying issue—themselves or with someone close they know—follow a pattern: denial, shock, anger, bargaining, depression, and eventual acceptance. Since her research first appeared, we have come to recognize that these stages are typical of other life processes, including the loss of a job.

Big events in life therefore are all-consuming. People instinctively resist change; few of us embrace it willingly. We cannot resolve events just by rationalizing them away. Our experience with people in our organizational change seminars and workshop presentations is that they want to talk about their feelings and motivations (soul); they want to share their struggles and searching for a new direction, meaning, and purpose to their lives (spirit); and they want to know how to stay healthy and not let the stress destroy them physically (body). On paper and in theory it seems easy to segment body-soul-spirit; we know that each of us is an integrated personal system. We do not live by head alone, we do not live by spirit alone, and we do not live by body alone.

The crossroads we are at now—the danger ahead—is that we may ignore or not even recognize these signals for the need for integration. While we can perhaps recognize the need for integration on a personal level, there is also this urgent need on corporate as well as community levels. We have found that people in organizations and in our communities are crying out for a sense of a worthwhile and sustainable future (spirit), for a transformation from a *work*place to a *worth* place (soul), and for connectedness (body) that will provide stability and focus. We have also become pragmatic in the process to achieve this ideal. We have found that a healthy community (well-being) requires sustainable development (work), and this is founded on achieving economic vitality (wealth).

We need to reimagine who we are and the value that our future needs to be. But we cannot do that exercise without a vision of who we are, a vision that is inclusive of body, soul, and spirit.

Before we can succeed in our revisioning, we must overcome some major hurdles. If, as we claim, wisdom is the balanced path, we must recognize that we suffer from idol worship, just as our ancestors did. Their idols kept them away from their true vision of where they needed to go as a people.

Our modern seductions or idols also take us away from the trusted path. We call them the four *P*s: **p**ersona, **p**rofit, **p**ower, and **p**restige. These four idols keep us from revisioning our future by cementing us to the old economic model based on the individual. Before we can embrace a new economic model based on the valued individual in the context of community, we must stop seeing an image of the old value system when we look at our present-day vision of leadership.

- *Persona* would seduce you by convincing you that you are your image, that how you want to show yourself to the world is the real you. To be seduced by your persona—or mask, as the Greeks referred to it—is to believe your own mythology about yourself. Are you perceived as a legend in your own mind? Do you believe that your role—for instance, of vice-president—is truly you? Many experts believe that Marilyn Monroe's personal tragedy hinged on her inability to be herself; she was unable to be free of her role or persona. Ask yourself: Am I completely identified with my role or persona? Can I be myself at work? At home? We do not mean to minimize the value of personas; we all need different personas for different situations. The secret to well-being is to know yourself and be able to wear the appropriate persona.

- *Profit* would seduce you by convincing you that your identity as a person is not *prophet* as well. A Chinese proverb says that you should beware of the person whose belly does not move when he or she laughs. You speak who you are, in other words. Ralph Waldo Emerson echoed those words as well when he wrote that "what you are speaks so loudly I cannot hear what you say." In our business culture there is a tendency to seek approval by speaking. There is also wisdom in learning to listen. Isn't the great cry of each of us to be listened to, to be understood? In this sense, then, your personal authenticity shows itself in your basic requirement to be prophetic as a person. By being alive, you are prophetic, you stand for something. What is your message? What is your vision of who you are? The saying "Actions speak louder than words" is very apt here.

• *Power* would seduce you by convincing you that you are totally in control. We're not talking about giving up all control. We simply mean that we are a dependent people; we don't run the universe; we live and work with the basic principles of the universe. Today we need to recognize that we are an interdependent people. This kind of thinking will be an attitudinal readjustment for many who think that if they have the right job, the right spouse, the perfect car, etc., then they will be "on top of the world."

• *Prestige* would seduce you by convincing you that by pursuing fame, you will feel and be significant. One of the most powerful motivators you can ever experience is that inner secure feeling that who you are and what you contribute makes a difference, has an impact. You have to be careful that your feeling of significance, of being important, of being worthwhile is truly genuine, rooted in you as a person, and not borne only by those around you. Otherwise you trade your value for the fleeting experience of prestige. Fame can be fickle. If you are chasing fame, you end up exhausted. Like shifting sands, your identity and worth are carried by others. If they change their mind, you're sunk. Your "fifteen minutes" are shot. None of us can live out of another's "psychological pocket." We have to carry and live our own humanity. We write our own human journey; we don't need to borrow someone else's book.

These seductions have given heartaches to many people in our society and offices. If the four *P*'s are the vision driving you, what does that say for you, your organization, and your community?

There is a better way to live and learn.

Blaise Pascal was correct in saying that the heart has reasons that the head knows nothing of. To feel and to be significant are rooted in the heart, in the holism of your body, soul, and spirit. Without that we live in a world of illusions, of smoke and mirrors. We live a false vision.

Today we are at a mental crossroads. We can include the "reasons of the heart" in our personal and organizational journey, or we can die from lack of oxygen (or spirit)—a quickly depleting personal and organizational asset that is absolutely critical today if we are to harness the potential and capabilities needed for the new millennium.

We need wise people today—people who can listen to their hearts and cope with life in a mature way. That is required for 20/20 vision. A vision of wisdom—as it has always been—is the first step on the Way, or journey. But wisdom is always preceded by *in*sight, not *head* sight. We need to develop what philosopher Bernard Lonergan calls "the distinct activity of an organizing intelligence" to provide us with a unique explanatory perspective. Insight does not come just because we desire it; insight is a gift. But we must hope for it and expect it.

We will not be sustained by continuing to build the tower of *head*strong technology ever higher at the exclusion of heart. Our community will be sustained only by including the breadth and depth of the heart of employees and their intellectual capital—what we call the spirit of enterprise. Breathing oxygen into the corporate human element frees up people, pride, and profits. Profits follow prophets; success follows holism. In that way we move to what Royal Bank of Canada calls a "more civilized workplace," where organizations move away from "the tough-guy primitivism which for too long has been held up among North American management as an admirable quality towards a more civilized society—one in which the 'basics' of work and love need no longer tear people apart emotionally." The formula for the new body of sense/cents is wisdom, well-being, and wealth.

Sensus Fidelium

The "sense of the faithful," "the pulse of the community that trusts." What a wonderful expression to remind us that even though some of the people go off track some of the time, not all the people go off track all the time. Human life and wisdom overcome even our most stupid blunders. The faithful keep the covenant. The faithful do not break promises. The faithful live the spirit of the Way. In Hebrew the word for *faithful* means "to trust," "to believe [a statement]." This same root gives us the word *amen*. A faithful person—or a faithful employee, therefore—is one who is trustworthy, dependable, trusting, and loyal. A faithful person or organization gives its "stamp of approval," its "amen."

For the ancients the *sensus fidelium* was always present in the integrity of the community, in the people. The early Christians were known as the People of the Way." They had a vision, a conviction of who they were. They had a corporate identity.

Today in our global community life is more complex and diverse, and the need to understand others more urgent. We need the reassurance of the *sensus fidelium*. We need to know that things will be okay—especially since loyalty and faithfulness have taken quite a beating.

But we have not been walking this path alone. The medieval center of the universe, Jerusalem, has always been the compass point, not just for Christians but also for those of the Jewish and Islamic faiths, who are also People of the Book. In the corporate community, which is local and global in nature, we need a similar "book" or vision to guide our corporate governance. Lewis Platt, Hewlett Packard's CEO, for example, emphasizes how "the H-P Way" guides the behavior of the company. Employees, rooted in a set of core values, can weather the storms of change.

We need to recover the story of the Way. We need to believe once again that people count, that relationships matter, that there is a better way.

Fortune magazine's 1995 Corporate Reputations Survey includes cases from many respondents who no longer believe that the short-term quarterly financials and shareholder expectations are the only things that matter. John Ginnetti, an executive vice-president of Hartford Life Insurance, emphasizes the role that management plays in creating the organization's identity.

This identity issue is similar to what parents do in the home with their families. The "family culture," if you will, flows out of the vision and values of the parents. The reputation of the family stems directly from that vision and its practical applications. Parents, and any children, foster and display the family's reputation. Our experience as professors suggests that students with a strong sense of self-worth have more confidence in themselves and perform at higher levels.

What leadership vision drives your family? Your organization? Your community?

In a similar way the corporate reputation, especially now in the knowledge economy, rests on more than just numbers alone. Andy Grove, Intel's CEO, believes that the human element in the corporate reputation gives employees that extra energy. From 1990 to 1995 Intel's annual sales increased to $11.5 billion from $3.1 billion.

Change may be the order of the day, but unless there is a vision of stability and continuity—what we have called the *sensus fidelium*—companies like Procter & Gamble (founded in 1837), 3M (founded in 1902), and Motorola (founded in 1928) could not have sustained the energy and drive needed to create the viable futures they have. Even in times of adversity vision is the leadership edge.

P&G believes very strongly that intergenerational management success is critical to building a sustainable future. As the world opens its borders and we open our minds, we will see this thinking is not a new revelation. Just as communities live and die, so do companies. For companies the challenge is even greater. We would do well to learn from cultures that see the value of generational planning. Many Japanese companies, Panasonic, for instance, have intergenerational business plans. This kind of vision can make the short-term pain valuable to the long-term gain.

What kind of new learning will it take for Western business culture, based on individualism, to build a shared vision of the future? A first step could be to value the corporate memory that has been cut out of a downsized workplace—the corporate story that has guided us in the past. To do that, of course, requires investing in taking time to pass on the corporate wisdom, the traditions, values, beliefs, ways of doing things—in a very real sense, its *sensus fidelium*. Our experience consulting to government and the private sector reinforces the need to consider seriously the long-term consequences of short-term decisions in letting good people go without listening to their collective voice. In the future that voice may turn out to be your competition.

Valuing the Spirit

What do we do, then, at this point? The ancients gave us the answer long ago: Where there is no vision, the people perish.

We need to relearn that vision is a valuable matter that gives meaning to our lives. It guides the Way. We need to stop believing our own hubristic myth that says we have all the answers. We need to listen to ourselves, to our employees, to the pulse called life, and to the breath of freshness called spirit. And then we need to value that breath or spirit as the empowering perspective of human and organizational life. The Chinese symbol for *to listen* includes three factors: ears, lips, and heart. If you understand these insights, then you understand the need to value the spirit.

The Hebrews use a word called *ruach*, which is translated as "breath" or "wind." To speak this beautiful word in Hebrew, one must *breathe out*. The Greeks used the word *pneuma*, or "spirit." We still talk this way today: "Breath of fresh air!" Perhaps our short-term decisions are leading to increased "pneumonia" and not to well-being.

When employees say, "You just can't breathe around here!" we know they are suffering from lack of oxygen; there is a crisis of spirit. Jesus told Nicodemus that the presence of spirit is like the wind: You cannot see it, but you can see its effects. In many organizations an amazing event takes place at quitting time: Employees come alive, talkative, animated, and purposeful! But it doesn't have to be that way for you or for your organization. The spirit of enterprise can breathe in your organization.

One organization that seems to understand the need for a spirit of enterprise is 3M. It encourages its seven thousand scientists and engineers to devote 15 percent of their time to developing their own ideas. Of course, it also spends $1 billion each year on research and development. Art Fry, inventor of 3M's Post-It notes, did what he did because 3M draws out the best from its employees. From Fry's perspective, he did it for the good of the company.

As we come to the end of learning the importance of this first pillar of putting visionary leadership into practice, see for yourself and reflect on how you would rate your "Corporate Ten Commandments."

THE CORPORATE TEN COMMANDMENTS

Does your organizational vision and decision making . . .   Check (✔)

Foster a leadership vision for experimentation and growth?
Create a healthy cultural environment where partnering is the norm?
Inspire people to learn to take charge?
Celebrate employees for who they are and what they do?
Encourage communication in leadership thinking?
Listen to the voice of employees to grow together?
Value trust to build people, pride, and profits?
Mentor leadership teams to achieve uncommon goals?
Invest in community development to sustain well-being?
Reward return on integrity in relationships (ROIR)?

These are the nuts and bolts of the thinking in vision-driven organizations. Like any family, group, or business, the spirit flows from the heart of the founder or the leader, just as in ancient times. In the beginning, according to the Jewish story of the Way in the Book of Genesis, the Spirit of Life "hovered over the waters." Later in history the psalmist records that he could not get away from the spirit, for that would mean annihilation.

That ancient lesson is one that we moderns need to heed. Today's leader is indeed the spirit maker of corporate values, vision, and memory.

PILLAR II

MAPPING

> "Roll up that map,
> it will not be wanted
> these ten years."
>
> WILLIAM PITT (1759–1806)
>
> [On a map of Europe, on hearing the news of the Battle of Austerlitz, December 1805]

IMAGINE A PATH TO THE FUTURE. Is your mental path an autobahn, a country lane detour, or a wilderness journey? Is your mental map sufficient to guide you on your journey through a world of change?

What issues will you need to respond to on your decision path? What new clear thinking will you need? What's needed to convince you to shift your mental paradigm?

Your "mental map" is shaped by your vision. In turn it helps you reach for your aspirations. But today our industrial-era road map is in decline. Its hulking, rusting smokestacks no longer correspond with today's knowledge economy. And its highly defended borders are irrelevant, as we move into a borderless world. A view of the earth from space shows no borders. Neither should our mental maps.

The ancient organizational mental map was easy to understand. It consisted of those who prayed, those who "slayed," and those who slaved. In our industrial-era organizations we created a somewhat more complex map of functional silos, what author Peter Block calls the ideal structure for command. Inside these functional silos or chimneys, employees have been trained for years to compete against one another rather than look outward to their external competition.

Like those rusting smokestacks, they remain a barrier to change.

And change we must—because we need to develop open thinking to respond to a borderless economic map. The new mental map will be an open systems model that will enable us to reach out and receive ideas and insights from anywhere. The new mental map is less about borders and individualism and more about connectedness and the process of work and relationships in the international marketplace.

The new mental frontier requires a innovative kind of pioneering spirit. Like visioning, the first pillar, our second pillar, mapping, requires us to use both hemispheres of our brains, the rational and the intuitive. Joining them will enable us to map out a journey that will align business, government, and educational thinking so that we can forge seamless solutions that let us rebuild our communities, sustain our economies, and endow ourselves with an enduring sense of self-worth.

The seven pillars of visionary leadership provide an archetypal visioning and learning process for individuals, organizations, and communities to make this future a reality. Pillar I, visioning, challenges you to reframe your thinking and embrace a new vision of the future. Pillar II, mapping, dares you to begin discovery planning with a map that will lead you on your journey to that future.

THE 20/20 LEADERSHIP PATH

Parting of the Mindsets

To shift our mental paradigms, we need to step out of our own cultural or organizational contexts. We did just that when we undertook an assignment with the United Nations Development Program as advisers on economic reform and privatization to

Poland. Our task was to assist the Poles in shifting their mental paradigm to reinvent their economic and organizational futures and align them with the changing global map. Our hosts thought it important to educate us in the history and traditions of their local environment—in other words, to understand *their* map.

To do so, they brought us face-to-face with an old landmark that had shaped their map. This landmark is one of the greatest fortresses in Europe, Marlbork, onetime headquarters of the Teutonic Knights. As we looked out across the Vistula River, we imagined what it must have been like to be an early "CEO" and leader of this growing organization, whose divine mission was to transform the local mindset to a higher vision. It put a Christian template on pagan thinking and substituted one spirit of enterprise for another.

The mergers and acquisitions strategy is not unlike the reality in the modern corporation. At each change of command, or with a merger or acquisition, CEOs bring out their mental maps and visions and often impose them as well on the organization. A few years back the Lotus Development Corporation of Cambridge, Massachusetts, and Novell Inc. of Provo, Utah, were discussing a possible merger. Their organizational maps were poles apart: Lotus, with its BMWs in the parking lot, eighty-hour workweeks, and company-sponsored sushi bars, just couldn't find a way to meld with Novell and its family values and Mormon ethics. After IBM's later hostile acquisition of Lotus, Lotus chief Jim Manzi quit the so-called marriage. What the *Wall Street Journal* called the enfant terrible of the software world lasted only ninety-nine days.

In our research into 250 companies we identified a direct connection between attitudinal mindset or map—its readiness to perform in a borderless economy—and organizational performance. Only 12 percent of these 250 firms had evolved their organizational vision to the geocentric perspective. The remainder of the firms we studied still had ethnocentric or regiocentric maps. Organizations with a geocentric or global vision achieved a minimum of 66 percent of their sales from international markets because the vision and attitudes at the top had led to the implementation of strategic direction to support a global capability. Firms without a global vision saw the world through limited windows of opportunity and achieved little or no success in international markets. This kind of bordered thinking doesn't prepare an organization to respond to external threats in a brutal global economy.

What's the connection between the Teutonic Knights "CEO" and the modern CEO? In both cases initially only the mental maps change; the organizational territory remains the same. It took several centuries of "blood, sweat, and tears" for the knights to transform the hearts and minds of the collective local mindsets. The borders came first; the passions came later. And that's similar in many organizations today.

Is your leadership map connected to the organizational territory?

It is important to remember that when a vision is offered a people, it not only must superficially touch or attract people but must also enter more deeply and transform their hearts and minds. A leader with a vision of a new map has a special responsibility for this teachable moment. Sadly, while the motivations of the leader knights were grounded in faith in their map, they lost their compass (their connection to heart and mind) and ended up killing the very people they went so earnestly to save.

So the new story of the learning organization is really an old story.

What's the connection between our vision and leadership change? The shared map.

History lets us recognize that the quest for a better way is part of the human condition. Without a doubt history confirms again and again that empires of the mind crumbled because the vision at the center wouldn't hold.

We can sympathize with the Teutonic Knights because their biggest battle, the Battle of Grünwald (Tannenberg) in 1410, was truly a dead reckoning. Because their head vision didn't hold, they became victim to the vision of their once-subjected people who now had heart and the courage to become free from an imposed map.

Our visit to the fortress at Marlbork may seem unconnected to the challenges facing us in today's organizations. Yet like the Teutonic Knights, many leaders have fallen victim to that same kind of military metaphor mindset and defensive map. Their command and control decision map is a legacy of outdated thinking that no longer fits a world in which relationships and alliances are the formulas for success.

It's time to drop our mental drawbridges and drain the moats so that our organizations are integrated into our community. We need no longer use the map we inherited from our Newtonian-Cartesian forefathers. For the first time, using the Internet and information technology, we can now connect and develop our own maps to suit our unique needs. Today's history and geography are in our head. If we develop a vision that lets us see that our intellectual resources are unlimited, we will find ourselves surrounded by abundance, and we can develop a mental map that lets us live locally *and* globally.

The lesson to be learned is that vision shapes ideology, ideology then shapes thinking, and thinking ultimately shapes how our institutions act. It is therefore critical, at this time of dead reckoning, that we truly understand what potential there is in imagining a personal 20/20 vision and organizational map.

At the crossroads of the industrial and the emerging paradigm we need to go beyond Descartes's logic of *Cogito ergo sum* (I think, therefore I am). We need to reimagine a future of *Sum ergo cogito* (I am, therefore, I think), which in essence turns our present thinking around 180 degrees to enable us to have a wider vision.

Sir Shridath Surendranath ("Sunny") Ramphal, former secretary-general of the Commonwealth of Nations, in an allusion to a similar theme in Winston Churchill's talk at Harvard in 1943, stated that the only empires we should continue to believe in are the empires of the mind. We must be careful that we don't become imperialist in our thinking. The new leader will recognize that helping people see the higher vision will require a personal transformation and commitment to learning. And the place to start that journey is within us.

Breaking Mental Maps

Like the grand masters of the Teutonic Knights, many have built a mental fortress on the eroding foundations of certainty. Perhaps you are carrying around in your head a siege warfare mentality about yourself and your organization—possibly with good reason. But it may be time to look in the organizational mirror to see whom you are really helping by living in this way.

As recently as the last decade, mainstream business advice asked us to become master business tacticians. One text encouraged the reader to learn to become "a master of strategy on today's corporate killing fields." The heroes and myths of the military mindset it endorsed were Genghis Khan, Hannibal, and Napoleon.

Is this the role model of leadership that will save the new inclusive organization? Is this whom you want as your coworker or neighbor? This strategic mindset urges readers to "mastermind the battle," "clobber the enemy," and "win the war." But what kind of future does this military mentality direct us to? Supposing that we have survived the restructured, right-sized, downsized, outsized, delayered, and who knows what next fad organization, do we really want to map out a future like this? To reach a healthy, worthwhile future, we need to break our mental maps and create new ones that value a life of work, wealth, and well-being.

Our organizational maps are crowded with management models and theories, but it has become readily apparent to us that existing methods of management learning are limited and not adaptable. They reinforce maps that limit us to institutional thinking, not inspirational thinking. The new map needs to be centered on three points: the individual, the organization, and the community. We need to look beyond our own culture to find and integrate the best ideas from any discipline or any place. This open map, in essence, is our compass and our "home page." It allows us to experiment and grow but at the same time affords us the freedom to "return home" or reconnect with our roots, if necessary.

The old map was linear and rational; it shaped our thinking; it was founded on certainty. The global map, as consultant and author John Naisbitt says, is focused on paradox, or uncertainty. Paradoxical thinking inherent in the Japanese culture, for example, serves to transform as well as sustain that community.

Let us take you on a simple learning journey. Using our archetypal learning process, look at a garden as a map and place where the paradox of change, growth, and transformation occurs.

In *The Dawns of Tradition* Gregory Clark, a scholar on comparative culture, states that when you look upon a Japanese garden, you experience a refined sensitivity with a balance all its own. In Japan the garden, or the natural way, has shaped a people's thinking. They live the paradox: By revering the beauty of nature, they have a way to integrate what happens around them.

There is an old saying that if you want a garden, then be a gardener. Clark notes that a deep simplicity supports Japan's refined culture. In casting about for reasons why Japanese culture has developed along these lines, he surmises that the Japanese have been able to take the instinctive side of their personality and refine it as a basis for their society. This mastery has given them an incredible step forward as they approach the twenty-first century. They are using both hemispheres to shape their map.

The Western approach has refined the rational and noninstinctive sides of human enterprise. We have ignored the instinctive side, much to our detriment. We don't trust instinct. Yet the ability to link our rational and intuitive minds, our intellectual and instinctive sides is a primary skill for all of us in the new economy.

Clark says—and our visits have confirmed—that in Japan there is a simple pleasure that is hard to find in the Western mindset: that of valuing quality in simplicity. This shared vision expresses itself in the concept of the work unit as the *unmei-kyodotai*, or the community with a shared destiny. This vision is relational, founded on imagining the pursuit of work and enterprise as one of an extended family or sense of community. These subtleties of the Japanese experience represent the shock absorbers of daily life. If we hold this mirror up to our lifestyle of individualism, how do our organizations compare? Who benefits the most? What paradox does individualism challenge us with?

The shock absorber example is an important lesson. It challenges us to invest in the human and the relational side of enterprise that change and transformation require. Without these shock absorbers, we lose the intimacies of good living and well-being. We miss the context that life is not just a pursuit of individual success, and we overlook the subtle insight and understanding that we are dependent on one another for the journey.

We, too, need to recover and learn to express the spirit of community, to reclaim it as an important landmark on our maps.

This appreciation of the spirit of community can happen spontaneously in many contexts if we are ready to see. An encounter by one of us in Kenya with Kikuyu tribesmen singing as they dug a ditch and chanting *harambee*—roughly translated as "working together"—sounded so much more rewarding than an organization of individuals chanting "TGIF" separately—or, as T. S. Eliot said so pointedly, measuring your life with "coffee spoons."

We have much to learn in order to leave our skewed value path and carve out a new, more holistic one. A new vision and a new map can serve as a compass. By identifying the critical issues on our personal maps and developing the inner core competencies for living, we will find our own true north.

Valuing Net Worth

Adam Smith, author of *Wealth of Nations* and intellectual godfather of the present economic system, wrote a lesser-known book titled *A Theory of Moral Sentiments*. In it Smith argues that a proper regard for others is essential for the functioning of a civilized society. To the surprise of many, Smith also argues that sympathy—what we call social responsibility—is just as important a concept as his "invisible hand" guiding the market toward efficiency.

In other words, the foundations of our present economic system started out not only with a rational but also with an intuitive framework for the development of work, wealth, and well-being.

Today many of the institutions that created this "sympathy"—that gave families and nations a sense of self-worth, well-being, and belonging—are deconstructing. It is not unlike the collapse of a beloved community or the death of a trusted old friend.

As we get older, it is harder to make new friends. But without the effort the breakdown of our social contract will leave us alienated and foster in us an unhealthy preoccupation with self; it will be like living in a cocoon. Civility today is indeed in short supply. There is a vacuum of trusted values. GE's Jack Welch says, "Trust and respect take years to build and no time at all to destroy."

Eberhard E. H. Weber, in his essay "Forging a New Economy," points out that although civility is not an economic term, it is a condition that allows economies to function and is an essential part of a society's stability and confidence. Civility is the link that makes civilization possible. It is a good value, and good values make good maps.

Corporate investments in community—indeed, in civilization—pay off. At Rhode Island–based Taco, Inc., a manufacturer of pumps and valves, the eighty-two-year-old chief, John Hazen White, has what he's always dreamed of: a learning center that invests money in employees on training, schooling, and citizenship. The payoff lies in not the return on investment but, as he calls it, the return in attitude.

Can attitude through training make you money? The National Center on the Educational Quality of the Workforce (EQW) studied more than three thousand U.S. workplaces seeking a relationship between investment in education and ensuing productivity. The results? The return on investing an average of 10 percent in employee education versus capital equipment gave a company an 8.6 percent gain versus a 3.4 percent gain! These findings, shown in Figure 2.1, reinforce the validity of investing in a map that puts people first.

Investing in people is the catalyst for creating and sustaining organizational transformation. Mapping and leveraging intellectual capital in the form of an educated workforce are the comparative advantage of the knowledge economy. Investing in technology will not sustain our competitiveness and well-being over the long haul, says Adrian J. Slywotzky in *Value Migration: Strategies to Preempt the Markets of Tomorrow,* because in many industries the rate of breakthrough technological innovation is slowing.

This investment in people and civility—in the values that sustain us, our net worth—can protect our sense of loyalty and trust from further erosion. In *The New Individualists: The Generation*

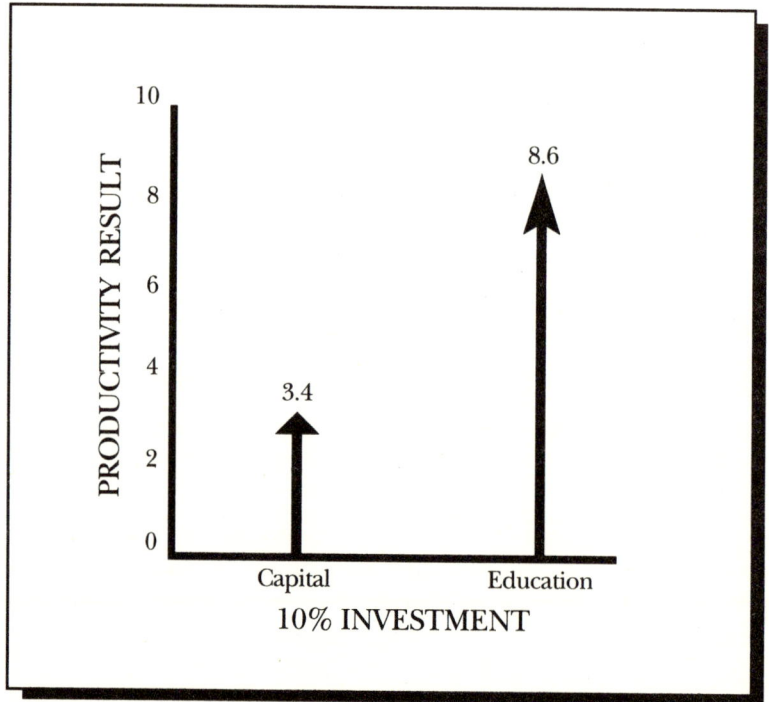

FIGURE 2.1

after the Organization Man, Paul Leinberger and Bruce Tucker point out that it is hard to be emotionally bound to an institution that keeps getting bought and sold. The "buy and sell" strategy doesn't *have* to be part of our organizational mental map. In order to journey to a new 20/20 vision, our internal value compass and shared mental map need to embrace the paradox of both I- and-Thou, of potential prosperity and posterity. The emerging 20/20 organization will need to come to terms with the net worth and added value of integrating the I (the beholder of self-worth), and Thou (the organization as collective ego). Valuing net worth means investing in a borderless map and intellectual capital so that our organizations are mentally tough and ready to act in a borderless world. Visionary leadership will be about learning how to empower team decision making and valuing dialogue to develop a sense of shared meaning as our next step on the journey.

We especially need to regain two inner-core competencies in order to succeed: *faith* and *trust.* Faith is what we value, and trust is how we act with one another, how we live out that faith. Trust really is the lifeblood in the new organization. It provides the antibodies to keep our organizational body healthy. Will we learn to trust or, as Charles Handy remarks, will our companies be no more than just a "box of contracts"?

It's always taken a heroic effort to change old thinking and start the new journey. In American mythology the Pilgrim Fathers were sustained by faith and built their economic way of life through trust in a work ethic founded on that faith. Their values served as their map into the wilderness of a new continent.

Similarly, our values must serve as our map through turbulent times. The path of the ancients will take us inward to assess our personal strengths that will make our leadership journey possible.

THE PATH OF THE ANCIENTS

People of the Way

We are not the first people in history to see our mental maps crumble before us. The ideological walls can come tumbling down, as they did at Jericho and at Berlin.

We are beginning to learn that walls can be double-edged, or as the poet Robert Frost says in "Mending Wall," we are learning that it is important to know the difference between what we're walling in and walling out. For too long we have walled out the wonder and serious creativity of the heart; we have walled off our hearts in favor of our heads. We have walled out what we thought was irrelevant, not contributing to the bottom line, but we have also walled ourselves in. We have limited our thinking.

This two-edged sword has imprisoned us and cut a huge swath through our mental landscapes. We are slaves in our own head spaces, in our own sterile paradigms of logic and quantification. We are now paying the price. We are cut off from the wellspring of personal and organizational spirit and enthusiasm that we need in order to imagine a 20/20 vision to reinvent the workplace as a new *worth* place that is connected to community.

Today many feel that they are between a rock and a hard place, exactly the experience of the people of the Way. Can you imagine what the early Israelites felt as they stood at the edge of the Red Sea, the Egyptians hot on their heels and Moses pointing to the sea as the way out? Can you share their feeling of impending doom when they realized they had only two choices: remain where they were at the edge, or take the plunge to an unknown future? They had to make a choice: stay where they were and die, or risk everything. They had to trust the new map.

A similarly stark choice faced the Greek hero Odysseus as he contemplated how to navigate between two sea monsters, Scylla and Charybdis. Scylla was twelve feet long and had six necks, each with a head with three rows of teeth. She would devour anything that came within her reach. On the other side of the Strait of Messina between Italy and Sicily stood Charybdis, the whirlpool that created shipwrecks. Three times a day it would suck in water and belch it out. Anything or anyone that came near would be engulfed. Odysseus was able to pass between the two, but six of his men were seized by Scylla and devoured.

To get through a rock and a hard place moment, we need awareness *and* a map. We need to be aware of the dangers, and we need to use our map to plan very carefully how to navigate the passageway. Our Scylla and Charybdis moments today are those where choosing to avoid one imminent danger exposes us to another. Andrew Stark, in the *Harvard Business Review*, says ethics today is not always having to choose between right and wrong but is often a choosing between two rights. If we're not careful, Scylla, or the rationalism mindset, will devour us and we won't make it through the passageway to 20/20 vision; Charybdis, or the whirlpool of the busyness mindset, will suck us into an artificial sense of managing even as we are being shattered. Andrew Grove, Intel's CEO, says we don't have a choice about working in a globalized economy or in an information society. In fact, we do. We can adapt, or we can die!

Such a decisional moment is upon us as we now ponder how to navigate the narrow strait between mindsets of rationalism and intuition and dare to choose the new holistic vision of mind-heart-body-spirit living. We have the choice of holding on to our mental chains as head space slaves or of taking a risk and experiencing liberation.

The Israelites faced a stark choice. But modern living confronts us with more and more gray zone decisions. Making them is not easy, and many would rather relinquish the task to others. However, full human development, what Jung called our unavoidable vocation to individuation—that is, to become who we must be—cannot be avoided without cost or without choice. We live our human journey willingly with choice or unwillingly with pain, in which case, according to Jung, we live it out as fate, at the whim of the forces around us.

Allan Bloom says that choosing is for people who ask real questions. Those of us who are worth our salt have personally confronted the big questions of life and death, being and nothing, eternity and time. To map our way into the future, we must choose true consciousness and true awareness. Awareness may bring pain, but when our backs are against a wall, like those of the people of the Way, we must have the courage to knock down the wall to get on our way to a better future.

Wilderness Journey

We have much to be thankful for from the thinking of René Descartes and Isaac Newton, but the old mental map is not the new global territory. The human spirit is broader, deeper, and more magnificent than our rational definitions of what it means to be human.

We must recognize that in many ways we have ironically been on a wilderness journey, but it's been an unconscious one that took us on a detour; it's time now to get back on a leadership value path.

Like everything else on the human journey, the wilderness experience can be either positive or negative. What makes the difference? Consciousness and choice. If we have the courage to choose and embrace risk and change to enter a new future, we can begin an authentic wilderness journey, one that gives us a positive experience of the new map. Left behind will be the known head marks and guides. The trusted certainties that brought us this far are too unsteady to allow us to continue into new territory. The wilderness journey for many will be to leave their safe, national maps and learn to live on the new global map. How well we do will depend on the depth of the confidence and trust we have in our ability to take charge of our lives. We don't know ourselves until we manage adversity. Adversity is a great teacher, and our maturity is best measured by how we manage what we don't like.

We urgently need a new vision of hope and a survival compass. One critical guide will be trust. Survival will also require a team learning effort and courageous leadership.

An essay on survival and society in *Time* magazine calls trust the machinery for "reciprocal altruism" and "the infrastructure for friendship." We cannot go through the wilderness journey without trust. Strategic direction requires strategic empathy. The outward-bound experience requires inward-bound competencies. Until we have been challenged by an authentic wilderness journey, we won't know if we have them or not.

What will light our mental path is the heartland inside us. At the conclusion of *Star Wars,* when Luke is flying in to break free, he realizes he cannot control his journey only with head stuff or technology. He hears his inner mentor tell him to trust his feelings, to go beyond a literal, head space resolution of his problem. When he listens to his heart and trusts his feelings, he makes it safely through his high-tech Scylla and Charybdis.

The frightening part of the wilderness journey for many today is that they don't trust or believe there is value in an intuitive component. This fear is paralyzing the courageous action we need to take. We have been trained in the logic of command and control. Our formal educations have focused us on a narrow intellectual theory of management and the achievement of meritocracy. We have not been taught how to include our emotions or trust in authentic instinct and spirit. These are critical elements of the learning map that will guide us on our human journey.

The heart has reasons that the head knows nothing of, and we need access to those reasonings now more than ever. The rational map has brought us this far on the journey. Today we are stuck. The traditional guides of quantification veneration have become limited. They killed the "prophet" by reinforcing the worship of "profit" exclusively.

As we enter the global wilderness, we need new guides—guides that come from within. The question is: How do we find these trusted guides within ourselves? They have been there all along. We have just built rational temples over our inner sacred ruins.

One key to laying out the map for this journey is to develop a shared vision of the challenges that face us. A shared vision certainly played a role whenever our ancestors successfully made stark choices or embarked into the wilderness. Before we begin our journey, we need to confront ourselves with valued questions and develop personal insight about our strengths and weaknesses. Our seven pillars provide a framework for the journey by letting us ask ourselves key questions before we start.

SEVEN VISIONARY QUESTIONS TO BEGIN THE CHANGE JOURNEY

Visioning	Do you know where you're going?
Mapping	Do you know how to get there?
Journeying	Do you have the strength to make the journey?
Learning	Do you have the willingness to begin?
Mentoring	Do you know who's done it before you?
Leading	Do you know who can do it now?
Valuing	Do you really care?

These seven initial questions avoid any surface solution or off-the-shelf formula. They encourage us to look deep within ourselves for solutions. When we include them in our workshops, these questions help participants give voice to their personal concerns, hopes, and wishes, what we have referred to earlier as "the voice of the organization." We teach our workshop participants the power of imagination in the visioning process. This visioning process raises to consciousness elements from the "organizational iceberg" or the "organizational unconscious"—that is, the hidden or "shadow side," what one author has called "the internal game."

Our experience shows that without our discussing the internal game, it is impossible to build the trust and commitment required to build a shared vision for the journey. The discussions and dialogue that result from this discussion tell participants that we value and trust everyone's voice in the organization.

Once we earn this trust, we structure a "value huddle"—an open, frank time in which we seek feedback and answers to map out the new corporate journey. These discussions result in real personal growth and nurture the "strategic empathy" and shared understanding of the tasks required of all employees to participate in the change process to move forward.

We have observed that people understand the need for change and realize that change requires learning. People don't resist change per se; they resist *being* changed. They need to see that their efforts and initiatives are supported and endorsed from the top. Failure to do this results in cynicism or what William J. Morin calls "silent sabotage." Using the value huddle process, we can discover, listen to, and guide the collective voice regarding the critical issues said to be blocking individuals in the organization.

In order to find its way successfully into the twenty-first century, an organization needs shared values for its wilderness journey. These leadership values support discovery planning for the new journey. They will be essential in the days ahead.

LEADERSHIP VALUES FOR THE WILDERNESS JOURNEY

Inspiring vision and focus
Building trust in one another
Valuing strategic empathy
Aligning work with common purpose
Letting people go
Remaining faithful to the covenant
Believing in the journey
Learning through adversity
Doing more with more

Our seven archetypal pillars represent the architecture and thinking of the leadership organization. These pillars will stand on a new global map. By understanding them, organizations can start to develop a 20/20 vision for the new journey.

DISCOVERY PLANNING MAP

New Architecture	Global Map	Global Journey
I. Visioning	Good ol' days are gone.	Reframe our thinking.
II. Mapping	Map is not the territory.	Realign our mental maps.
III. Journeying	New workplace.	Reinvent our future.
IV. Learning	Knowledge economy.	Relearn continuously.
V. Mentoring	Spirit of enterprise.	Remember connections.
VI. Leading	People, pride, profit.	Reward imagination.
VII. Valuing	Work, wealth, well-being.	Recognize community.

PREPARING FOR THE JOURNEY

Let us give you an archetypal lesson for the journey. A journey requires a compass as well as a map. Richard Leviton says that our journey's compass consists of eight things: a body; an alms bowl; a star; a mirror; an apple corer; a sword; a notebook; and patience. These factors can easily be applied to the corporate journey.

- *Body*—an inner sense of ourselves as a corporate body, where matters of importance are pondered and important issues for all employees are tabled in order for the body to find relief, refreshment, and re-creation.
- *Alms bowl*—a symbol of an attitude of receptivity, of openness to life and opportunity. A corporate alms bowl, therefore, is a metaphor for attitude realignment and adjustment to the priorities of the big picture of well-being: people, pride, and profits.
- *Star*—the compass, par excellence, that guides and illuminates the path. In modern corporate terms, the star is the centred organization that is guided by its core values.
- *Mirror*—the ability to look at ourselves as we go through this wilderness, by checking our motivations and the geography of our inner road. The mirror reminds us of who we really are. It is the skill of not being betrayed by our own hubris, of

not believing our own mythology at the expense of feedback.
- *Apple Corer*—or the peeling off of the layers of stuff that keep us from knowing about and relishing the centre of who we are. Going through the contemporary process of corporate delayering is very much in the spirit of the apple corer. This process would not feel as rough if we had tended to it on a daily basis.
- *Sword*—an item for protection, symbolically understood as the keen edge of discriminating insight. We read of companies being on the cutting edge! In the global economy this discriminating insight will refer not only to a company's position or its products and services but especially to its human resources, its intellectual capital. Employees in smart companies carry swords as well as alms bowls. Smart companies honour intelligence and thinking.
- *Notebook*—or careful, detailed notes and record keeping. Ideas are critical, but the execution is in the attention to the details. In today's corporate environment, we literally have notebooks.
- *Patience*—the ability to undergo, to endure, to suffer, if anything. Executives often say, after going through an organizational transformation, "We really went through a lot, but it was worth it." Patience allows us not to lose sight of the goal and to stay on the path.

We have now come to understand the second pillar, the need for vision and mapping. Let us proceed, like pilgrims to the appointed place, to the next step: the third pillar, journeying.

PILLAR III

JOURNEYING

"King Tamatoa realized that there came a time on any voyage when a man and his canoe had to trust the gods and to run forward, satisfied that the sails had been well set and the course adhered to whenever possible; but when all precautions failed to disclose known marks, it was obligatory to ride the storm."

JAMES MICHENER, *Hawaii*

IMAGINE IF YOU HAD TO JOURNEY through the wilderness with your present organization. Would the people in your organization survive? Would there be enough faith and trust in the leadership for the center to hold?

The third pillar of the new organizational architecture is the journey. The archetypal theme of journey has been part of the human experience since the dawn of humankind. In all cultures and in all times and places the archetypal journey has always meant the same: the transition from one state of affairs to another. It is the eternal quest for the center.

For the ancients, heroic journeys meant crossing the sea of life, a feat that included meeting life's challenges, trials, and dangers with courage and endurance. Endurance meant having the ability to be patient—that is, to undergo an experience, even to suffer. Only heroes and heroines could endure because only they had the patience; only they could undergo any suffering to meet their goal. They also knew, like King Tamatoa, who eventually reached Hawaii, that once you set out on the journey, you don't look back.

In ancient Greek mythology, Orpheus journeyed to the underworld (the inner journey we all must take) to find his lost wife, Eurydice. He was permitted to return with her from the underworld on one condition: He was not to look back until he was out of the underworld or he would lose her. He had to be patient enough and resist any impulses to do otherwise so that he could get through this part of the journey. He had to tend to his mission single-mindedly and single-heartedly. He failed and lost his beautiful Eurydice. In another story it is recorded that in Israelite times, when Lot's wife looked back, she was turned into salt.

Dedication; perseverance; endurance; single-mindedness; commitment: These are all qualities that the sojourner needs. It is little wonder, then, that a person's send-off on the journey has often been accompanied by a sacred rite or by a symbolic ceremony. In the Eastern world the potential Zen monk raps at the monastery door three times before being allowed in to join others on the monastic journey. Zen wisdom says that for someone to come back three times and rap at the entrance is probably a genuine sign of a person's desire for membership.

The journey into the wilderness can drive one mad or return one to oneself. During the second century A.D., the desert fathers practiced their vocations alone in the desert. Not every monk could endure the vicissitudes of the wilderness. The modern monk who has captured the Western imagination is the late Thomas Merton. Professor Michael Higgins calls him "the ideal pilgrim." Why? Because he was constantly en route, always looking for the perfect home. As the ideal sojourner Merton traveled throughout his life in a quest for inner peace, for wisdom and for final integration. Higgins writes, "Unless we can be brought to see with the Spiritual Eye of the Imagination we will only see with the Temporal Eye of Abstraction."

The wilderness is not a glamorous place, but ironically it has been associated with the theme of journey for centuries. Perhaps this accounts for the few who accept their journey—their destiny—in life, because only a few are willing to experience the wilderness: the loneliness, cold, heat, terror that will be part of it. It is said that it is lonely at the top; it is lonelier in the wilderness because even the power of the "top" is stripped away from every sojourner.

The archetype of the journey always includes a crossroads. One has to choose a path, either to the left or to the right. The journey moment is a decision moment. Robert Frost, in "The Road Not Taken," writes that he made his decision at his crossroads on his journey: He choose the road less traveled by, and for him that made all the difference.

From an archetypal point of view, according to the Spaniard J. E. Cirlot, a former art and literary adviser for Editorial Gustavo Gili, S.A., of Barcelona, the journey

> is never merely a passage through space, but rather an expression of the urgent desire for discovery and change that underlies the actual movement and experience of travelling. Hence, to study, to inquire, to seek or to live with intensity through new and profound experiences are all modes of travelling or, to put it another way, spiritual and symbolic equivalents of the journey. Heroes are always travellers, in that they are restless. Travelling, Jung observes, is an image of aspiration, of an unsatisfied longing that never finds its goal, seek where it may. . . . Primarily, to travel is to seek. The Turkish Kalenderi sect require their initiates to travel ceaselessly, since . . . travelling is often involved with a higher, sublimatory significance.

For the Greeks the hero's journey was the search for and discovery of oneself, such as the journey Odysseus made, as recounted in Homer's *Odyssey*, or that of Hercules who, even as a child, accomplished heroic feats; or that of Jason and his band of heroes, the Argonauts, who accompanied him on his quest for the Golden Fleece. Interestingly, in California's gold rush of 1849 those adventurers who were seeking riches were often called argonauts. For the early Christians the idea of journey always meant the transition from death to resurrection. Only by "dying" could one find life. The hero's journey was also reenacted with King Arthur's Knights of the Round Table. Fairy tales over the centuries often recount strange and harrowing stories of people journeying. They, too, describe a transitional dynamic. Only the brave and those willing to risk all found what they were searching for.

Each of these journeys started out with a visionary destination like the golden road to Samarkand. It is a personal search, not unlike the Crusaders in their search for the Holy Grail. The global map we see today is the result of the weaving of the rich tapestry of two thousand years of personal exploration. As St. Augustine implies, the person who never leaves home reads only one page in the book of life. A Chinese proverb says it is better to walk ten thousand miles than to read ten thousand books. Augustine also states in his *Confessions* that we will be restless until we find a satisfying higher vision.

A question here then is: Can we afford to continue our present journey? We believe that the journey of the past fifty years has not really tested the spiritual mettle of the generations that have been raised on the individualist consumer ethic. The Western individualist ethic has made our homes, workplaces, and communities dysfunctional. Many see this reality in our compulsive acquisitiveness. We have learned to define achievement as the acquisition of things. To do this, we have reinterpreted and realigned what it means to be happy, to be successful, and to be worthy. We have learned to worship at the altar of false images and idols. We are what one writer calls the new "Church of the Shopper." We need to get back on track. The future mandates that we work together.

Fortunately some leaders see the bigger picture and are taking the necessary action. Matthew Barrett, chairman of the Bank of Montreal, says we need a new corporate journey with a new corporate culture. Barrett is the new kind of visionary leader, a radical banker, who is letting his people go and has taken his organization internationally on a learning journey. Together with his president, Tony Comfer, Barrett has steered his corporate ship into global high seas. This means the B of M has developed a new map: It has aggressively moved into the U.S. market with its Chicago-based subsidiary, Harris Bank, and with a 20/20 vision in mind has also recently expanded into China.

Corporate journeys are often an expression of learning from personal journeys. Coming from humble roots, Barrett has learned the value of being tested on the corporate journey in that he rose from the position of teller to his present position as chairman. This personal endurance guided him eventually to build a $50 million Institute for Learning to transform the bank.

What archetypal passion drove this idea into a reality? In Barrett's mind, big business is giving capitalism a bad name. The B of M is transforming into a learning culture. It has decided that structuring and functional mediocrity creates a short journey in today's marketplace. Barrett has developed the vision to see that knowledge is power and the key to human survival.

At the center of his bank's vision is an obsession to avoid obsolescence. Change requires learning. Barrett remarks. "This is very much a journey—the destination is not yet clear."

Question: What's at the center of your vision? Barrett learned what needed to be at the center of his vision after he had been tested on the journey of learning with his advanced management studies at Harvard. After he had completed a case analysis, his professor stated that the result was a good technical piece but missed the "big picture." What did Barrett learn? "You've got to try to be a Wayne Gretzky, to be aware of the whole game."

Like individuals, communities and corporations go on journeys. New York City's efforts to move away from the edge of bankruptcy is one such community journey. The journey that the former Soviet Union took its people on for seventy years ended in paradigm paralysis and economic and spiritual bankruptcy. GM, Chrysler, and Disney are good examples of corporate journeys taken through the wilderness. To make these survival journeys, new learning, time, and energy are required. So is the development of visionary leaders. CEO Wayne Calloway of PepsiCo has invested substantially in his people. When he speaks of corporate survival, he says, "I'll bet most of the companies that are in life-or-death battles got into that kind of trouble because they didn't pay enough attention to developing their leaders."

"Our job is to set an environment that allows risk taking, creative thinking, continuous process flow, trust in people and respect for people," explains Hewlett-Packard's Dan Branda in commenting on the journey H-P sets its people on. "If we can do this, it's going to be a lot easier for the company to move as the pace continues to quicken." At a CEO "Thought Summit," a roundtable sponsored by Price Waterhouse and the MIT Sloan School of Management, participant Richard A. Goldstein, the president and CEO of Unilever United States, Inc., commented on the need for companies to build cultures that include more risk taking as part of their journeys.

As we move on the journey from a local to a global reality, uncertainty will be the norm. It will be a continuous learning journey as the vision of the new map unfolds. For leaders who have traveled on linear journeys from A to B, the new inner voyage promises to test the real substance of their visionary leadership.

THE 20/20 LEADERSHIP PATH

We have come to the end of the old road, and it's time to find a new one; however, the new one will be filled with ancient echoes. We carry their voices and thinking in our head.

The global journey requires a higher vision. The old rational model just won't work. Companies may be showing huge profits, but they take on a different perspective when examined with a more holistic 20/20 vision of individual and community well-being. It is almost as though our corporations have been on a different path from that of our communities. Our hospitals are overflowing; our streets are unsafe; workers are overstressed; loyalty and commitment are in short supply; and suspicion, fear, and anxiety fill the boardrooms and bedrooms. In Canada, rated the number one place to live by the United Nations Human Development Index, depressed workers are costing employers $300 million annually in long-term disability. When we multiply this number by a factor of ten to apply it to the United States, it is easy to see that we are failing. We cannot afford to maintain the staggering costs of not addressing the real problems: relationships and trust at home, in the organization, and in the community.

In response to our changing world, many corporations are trying to transform through a restructuring and reorganizing journey that attempts to leap from one paradigm to another. Many times these changes entail wholesale reductions in force. Management thinker Henry Mintzberg of McGill University says the "layoff craze" is taking its toll on managers, families, and society. He finds many of the layoffs "unconscionable" since the organizational "fat" was created by senior managers in the first place. "I'm with Henry," says Tom Peters, in agreeing with this assessment. In a conference in Montreal Mintzberg quoted a *Fortune* article describing the hard-line attitude toward downsizing within the U.S. giant IBM, "where not laying off people was like maintaining their virginity."

Laying off people is not a transformation; it's equivalent to throwing bodies off the lifeboat. Some of us will survive the journey, but we will never recover the loss of trust that we have tossed away forever. Transformation requires a new journey, a new spirit, and a new set of values that recognize that we're all in the same boat together. The role of the leader is to install a spirit of enterprise and inspire hope in the crew.

The corporate journey we currently face is seducing us to put our faith in technology as the deus ex machina of transformation. Technology is indeed shifting the organizational paradigm; it is driving thinking and it is leading us along an economic path that still uses old strategic mental maps and management leadership models that are counterintuitive to the logic of the spirit of enterprise. Under these old models, people are placed at the periphery and machines at the core. Will this kind of center hold?

A new corporate journey will free our imaginations to reimagine a world with different results. Instead of entering the twenty-first century with nineteenth-century thinking, we need to take with us on our corporate journey a 20/20 vision and a map that places people at the center. When we allow our organizations to nurture the spirit of the human side of enterprise, we unleash the power of imagination and innovation that leads to enduring growth and well-being.

A clarion call about our present moral crisis cries out to be heard. A mounting tide of silent sabotage is building in organizations. These are the people who have given up the journey. The silent voices are waiting for release from the bondage of a life based on ROI (return on investment) and a liberation of thinking to shift the corporate journey and spirit of enterprise to ROIR (return on integrity in relationships). The search is on for spirit in the workplace.

Revolution of Imagination

Only by undertaking a personal revolution of the imagination can we begin our journey to individual, organizational, and community transformation. We need to leave behind the skewed value path that celebrated the separation of work and well-being and re-create a culture in which imagination, innovation, learning, and mastery of work are perceived as labors of love. We need to shift our thinking and find new ways to authenticate individual self-worth in the new organizational age. Only by freeing our imaginations can we loose the spirit of enterprise we need to build people, pride, and profits.

Reimagining the future of work will require much more, however, then retooling corporate mindsets to meet the challenge of increased global competition. It will also require understanding the very important changes taking place on our three mental maps: our personal map, our organizational map, and our global map. To embark on the new corporate journey, we will need to align our personal map with the other two; in other words, we will need "to get all our planets in a row!" A human journey such as this will provide a vision of abundance so that we can do more with more.

Transformation is not a top-down solution but a shared corporate journey. This inward journey across our stale mental mindscapes will lead us toward a higher vision of organizational learning to sustain people, pride, and profits. Our role in the new organization must be infused with archetypal energy—or meaningful connectedness—and learning, in order to carry personal value. We need to rebuild the corporate psychological infrastructure so that it can sustain people's hopes, aspirations, and working relationships.

The emerging 20/20 vision of a leadership value path is one that is spirit-filled and anchored in visionary archetypes and value metaphors that empower people, pride, and profits so that employees "burn up, not out." The 20/20 leadership value path sustains the way, leads the path, creates livelihood rather than just "jobs," and sustains work, wealth, and well-being in an age of unrelenting economic change. The alternative, as Thomas Hobbes said, is that life can be nasty, short, and brutal.

Seeing the Vision

If we had the sense to see, we would see what the present journey is doing to our individual, corporate, and community bodies.

Like a body that has suffered a fracture, our current workplaces and communities are suffering. But the signs of fatigue, the poor breathing, and the performance are not caused by a simple fracture. Underneath the visible symptoms is a serious heart problem that is weakening the whole of the body structure. If we had listened more carefully, we could have been alerted to this problem much earlier.

Many of our organizations are like this. Current "medical" case studies of clients that we have assisted show a similar heart problem, even though the initial symptoms showed only an external fracture. We know that recovery for the organizational body will be rapid and sustainable as soon as it is recognized that health is dependent on body, mind, and spirit.

What is needed to see what is not seen—that is, the corporate unconscious affecting the health of the corporate culture—is *new clear thinking.* This kind of thinking connects the rational with the intuitive to develop congruent decision making with sufficient insight to provide real solutions. In many organizations we have found that decision making is not connected. The head doesn't know what the heart is doing; the body doesn't see the big picture. Visioning is the leadership edge that provides the archetypal images to rebuild the architecture and spirit of the organization. In *Built to Last: Successful Habits of Visionary Companies* James C. Collins and Jerry Porras show that successful companies believe passionately in a set of core values. These companies then design ways for their employees to follow through on these values in their actions. "Companies that take an architectural approach, putting in mechanisms to produce the right kind of behavior, don't need to look outside for leaders."

Value Path to 20/20 Vision

It is time to get back to common sense. It is time for a revolution of the imagination. It is time to break away from the tyranny of old thinking and to embrace congruent thinking that lets us see how the complex patterns of change are affecting the health and wealth of the whole community.

The thinking we need for this new journey must be bold and courageous. Great institutions and organizations are built on the courageous and revolutionary thinking of people who dared find a better way. This kind of thinking is a spirit-filled vision. In a time of change and uncertainty, when one map is replacing another, visionary leadership is essential.

One such visionary thinker was Thomas Paine. His pamphlet *Common Sense* published on January 1, 1776, sold more than five hundred thousand copies, and his thinking contributed directly to the eventual printing of the Declaration of Independence half a year later. George Washington ordered another of Paine's works, *The American Crisis,* to be read by his troops to improve their morale; this work began with the famous words "These are the times that try men's souls."

Here was a value path and a vision of a worthy journey. It didn't have to look at quarterly results to achieve its revolutionary objective; it believed in its cause and had faith in its purpose. We desperately need a visionary leadership that is audacious to shift our minds and hearts to a new enlightened horizon.

Paine wrote about the American crisis. Today we have what Francis Fukuyama, formerly of the RAND Corporation and the author of *Trust: The Social Virtues and the Creation of Prosperity*, calls the moral crisis. As the twentieth century draws to a close, Fukuyama says we have stopped trusting one another. We have handed over our trust in God to trust in lawyers. The result is obvious.

The issue of the moral crisis we are facing is one of public and private trust. We need a moral community, one that has common purpose and a common culture. By this we mean we need to respect one another's differences but recognize that a moral coherence is essential to build trust and community.

The United States holds the position of leader of the global community. Vice President Al Gore says, "Ever since the great voyages of discovery five hundred years ago, the political imagination of Western civilization has been focused on the New World, the place where hope has a second chance and where, in the words of F. Scott Fitzgerald, 'for the last time man came face to face with something commensurate to his capacity for wonder.'"

We need a new archetypal destiny, a New World inside our head that brings into sight a value path for 20/20. The New World has always had a strong hold on our imagination. It is the image of a better place. What's stopping our generation from discovering this better place? We believe it's a lack of faith in a future worth journeying to. Paul of Tarsus, in his letter to the Romans, reminds us that endurance frees our souls. The spirit of his words is as meaningful and needed today as when they were first written nearly two thousand years ago. We have become a society that lacks endurance in our relationships, in our tasks, and in the value of our journey. We have been hardened and consumed in the school of immediate self-gratification. One of the key factors in emotional intelligence is the maturity to handle delayed gratification.

If we have hope in our future, we would do well to meditate on Paul's words; if our center is spirit-filled, then we can "rejoice in our sufferings, knowing that suffering produces endurance, and endurance produces character, and character produces hope, and hope does not disappoint us."

It's time to heed the call within for a rejuvenated workforce. It's time to liberate spirit. It's time for the voice of the "prophet" to speak in the boardroom so that the spirit of enterprise can finally take hold and sweep us into the 20/20 vision of a new worth place. This is a shared goal worthy of our endeavors.

THE PATH OF THE ANCIENTS

A new clarion call tells us to "step inside" and heed the spirit.

When we look back to the path of the ancients and the cleansing by the spirit from Jericho to Berlin, what is the lesson that stands out? The lesson is simple and profound: The spirit of people cannot be suppressed forever. Ideological walls crumble when values shift. It was not guns and bombs that finally tore down the Berlin Wall, but the relentless need of spirit that people have for community.

In the clash of the rational mindsets, the walls have come tumbling down. The critical mass of those who have heard the clear call for spirit has grown too large to be ignored.

For organizations to grow, a new spirit of enterprise must begin from the inside out. The learning formula for this change, this growth, this tearing down of walls is simple and has been known for centuries. It was carved on the entrance to the temple at Delphi temple: "Know thyself." On their journey to the temple, which, for them, was the center of the universe, the ancients made the connection between "Know thyself"—as the fundamental principle of learning—and the need to "step inside" to understand the meaning of life.

Yet we moderns fail to heed the voices and experiences of those who have gone before us and provide the wisdom we so badly need today in the knowledge economy. Maybe we fail to heed these voices because we haven't studied them. Our corporations and institutions are not connected to their classical roots. On our modern journeys we often fail to "step inside." We need "to go forward" with the ancients. What made our civilization great was an appreciation of the humanities as essential to being educated. Without an understanding of the humanities, decisions are made recklessly in a vacuum. There's no value context.

In *No Man Is an Island,* monk Thomas Merton aptly summarizes the introversion and "inscape" that must be a part of us on our wilderness journey:

> There must be a time of day when the man who makes plans forgets his plans, and acts as if he had no plans at all.
>
> There must be a time of day when the man who has to speak falls very silent. And his mind forms no more propositions, and he asks himself: Did they have meaning?
>
> There must be a time when the man of prayer goes to pray as if it were the first time in his life he had ever prayed; when the man of resolutions puts his resolutions aside as if they had all been broken, and he learns a different wisdom: distinguishing the sun from the moon, the stars from the darkness, the sea from the dry land, and the night sky from the shoulder of a hill.

When, as now, the trusted learning formula gets twisted or reversed and becomes profit first, people second, then the "produce or perish" industrial values map becomes the territory. Educational institutions simply become industrial warehouses to feed this insatiable machine. The spirit dries up.

We must leave our old mental baggage by the road, in order to start a new spirit-led vision-filled journey of self-worth redefined in a new community worth place. The place to start is in the home, the school, the organization, and the community.

The Inward Journey

The first task on our journey begins with an inward-bound orientation, what the ancients called metanoia, a conversion of heart, a turning around, a turning inside out. All authentic change occurs inside out. Essentially learning is an inward journey. Then true education—understood by the ancients as "to lead out" *(educare)*—can occur.

To change direction, we must dare to reimagine. We must believe, as people did in the time of the prophet Ezekiel, that the "dry bones" of the organization can come back to life. As in the time of Ezekiel, the breath of vision can enter organizations today. "Tendons" can be reattached, and there can be new "flesh" and new "skin" to give meaning to the corporate experience.

Metanoia, or personal transformation, is the initial step to new flesh and new skin. It is the first "step inside" for the beginning of the journey after a crisis, or a decisional opportunity, has been confronted.

Organizations are born in the imagination, just like everything else. Whether they grow and develop depends on the way they handle their stages of transition. The vast majority of organizations don't survive the middle-age crisis; most collapse before reaching the forty-year mark. If we see organizational life as a journey that organizations travel on, then it follows that at different stages on their way they must pay attention to rethinking and relearning if they are to survive. Each of these critical stages demands a metanoia, a turning around, an about-face, from the old to the new. An example of this is the present needed shift from the adversarial model of human and work relations to a participatory culture.

In ancient Greek literature *metanoia* meant "repentance" after one had committed a misdemeanor. In the Greek version of the Old Testament, *metanoia* translates the Hebrew idea of "to be sorry" or "to be moved interiorly with sorrow or pity" (the

Hebrew *nihām*). In the later Hellenistic Jewish literature, the Greeks used *metanoia* to translate the Hebrew idea of "to turn" (the verb *úb*). In Hebrew, "to turn" was often used by the prophets to get Israel refocused on God and away from focusing on themselves or on other idols.

What becomes very apparent in an etymological journey and meditation on the word *metanoia* is the Jewish emphasis on the deeply interior attitude and disposition of repentance that was contained in the metanoia experience. Later in history Jesus insisted that any kind of forgiveness had to be preceded by an inner turning or repentance. We recognize instinctively today, for instance, if someone is truly "sorry" *(metanoia)* when he or she asks to be forgiven. If metanoia is lacking, the request for forgiveness is strictly artificial and usually a sham. Lack of metanoia has undermined many of our institutions today. The average person sees through the sham; the result is a loss of credibility and trust. We also believe we need not only individual but business, community, national and international metanoias.

Some of the numerous metaphors that scholars have highlighted to profile more clearly this idea of individual (and national) journeys to conversion in the Old Testament include seeking and asking for a higher vision, humbling oneself, aligning one's heart with this vision, learning to do good, acquiring a new heart, and turning from wickedness and loving the good. These metaphors show that conversion was conceived as a genuine interior change of attitude that brought about a revolution in one's personal conduct.

In summary, when we experience metanoia, our hearts are changed, we think differently, we develop fresh attitudes to life, but we also change course or direction. Hence metanoia is an inner (profound) change accompanied by an outer (profound) action. Depending on circumstances, that is why an outer activity of repentance (such as confession of guilt, fasting, going on a pilgrimage journey, making restitution) accompanies genuine metanoia.

As with the individual journey, so also the corporate journey begins with the call for metanoia. Some organizations have an ongoing commitment to renewal and learning. Federal Express is one such company with its transformational leadership program known as LEAP (Leadership Evaluation and Awareness Process), which aims to help employees understand what the company expects of those in management positions and to decide whether they have what it takes to be in management. At Hewlett-Packard, developing employees is directly linked to the company's overall business strategy.

When the commitment to renewal and learning is an ongoing experience, an orientation and posture of openness are already built within the corporate journey. This does not preclude potential crises; however, it does build a competitive edge. It is said that success is the intersection of preparation and opportunity. This attitude cannot be shaped without a disposition, or ongoing metanoia to become the best one can be.

Let's assume for a moment that organization X does not have this disposition or metanoia ethic on its corporate journey. This ignorance or blindness does not shield the organization from the stages of the journey. The crisis, or crossroads, will happen to it, as to every other organization or individual. What will be missing is that critical inner "shock absorber," or metanoia orientation, that would quickly remind it that it needs to change focus, attitude, and direction. A metanoia ethic allows the organization to respond more rapidly to changing conditions. Company X without this ethic will more likely react to the changing conditions and, in so doing, be at the mercy of its impulses and not act with the integrity of its corporate vision and journey. Responsiveness is supported by a conscious awareness of options; reactiveness is the result of fear and threat. Response profiles character; reaction highlights lack of control.

But by the same token, if you and your organization do have this ethic of metanoia, it doesn't mean that you will be spared upheaval or testing on the corporate journey, but you will be able to look yourself in the mirror and make the necessary adjustments. This time of testing is the trial by ordeal. Organizations will often look back later and reflect on this period of their journey and say, "But we did it. We got through—together."

This is where endurance is critical. By getting through, they "passed the test" because they allowed the process of change, or learning, to occur and, as a result, are able to return, as Thomas Merton says, as if for the first time. Their journey has brought them "home" to their "center." They are now renewed; they can press forward and meet the challenges ahead. If we could apply this thinking in our lives, we would see the benefits of facing adversity on the journey and the folly of walking away.

Stages of the Journey

The four stages of the archetypal journey are *crossroads* (or crisis), *test* (or threshold), *change* (or learning), and *return* (or incorporation).

In their effort to deal with the challenge of a crossroads (or crisis), many organizations, in their confusion, may not see where the difficulties or threats of their new journey are taking them. They have not had the experiential learning to become all they can be; they are still untested. They may rush headlong into another crisis by not acknowledging or acting on the need for personal metanoia. Like the ancient Israelites, they may panic unless a leader has the vision to lead them safely through their organizational Red Sea crossing.

What they fail to realize is that this crossing from the old to the new territory is part of the journey and unlike any other they have ever taken. Once they have made the choice to part from the old and risk following a new vision, they then need to learn to retreat inward in order to go forward! They need the personal mental experience that is equivalent to the wilderness journey, as did the ancients who came to know themselves in a renewed spirit-filled way. Because of this experience, they came to trust themselves and hence one another. This introversion to "Know thyself" is the only path to transformation. Managers today need to realize that the step of transformation first takes place in their heads and hearts and then expresses itself in their organizations.

The wilderness journey is the decision to take time to "waste" time. This is a real challenge in our Western management culture because of the ethic that insists that time is money. If time is money, then renewal or reflection is simply seen as a waste of effort and not meeting the bottom line. But if we don't have time to do it right, how is it that we somehow always find the time to do it over?

From an etymological point of view, it is interesting to note that the word *waste* has the ideas of "desert" and "wilderness" within it. "Barrenness" and "uselessness" are also associated with "waste." From an Anglo-Saxon root, we also get *waxon*, which means "to grow." Wasting time can also be essential growth time.

It is little wonder, then, that our action-oriented culture instinctively shies away from "taking time to waste time." Something in us at some preconscious level tells us that wasting time will bring us into our own personal desert or wilderness and that it will be in that "place" that the real test of life will begin. We may not want to take that test. In the "test" stage we face ourselves, individually or corporately. Ironically, however, unless we do set aside time each day for the inner journey, we will be forced into the wilderness by sickness, accidents, or a great listlessness about life, and we will have to undergo (or suffer) a more severe testing of who we are.

This state of affairs often happens to men between the ages of forty to fifty-five. No longer do they find fulfillment in holding up their trophies of personal, academic, financial, and business conquests. More and more they become meaningless, and a different enthusiasm—often threatening at first if these individuals have not allowed for introspection or time for the inner journey in the first half of their life—breaks through. This is the enthusiasm for meaning, for purpose, for a spiritual center. The search for spirituality is apparent now. Since many in our society today are in midlife crises of identity and meaning, it follows that our organizations are as well. The old outer enthusiasms won't work now to fix the demands of the new inner journey.

Fortune magazine was so convinced of this need for reflection that it devoted a six-page article to it called "Leaders Learn to Heed the Voice Within." Right up front the article shouts: "In the fast-moving New Economy, you need a new skill: reflection." And then it goes on to highlight companies that are including this creative dimension of reflection for their leaders: AT&T, PepsiCo, Aetna Life and Casualty, Wisconsin Energy, Silicon Graphics, Du Pont, TRW, Booz, Allen & Hamilton, and Chrysler Corporation.

At this juncture in our history the unexamined life that Socrates told us was not worth living has become a liability. Self-awareness is a critical factor in the globalization of our minds. Hubris has no place in the global marketplace. Teamwork is in. As companies seek to engage both the hearts and minds of the employees to have the competitive advantage, they are realizing that this requirement for personal awareness, change and transformation has to occur right at the top. Both the rational and the intuitive (doing more with more) must now work together.

The new individual, corporate, and community journeys need to include emotional insight in their equations. What many are struggling with, however, is whether, as *Fortune* puts it, "everyone is capable of facing down their [sic] inner mysteries. If not—if the bull-moose go-getters aren't capable of successful introspection—presumably they must be replaced en masse before their employers can adapt to the new corporate environment." Stanford's James Collins asks, "How do you get people to share your values? You don't. You find people who share them and eject those who don't." The road ahead for some will be continue to be bumpy. To prepare for this new journey of introspection, leaders need practical discernment to develop new clear thinking skills.

Our bodies do not live independent of our souls. We are flesh-and-spirit human beings. It would make sense, then, that if we neglect our souls, if we neglect taking the journey to "Know thyself," eventually our bodies will try to get the message to us. That effort by our bodies should tell us that it is now time to take time to "waste" time. It's time to take time to ponder the inner realities. Illness will often function, as noted surgeon Bernie Siegel reminds us, as an escape from a routine that has become meaningless. In this sense, says Siegel, illness might even be called "a western form of meditation." How often it is that when we don't take care of ourselves, when we put too much on our plates, we come down with colds, we have to stay in

New Clear Thinking	New Leadership Skills
See ourselves as others see us.	Be open to others.
Be open to change.	Learn from experience.
Welcome adversity.	Prepare for the unprepared.
Honor the principle of duty.	Take a moral stand.
Respect paradox.	Invent your future.
Seize the moment.	Take action this day.
Embrace both-and thinking.	Live inner and outer journeys.
Do more with more.	Be intuitive and rational.
Silence the mind.	Take time to "waste" time.

bed, we have the flu. We're all like that. If we're honest with ourselves, we all can admit that we wait till the body tells us, "Enough is enough!"

Vision is about taking time for reflection. It is the "top line" that strengthens and gives depth to the bottom line. Crossroads and crises force each of us, and organizations as well, to take stock. Crossroads and crises force us to reconsider the journey we're on and to see if we have lost focus of which center we're really working toward.

The wilderness journey is also a time of corporate cleansing. We all know that if we do minicleanings throughout the year, the task, come spring, will be quite easy. There will be a more natural flow to work and events. The five-thousand-year-old Chinese *I Ching: The Book of Changes* talks directly to us when it asks, "When spring comes, does the grass plan to grow?" We try to control so much. Many have never made a retreat or done "wilderness spring cleaning." Like anything else, it is not difficult if made part of your daily, monthly, and yearly living. When mapping out a new leadership journey, we need the wisdom to reflect, renew, and relearn.

The "cleaning house" or change (learning), phase of the journey can also be the most dangerous part. Two thousand years ago Jesus was clear about this point in a person's life: After cleaning house of one's adversary, he told his friends, a person has to realign priorities quickly because seven, even more deadly adversaries can swiftly appear and take up residence. Nature abhors a vacuum, and business has to move in rapidly with a more holistic vision of enterprise to capture the spirit-led yearning in people to experience work again as a labor of love. Learning must occur not only in the traditional "head space," but, more important now, in the "belly."

From a contemporary point of view, we must be genuine in our response to the spirit call and cautious about the new fads that would simply act as corporate window dressing that promises transformation but leads to disappointment. Organizations may feel good that they have "cleaned house"—i.e., downsized, delayered, dehired, etc.—but if there is a spiritual bankruptcy in its core, then seven new, and more powerful, adversaries—i.e., problems and dysfunctions—will take over.

Finally, when we have confronted the crossroads, passed the test, changed our focus by realigning our priorities, we are now ready to return. Instead of the "old self," there will be a "new self." Instead of the old ways of doing business, passing through the stages on the corporate journey has brought the organization to a new horizon, with its attendant duties and privileges. Anthropologists refer to this stage as incorporation, when one actually "takes on a new body." We can see that the abbreviation *Inc.* can now take on a new meaning for an organization. Without going on the corporate journey, an "Inc." organization is one in name only. It is simply a legal and contractual reality. When an "Inc." organization "returns" from the journey, however, it now has *vision* (it can see); it now has *soul* (it can breathe); it now has *body* (it is incorporated); and it now has *energy* (it is empowered).

A Pilgrim's Progress

We have wandered now through the valley of the rational side of the intellect for three hundred years. We know what dry bones feel like. This pain of the brittle, dry bones of dispirited employees can end. We can dream a new dream. We can go on the transformative journey. We can let the old world die because we believe in the freshness and opportunity at hand to free up the intuitive and to liberate people, pride, and profits. We have the power within us to transform; we just need the leadership.

Fishery Products International Ltd., in a classic pilgrim's progress of an industry in decline, met the challenge for organizational transformation. Victor Young, voted CEO for 1994, realized that as a producer FPI was dying. It had to "reinvent" itself. Like the ancients, it confronted its "Red Sea cinch point" (the crisis or crossroads stage). It developed an innovative survival strategy and took the risk by transforming itself into a procurer of seafoods from around the world. It went from producer to procurer. It looked in the mirror, faced who it was—i.e., being producers (the test, or threshold stage). It underwent its transformation to being procurers (the change or learning stage). And it began doing business in a different way; it had reinvented itself (the return or incorporation stage).

A new mindset, a new vision. The result? A sizzling 107 percent gain in the company's share price in one year (1994), or a 325 percent improvement in its operating earnings during the first three quarters of 1994. A new worth place and a secure future.

When FPI took the risk and went through its symbolic Red Sea, it entered its wilderness journey experience. In order to go ahead, it knew it had to retreat to develop a counterintuitive sense of problem solving. Victor Young said that it took some of the senior salespeople and told them to turn themselves "inside out." That meant that instead of their seeing themselves as sellers of fish, their new mindset would be that of buyers. Ironically, at a time when FPI lost 90 percent of its traditional core business, it also increased its sales. Young is quite candid when he describes its situation at the time: Its alternative was unthinkable; it had to have a survival and transition strategy. It had wrestled with its corporate "Red Sea cinch point," made a decision to keep on the journey, and came through with flying colors. Like the ancient pilgrims, FBI went to the brink, crossed over, and, for taking that risk, became wiser and stronger.

Tribal Tensions

We are at the crossroads. We started the ancient journey as the tribe; we became communities that embarked on national journeys. We are now moving from national journeys to a global journey. The path ahead can be one of conflict or cooperation. The choice is ours.

T. S. Eliot in "The Waste Land" asks what it is that grows in our modern societal wilderness or "stormy rubbish," as he calls it, of contemporary living. According to him, it is not much: "A heap of broken images, where the sun beats," where "the dead tree gives no shelter, the cricket no relief. And the dry stone no sound of water. . . ." Surely we need a future more inspiring than that.

In similar fashion in "The Hollow Men" Eliot writes that the modern facade called living—and we can say working as well—heaps together "hollow men . . . the stuffed men" with headpieces "filled with straw." Sadly sojourners in the modern corporate wilderness can relate to what Eliot is writing about when he describes the "dried voices" that are "meaningless as wind in dry grass or rats' feet over broken glass" that "whisper together."

On your learning journey, you will often feel like a stranger in a strange land. You should not be surprised if tensions abound almost at every turn. Your situation will not be unlike that of the ancients, who also moved from slavery to freedom. They were always under tremendous temptation to return to the old ways and back into the arms of their slave masters. For some, a known slave master was better than facing an unknown but free future.

You may face new and different tribal tensions, but like those who have gone before you, you must pay attention to some key things in order to rebuild community. The Israelites, for instance, were saved through realizing their helplessness and utter dependence on Life. Technically this was referred to as having an attitude of poverty. *Poverty* is a misunderstood word today. Initially it meant an attitude of openness to what life would bring the tribe and an understanding that all life depends on a higher vision. One's journey, therefore, was nothing if not tied to a higher purpose and sense of community.

Today we would say that a corporate attitude of poverty shows itself by keeping perspective, keeping things in balance, getting priorities straight, and balancing the many conflicting demands with grace, dignity, and magnanimity. It is management on bended knee.

For the ancients, life was the animating force and source for everything. To refuse to acknowledge that was to adopt an attitude of arrogance. Idolatry was wrong because idols were dead in comparison with the Source. Even the idols depended on life! Later the psalmist and Job wrote that if life were to withhold breath or spirit, we all would die.

The ancients gratefully showed their poverty or the awareness of their true standing in the grand scheme of things in the manner in which they accepted and treasured the community to which they belonged. They had to come to terms with their true condition, and they did this as a people. They needed their tribe. They were people of the Way.

Today we all need to rediscover trust and community more than ever. Foresight and 20/20 vision embrace community as its mental map and value compass on the learning journey. What we need to do now is to understand the critical issues that can be seen as beacons or hurdles on the leadership path. The third pillar on our path, journeying, throws light on the horizon of today's issues in order to prepare us for tomorrow.

Francis Fukuyama describes what he calls the "radius of trust" as the size of the trust circle that different cultures are willing to extend. Because, as he argues, we have stopped trusting one another, we are in a very dangerous situation. When people and communities don't trust one another, their economies begin to suffer and erode. Social capital, the building block for communities and hence economies cannot be established without trust or internal cohesion. Fukuyama illustrates his thesis by depicting how the radius of trust in different cultures limits their economic opportunities. Lack of trust "imposes a kind of tax on all forms of economic activity, a tax that high-trust societies do not have to pay." Defensiveness, in other words, restricts wealth. While not saying that culture is the equivalent of economic destiny, Fukuyama does highlight the comparative advantages stemming from the interface of social capital and cultural differences.

In summary, ROIR—return on integrity in relationships—is both the real "top line" and "bottom line." Hewlett-Packard, long noted for its founding vision and culture of values, is classic proof of this. Since 1961, when its stock was first publicly traded, Hewlett-Packard has increased its stock value 7,885 percent! Its top line—the values, or "soft stuff"—makes the bottom line—the financials, or "hard stuff"—grow and increase.

The modern personal and corporate pilgrim knows that a 20/20 vision must include the honoring of classical roots to find the wisdom of the ancients who have already trod this path. The Aspen Institute in Colorado includes Plato, Aristotle, and the Old Testament, for example, in its syllabus for senior executives. Yotaro Kobayashi, currently chairman of Fuji Xerox and successor to Sony's Akio Morita, discovered from his time in Aspen that in a global economy it is important to globalize the mind as well. This globalization of the mind includes understanding other cultures, particularly their values and how they make their judgments. At the time of World War II there were only 38 nations on the map. Now there are more than 160. The map is always changing. These 160 have gone on a journey and taken charge of their own destinies.

Like those before us, our contemporary leaders will have to include in their journey time to build and nurture a visionary corporate philosophy. This will necessarily mean building a community-based plan for well-being that has, at the center, business as the provider, not reaper, for society.

Philip Dorrell, a computer programmer with a lifelong interest in science, mathematics, logic, and philosophy, asks a very pointed question in an essay titled "Bankruptcy as a Metaphor for Depression," What does a business do? He gives an archetypal answer: Business is really "a metaphor for consciousness." That is, in doing business well—in our terms, living the genuine corporate journey—one develops the *being* and *having* of the human journey. One can grow as a person—"Know thyself" (being)—and one can achieve as a person—accomplishments (having). Both the intuitive and the rational. Both discovery planning and strategic planning. Both the top line and the bottom line. Both prophet and profit.

If, as Dorrell also claims, bankruptcy acts as "a metaphor for depression" in the activity of business making, we begin to realize that in business as in personal life, nature itself imposes limits on our strategic plans for growth, expansiveness, and doing at the expense of being. Depression, in both cases, acts as a "psychic brake" on unrestrained activity, on an outer-directed lifestyle that takes no time to waste time. Dorrell writes: "Depression is essential for the successful operation of the conscious mind, acting as a required constraint on behaviors that gain too little reward for too much cost. The mind not subject to the constraining possibility of depression is subject to mania, a tendency for behaviors to go out of control, unable to control themselves, but going off in crazy directions that have little to do with the needs and wants of the body controlled by them." When a profound depression happens to an individual, the person is forced to do nothing, to "waste" time. If this forced introversion is managed well, there is often a profound conversion experience, a change in the basic direction of one's life.

A business going into bankruptcy is analogous to an individual going into depression. Like any individual, the business has to go inward, go through the experience (depression, bankruptcy), and come out a changed reality.

The lesson here, of course, is that managers and executives may be able to ignore the archetypal dimensions of the journey for periods of time, even years, but eventually, as when the sick body puts the brakes on for individuals by pushing them into depression to get them to find their true centers again, so nature (and market forces) put the brakes on the sick corporate body, and it falls into bankruptcy.

We maintain that the new vision of the corporate journey must include a realignment of the individual, the organization, and the community to produce work, wealth, and well-being. No longer can we nurture growth if thinking is not anchored in a sense of community development and well-being as the raison d'être of economic purpose.

A summary of some of the key points that we need to keep in mind for our "pilgrim's progress" on the 20/20 visionary leadership path includes:

• *A metanoia of heart and mind.* We need this about-face personally, organizationally, and in our communities. We need to remind ourselves that we're all on the human journey together, that life never discriminates against anyone in its demand for each of us to become all that we can become. This is an ongoing process and journey; there are ebbs and flows, but like any journey, human and corporate journeys have a beginning, middle, and end.

• *A humble acknowledgment of our* hamartia. The ancients referred to this as "missing the mark." We use the expression "being off base." When the Old Testament uses the word *hamartia,* it personifies it as a malevolent agent thrust upon human history at the time of Adam and Eve. *Hamartia* was a religious concept to begin with, a power experienced as hostile to God, which alienated people from God. We might call it defiance in the face of overwhelming evidence. In the Adam and Eve mythic account, this defiance was hubris: to be like God—that is, to try to overstep one's legitimate and life-affirming boundaries. These considerations are critical for managers and executives on the corporate journey. Without a realistic perspective—hence the value of 360-degree feedback—on themselves, it is easy for them to "miss the mark" and pretend that they are God-like. They fail to do what needs to be done and do what shouldn't be done. It is little wonder that corporate ethics has become such an important topic these days.

• *The rebirth of community.* We are crafted in relationships; we find our identities in relationships. Relationships hold up a mirror to us. A loving relationship mirrors a positive and healthy self-concept; a negative relationship, a destructive and life-denying one. Healthy relationships bring out the best of who we are;

we can become all that we can be. The crucible or container is trust. A healthy community, by extension, is one where trust is the connecting fiber, for a community's wealth and well-being are frequently an outgrowth of the trust among its citizens. Trust grows social capital; social capital is the foundation for wealth. We are social beings by nature, and we discover our uniqueness in community in service to others. In order to do this, we need to foster what Royal Bank of Canada refers to as the duty of civility. United States Senator Bill Bradley says, "Civil society . . . is the sphere of our most basic humanity, the personal, everyday realm that is governed by values such as responsibility, trust, fraternity, solidarity, and love." We cannot lose what Bradley calls "the fragile ecology of our social environment." The exercise of democratic citizenship must become more evident, but it can be only the fruit of a journey to civility and the rebirth of community. David Mathews, president of the Ohio-based Kettering Foundation, which works on problems of governing, says that "there is a deep and untapped reservoir of civic desperation." A critical mass is needed. But there is hope. At the New Communities Corporation in Newark, New Jersey, people spend their energy building this new community. Franklin Thomas, president of the Ford Foundation in New York, says that the rebirth of community is happening and is "the equivalent of a nonviolent revolution." Communities and neighborhoods are realizing that if they don't build together positively, they will surely fall together.

- *Business as the provider and agent of change.* This is the century of the organization. Like the monastery in ancient times, the hub of the value code and center of transformation, today's organization is a force for providing 20/20 vision. Gary Hamel, author of *Competing for the Future,* says that it doesn't matter what size company you are because you need an aspiration greater than your present existing resources. This need will create a "stretch," a tension dynamic that will inspire creativity and let your people commit themselves to something bigger than themselves. As a leader you need to craft the corporate journey with this creative tension to accomplish great things.

- *The integration of know-how with know-why.* The pilgrim's progress has to include thinking and wisdom. American business culture has succeeded predominantly on know-how—which is a "can do"—and not on know-why—which is a reflective philosophy of doing business. In the global economy we will need an integration of both these strengths. Understanding these dynamics will make trading relations between Occidental and Oriental cultures more effective.

- *Reflecting and balancing a shift of the Protestant* work *ethic to a reflect the* worth *ethic.* Thomas Moore, in *Care of the Soul,* says we need to begin asking ourselves new questions about our work: "What is the spirit in this workplace? Will I be treated as a person here? Is there a feeling of community? Do people love their work? Is what we are doing and producing worthy of my commitment and long hours? Are there any moral problems in the job or workplace?"

- *Going beyond strategic planning to strategic empathy and discovery planning.* In a response to rebuilding social capital and long-term profit, we need to "round out the corners," so to speak, of how we think of business. The corporate journey, as we've indicated, needs a more authentic realignment with the human journey. Discovery planning allows one to put hubris in its place and admit the dilemmas of life more easily. As we know, life does not always go in a straight line. The rationalist mindset would, of course, disagree. We have to change; the price is too high. We do not live by head alone.

- *Reawakening the principle of duty.* In its emphasis on individualism and rights for the past thirty years, society has made a corrective from a top-down, hierarchical approach to life to one that embraces equality in a greater way. However, we have forgotten along the way that individual rights are connected to responsibilities or duties. It was the "corporate individualism empires" that created great drive in the past, but now they are a hindrance. Indeed, they militate against growth and building a healthy future. The global reality demands a team synergy. Only those who share a common belief around the principle of duty can work in such a context. The Bahá'í International Community's Office of Public Information, in a statement called "The Prosperity of Humankind," points out we will have to recover "the devotion to duty" that until recently was essential to being a full human being. Indeed, such a recovery of a genuine devotion to duty will bring needed feelings of self-worth.

• *Focusing on holistic well-being.* The renewed value code for the 20/20 economy will, of necessity, have to include a commitment to individual, organizational, and community work, wealth, and well-being. Little by little, from the time of the Industrial Revolution on, organizations failed to make their connections to the worth of the individual and the community. As a result, they became isolated, entities unto themselves. Many, however, like IBM and Hewlett-Packard, did maintain a social conscience. But in spite of socially minded companies, the topic of business social responsibility did become a debatable item in ethics, with some, like the University of Chicago's Nobel laureate Milton Friedman, declaring that the only ethical responsibility of business was to make profits and not to break the law. Social responsibility was for social workers, not for business. Many, of course, disagreed with this premise. Capitalism, and the leaders who steer its dynamic, will have to develop an individual, organizational, and community-sensitive conscience if they are to build a 20/20 future worth journeying to. Peter Drucker reinforces this view when he states that even though business would be socially irresponsible by ignoring return-on-investment and getting involved in social action beyond its scope and competencies, it nevertheless has "a responsibility to find an approach to basic social problems that can match their competence and can, in fact, render social problems an opportunity for the organization."

Breath can once more enter the corporate dry bones. Employees can come alive again. The 20/20 journey to the leadership value path does shift the old mental paradigm to learning the value of visionary leadership. The path of the ancients is a call for the reawakening of the spirit of enterprise in the workplace. It is the vision and foresight to set us free and advance the concept of the learning organization.

The future is to be inherited by those ready to learn. The 20/20 vision, the global map, and the new corporate journey have been our way thus far in building the new architecture for transformation. We are now ready to proceed to construct the fourth pillar, learning. This is the path to visionary leadership. The new learning competencies we all will need for the twenty-first century will be our new curriculum. The world is your classroom, and your thinking can now be world-class!

PILLAR IV

LEARNING

> "In a time of drastic change
> it is the learners
> who inherit the future.
> The learned
> usually find themselves
> equipped to live in a world
> that no longer exists."
>
> —ERIC HOFFER (1902–1983)

IMAGINE THE JOY in a child's face in learning the ways of the world. Imagine the potential for fresh thinking to expand his or her mental universe, to invent a yet unseen future of work, wealth, and well-being.

Learning is an essential pillar in the architecture of the new institution. Unlike the institutions of the past, which have stymied our creativity and paralyzed our spirit for enterprise, the new organization needs to be a learning organization, one that values knowledge as the principle for change.

We have discovered the inner journey that is required to develop the learning that provides the wisdom to change. We now stand at the mental path that leads us to visionary leadership. To travel this path, we must open the doors to our mind to set free imagination and innovation.

Opening the mind will set free our preconceived vision of

what learning really is. Think of the power of learning from ancient wisdom. Ancient wisdom is at the core of what we call archetypal learning. It goes beyond words, languages, and formulas. The seven pillars support this archetypal learning journey. We need the art of learning before we can implement its practice.

Archetypal learning follows a Socratic journey; it is a walk through the great thinking and ideas of the past that shape our imaginal worlds today.

Let us take you on that journey so you understand the power of the art of learning. A virtual library of insights and knowledge will provide the foundation to hook and anchor your thinking. In that sense your thinking can be both strategic and intuitive. Those are qualities we need, first, to unleash our imaginations and, second, to think out a strategic direction.

What are the "hot buttons" of learning that we need to press to transform our hearts and minds?

They are *vision, leadership, learning, change,* and *spirit at the center* (Figure 4.1).

We need vision to have perspective to see.

We need insight to inspire leadership.

We need images to visualize change.

We need spirit to guide the transformation.

Most of all, we need people with a passion for learning to mentor the new learning. The place of change is in the heart and mind. To change an organization rapidly will require a new approach. Leaders will be the inspirational guides who help mentor the seven pillars of archetypal learning. They are the new architects and the change agents.

Organizations today are seeking ways to harness their intellectual capital. We prefer to set it free.

The Art of Archetypal Learning

Throughout human history our minds have been shaped by patterns learned from an early age. Today a new pattern, or archetype, for learning and thinking can provide the visual imagery

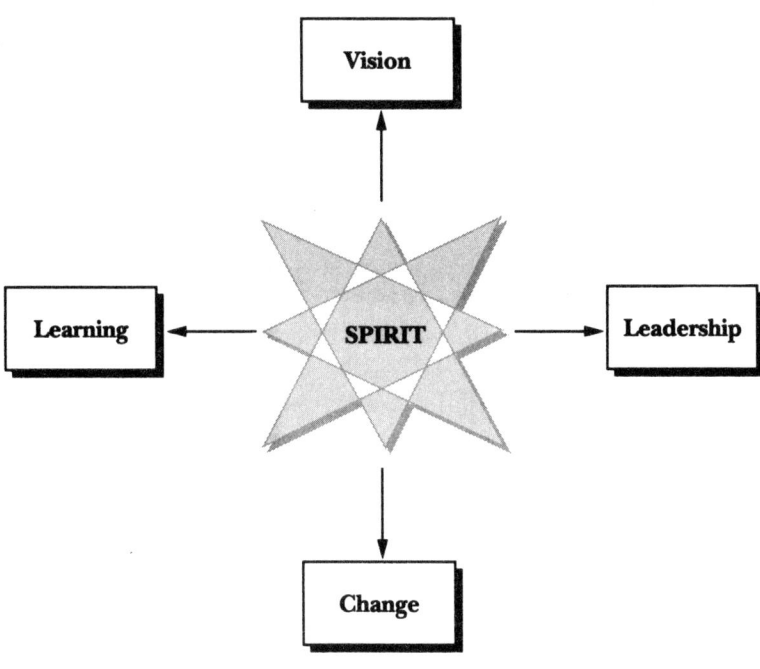

FIGURE 4.1

we need to see the steps required for personal, organizational, and community transformation.

People learn best when they learn archetypally, when they can embrace images that capture their passion and illuminate important lessons. These images often unconsciously hook or propel us to latch on to something powerful. A newborn baby, for example, evokes an archetypal response from us. We automatically respond by reaching out and mothering or fathering the infant.

According to Carl Jung, an archetype is a natural imprint, like the instinct that sends birds south in winter. The Greek for *archetypal* means "first." It is a primal, inborn pattern. The mother archetype is released when a woman has a child. The father archetype is released when a father is created. Likewise, the archetype of learning, of wanting to change and discover, can make us determined to endure whatever it takes to transform ourselves and have a new vision. Archetypal images and archetypal learning release passionate energy.

Archetypal learning is the powerful imagery that can help crystallize our thinking to enable our transformation. For example, an archetypal lesson on visioning might be taught by a reading from Susan George and Fabrizio Sabelli's *Faith and Credit: The World Bank's Secular Empire.* Their essay "The Savage Mind" provides a vision that archetypally illustrates what is required for each of us to learn to change. In the essay, "Yali," an authentic primitive and noble savage, sets out to discover why some societies are richer than others. He's particularly curious about what he calls "cargo"—that is, commodities like motorcycles, matches, canned meats, wristwatches, rice in bags, and steel tools—that his tribe doesn't have. His vision of the promised land is that one day a plane will land with these items and there will be heaven on earth.

Yali's worldview has been expanded by his radio, his most cherished possession. He believes that the radio people were very strange. They never talked about the most important things in life: family, yams, pigs, ancestors, or indeed cargo itself. And when the radio people weren't talking about wars or the weather, they went on about money and where it was kept: stock markets and banks.

Leaving his tribe in Australia, he journeys to Washington because he's heard about a "World Bank," a group Yali thinks should have the greatest cargo of all. He wants to meet the big men in the World Bank to find out how to get some cargo for his tribe. Yali is clearly on the right track. He has the vision to transform his tribe's destiny.

How does this connect to your organizational learning journey? Imagine that your corporate tribe has also nurtured a "savage mind." In place of the radio you have the Internet. The "World Market" is where you are journeying to to find better cargo.

We may believe we have the vision, but like Yali, we don't quite have the new mind map to comprehend the learning required to acknowledge the subtlety of the new world we are entering. We must recognize our learning disability before we, too, can develop a global vision to interpret opportunity.

We must never forget that we all once started out from the same "tribal place" as Yali. To forget that archetypal world of our ancestors is to be disconnected from the stewardship of the earth that we share. We must keep this moral vision alive as we develop a future together.

Lesson learned: We need to keep one eye on our traditions and one eye on the future.

THE 20/20 LEADERSHIP PATH

ASSESSMENT OF OPPORTUNITY

Much change means a great opportunity for learning.

But we have grown overly dependent on institutions and institutional thinking to solve our social and economic problems. We desperately need leadership that values learning. We need to put people first.

We need a fundamental shift in our thinking to grasp the deeper meaning of learning. We need "institutes of leadership and imagination," not just of science and technology. Individuals and organizations have to relearn what learning is all about. Real learning is at the heart of being human. Through learning we re-create our universe; we do what we have seldom done before: We reenvision and reroute our purpose in the world, and in so doing, we extend our capacity to serve.

Everyone wants to leave his or her "mark" in life. One doctor in Southern California has a wall for children to "leave their mark." Noted psychoanalyst Erik Erikson lists "generativity" as a critical stage in all our lives. The need to be part of the generative process of life is true for each person, whether that process means having a child, writing a book, or planting a tree.

Imagination *does* rule our learning. Cliff Hakim, author of *We Are All Self-Employed: A New Social Contract Affecting Every Worker and Organization,* sees a better future for American workers, but only if they are willing to continue to learn and change. He encourages individuals and organizations to see themselves on a journey that is filled with adventure and responsibility: "Now, more than ever, we need to stretch our imaginations and open our minds to new questions and unexpected obstacles. We all have a responsibility to, first, know ourselves, and, second, add value in some way—in our way—to the world, despite the obstacles."

This is a new assessment of opportunity—the opportunity to recognize that we all are leaders. The beginning of leadership is self-knowledge. That is why our challenge is to learn how to "Know thyself."

Peter Drucker reminds us that self-renewal is found not outside the individual but *within.* Unfortunately many of us, as well as our organizations, do not look within, so do not know ourselves. We focus so exclusively on rational thinking and teaching methods that we exclude other sources of information and intuition. As we leave the industrial era for the information age, we need to replace our old ways of learning and thinking. At the root of change is the mind.

During the industrial age we needed information about production. We used rational thinking to find solutions to business problems, while government and education focused on argument in place of finding solutions. Intellectual and social capital—the knowledge, wisdom, and people in our communities—is the currency of the future. In the postcapitalist economy it is knowledge that brings the cash. In a system driven by knowledge wealth will be generated by superior performers who deliver much more than average performers. These are the people who have the wisdom to change.

Learning in the new workplace must now include valuing new inner-core competencies, the competencies of the knowledge worker. These competencies include congruent thinking, seamless learning, conceptual research and development, emotional intelligence, innovation, and creativity. This hemisphere connects with rational thinking to provide a powerful mind map and a higher vision.

It is important to realize the limitations of the rational corporate mind. The university and college management curriculum has been blinkered by the scientific vial of rationalism and by overdependence on using one hemisphere of the brain. As a result, we have developed specialized management professionals who lack the core "inner competencies" required for "learning across the organization."

This becomes apparent when we contrast our learning myopia with the Japanese experience as outlined by Eamonn Fingleton: "Since the mid-1980s I.B.M. has got 'lean and mean' by eliminating 150,000 people from its workforce: Hitachi has hired 5,000 people and become the world's largest high-tech company. Even with Japanese labor costs so high, companies like I.B.M., Boeing, Xerox, and Apple increased their purchases from Japan in the early 1990s; they couldn't find the components at home." The rational mind has valued only the mathematical solution.

The issue at stake for "learning across the organization" is the question of a wider vision of what we value. Is what we value about work simply profit? If we have no reverence for intellectual and social capital and no commitment to what we leave future generations, what are the essence and spirit of the moral imperative that motivates us?

On our journey to servant leadership, we are undergoing a time of metanoia, of turning around old thinking and slaying the old ideological dragon with a philosophical value lance. The death of old thinking is essential for the rebirth of common sense, visionary leadership, and the resurrection of the spirit of learning that is founded on a holistic value path. From our metanoia of learning, the knowledge worker will be reborn—from the inside out.

The major paradigm shift in learning took place in the seventeenth century with the rise of the scientific-rational worldview. It shifted again with Frederick Winslow Taylor (1856–1915), best known as the father of the industrial workplace. According to Peter Drucker, Taylor's "Scientific Management" theory has been poorly understood. As we do with many things in life, we have taken only part of his thinking, the quantitative, and ignored the intuitive. For Taylor wrote about a "Fourth Principle," by which he demanded that work study be done in consultation, if not in partnership, with the worker. Radical for its time, Taylor's thinking brought about a mental shift in the way of learning to do business. It enabled the United States—the "New World"—to train people in a few months, compared with the European "Old World" mindset, whose job-specific apprenticeship system took three to six years.

Taylor's theory represented a learning paradigm that showed that trained people have the potential for self-development. It was an early crude example of harnessing intellectual and social capital. The challenge at the mental crossroads of today and tomorrow is in *learning how to apply knowledge to knowledge.* What we mean by this is that knowledge in an organization creates the future. Why? Because the current knowledge will be the foundation for the future thinking that will give the organization the products or services that will be invented. Knowledge building on knowledge is the recipe for cooking up new ideas, products, and services. Our fourth pillar of learning does precisely that: It puts the knowledge worker first in the learning equation.

Tony Buzan in *The Mind Map* makes observations on mental development that provide for sobering reading at the parting of the industrial and postmodern mindsets. He states that for the first time in its 3.5-million-year history, human intelligence has learned how to understand, analyze, and nurture itself. Now it can begin to apply intelligence to intelligence and develop new and creative ways of thinking that are more flexible than the traditional models of thought currently used in the world. The cumulative effects of these quantum leaps are just now looming on the horizon.

The visionary leadership value path for 20/20 vision mandates that we rebuild the temple of learning focused on both organizational and community well-being. The architecture of this archetypal temple is at the center of healthy community, economic vitality, and sustainable development. To build this temple will require the whole community working together, the thinking of government, business, and education in a partnership for change.

Measuring the Costs

Change we must, for the costs of *not* changing are far too high.

If we stop to measure the costs of learning and conducting business the old way, we will see that these costs cannot be sustained without increasing social and economic crises. In the early days of the United States, the rugged individualist was the archetypal hero and myth to learn to live by. In a series of extraordinary articles on reinventing the individual, the organization, and the community for citizenship, the *Dallas Morning News* on the Internet described the shift from rugged individualism—what Dr. Amitai Etzioni, professor of sociology at George Washington University, would argue was saddling up the horses and riding off into the sunset—to the recapturing of the impulse to form communities, which is as old as the pioneers. As Etzioni contends "You don't circle the wagons when you have just one wagon." Today's "one-wagon organizations" are compelled, for survival and ethical reasons, to relearn that lesson. In essence we're new pilgrims. We all arrived on different boats to find a better land. We must recognize now that "we're all in the same boat together."

Shifting to learning this mindset is hard to do.

Ancient wisdom grounded in common sense is the value-added mental tools of the knowledge worker. The costs of not accepting the challenge and realization—that we are spiritual beings having a human experience—can be measured in hard numbers like lost profits, absenteeism, drug addiction, and the disintegration of the family and community. A comprehensive examination of one hundred studies on the impact of innovative workplace practices on corporate financial results by the U.S. Labor Department, conducted by researchers at the Harvard and Wharton business schools in partnership with Ernst & Young's management consulting firm, showed that investing in best practices in the workplace correlates directly with the organization's financial results. Indeed, Labor Secretary Robert

Reich often preaches that employees should be regarded as "assets to be developed, rather than as costs to be cut."

In contrast, companies that have begun to transform themselves into learning organizations are achieving better results. For instance, the Cigna Corporation of Philadelphia turned its property and casualty division's business loss of $251 million into an $87 million profit in just twelve months. The key? Realizing that while making operations efficient is critical, learning to make more knowledgeable choices is central to achieving results.

The question is: Are our educational institutions in their present form ready for this learning challenge to support a vastly different organizational reality? Walter Wriston, a former chairman of Citibank, once said that the job of management is to create wealth, not to allocate shortages. You don't shrink yourself to greatness! Our educational institutions seem to have been using a different strategic map. Carol A. Twigg, in an essay titled "Toward a National Learning Infrastructure: Navigating the Transition," makes these observations:

> Without creative approaches to the cost-quality-access nexus, our colleges and universities will continue to flounder. We need a better system of learning to enable students to acquire knowledge. It is time to turn our attention to creating something new. It is time to move beyond the walls of our individual colleges and universities to join forces with other institutions, with corporations and with public policy makers to revitalize American higher education. Together, we can create wealth; together we can create a national learning infrastructure that will serve the learning needs of our nation as we enter the twenty-first century.

By not taking this bold action for rethinking our learning strategies, we will continue to create untold stress and mental anguish for many in our changing workplaces. In one of our workshops a vice-president with forty years' service in the manufacturing sector shared the sense of hopelessness that he felt in a spiritless workplace. He told us, "Things have become so bad around here that the Resurrection now happens at four-thirty each day when everyone goes home!" David Noer, an expert in organizational behavior at the Center for Creative Leadership in Greensboro, North Carolina, calls the misery of those left clinging to the big fish "survivor sickness." As Noer says, "No one knows for sure how many executives suffer from it. Companies aware of the problem in their midst are not eager to talk about it. But a striking increase in the number of disability claims for mental and nervous illness may be an indicator."

We pay a price when corporate loyalty, values, memory, and skills walk out the door. "There is, indeed, a price for broken employee morale and shattered loyalty. . . . There is also a price for lost skills. By eliminating middle managers who once trained workers . . . manufacturers now pay five times what it cost to train new workers in 1985. . . . The training costs have jumped from $2,000 to $10,000 (U.S.)." Observes Daniel Yankelovich, the public opinion scholar whose organization recently completed a survey of top executives on the tactics of reorganization: "Most managements don't have as firm a hand on the human aspects of restructuring as they do on finance and technology. That shortcoming can wind up costing employers greatly in lost talent and lower sales."

WHAT DO WE NEED TO LEARN?

- We must learn that business is a moral act, a cultural expression of self-worth.
- We must learn that leadership is about stewardship guided by a leadership value path.
- We must learn that organization is about good governance, not simply management.
- We must learn to listen to the voice of the people, the bearers of our future.
- We must learn to promote the development of the human individual.
- We must learn that visionary leadership is found in the depths of our being.
- We must learn that leadership is based upon participation and anticipation.

- We must learn that learning is a leadership principle of duty that never ends.
- We must learn to create visionary centers for dialogue on alternative futures.
- We must learn to include the imaginations of our younger generations.
- We must learn that a new clear thinking is indispensable for our future.
- We must learn that only a new spiritual-economic path can sustain our organizations.
- We must learn to value our citizenship both locally and globally.
- We must learn to create human organizations and communities.
- We must learn to integrate civility, trust, honesty, and loyalty.
- We must learn to appreciate our similarities, not just our differences.
- We must learn to demand more accountability from those with the privilege of leadership.
- We must learn to create a learning consciousness in our educational systems.
- We must learn to celebrate what *can* be, not just what is as a shared vision.

The visionary leader on the path to learning will measure the costs of the current methods of learning as appropriate to developing a holistic sense of business. We see this consciousness arising in such fields as management, environment, and health care. We're seeing this new consciousness because the old way is not working. The old way presents simplistic solutions to complex problems. A better way is to see the whole vision as our decision-making map both shrinks and expands. We need a new vision of both local and global community.

Key questions at this learning crossroads are: How many institutions can stake a claim on an untapped mental resource that they may have been using as a landfill? What kinds of learning are we trusting to build the learning organization? Whom are we trusting to shape learning in our institutions to set free a spirit of enterprise?

Learning to travel on the leadership value path strengthens organizational well-being, which in turn mentors new meaning in a learning organization. We *can* think and learn beyond our culture. Our experience is that our mental maps are shaped partly by culture—which is irrational—and this in turn enables some people to think that their irrational actions are rational in that context. Our mental maps are like icebergs: nine tenths in the unconscious and one tenth in the light of consciousness. It is important, during the change process, not to be like the *Titanic* but to keep all hands on deck, so that the change process is not driven by hubris and sunk by the organizational iceberg.

Our learning today needs to be synchronistic. Synchronicity is letting go. Synchronicity is letting things happen. Synchronicity is seizing the moment.

Why is it that we think that strategic planning is the only way to accomplish something? Why is it that we don't see that strategic insight, such as being open and seizing the moment, can allow even greater things to happen? Strategy and planning don't happen in a linear way. Synchronicity lets the spirit of enterprise take charge.

An example of synchronicity's achieving a goal would be the interplay and unexpected outcomes of being open to the best thinking from both the rational and the intuitive. One could combine two different but valuable, mental paradigms to create a seamless learning experience that integrates knowledge from different perspectives.

As we come face-to-face with our own limiting economic ideology, we need to learn to build relationships, share information, and create values for a world that needs cooperation, not always conflict. Edward Hall argues there are two related crises in the world that we must come to terms with if we are to survive as a species: (1) the environmental crisis and (2) the crisis of humankind's relationships to one another. For Hall, both crises are lethal and can be solved only in relation to each other. If we don't work at them, technology and technological solutions will not solve them for us. He remarks, "There are no technical solutions to most of the problems confronting human beings." The core values we hold guide our destinies. In a community of nations we must focus on the core humanity that unites us. Without this focus the center will not hold, and like our cities, we journey, mentally and physically, to a "suburbia of the mind."

Harvesting the Benefits

We reap what we sow. We are now reaping the "benefits" of previous solutions. The cost is apparent.

To change directions demands passionate archetypal energy.

In order to achieve enduring success, we must transcend the intellectual barriers imposed by our institutions, our philosophies, and our cultures—barriers that have, in many cases, stopped our learning. We must undergo nothing less than an inner Copernican revolution of the mind map. Like Copernicus, we need to determine who is revolving around what. Like Copernicus, we must realize that we are not the center of the world.

In the place of our self-centeredness, we must cultivate a new attitude, an attitude of *servant* and *leader*. Attitudes are navigators for our value system. They give us permission to act a certain way. They shape our decisions, and they provide the windows of opportunity to transform individual and institutional thinking.

Leadership attitudes can affect the health of the organization for good or for bad. Attitudes are analogous to oxygen: They help the corporate body breathe to help achieve a positive or negative shared vision. It could be argued that there is a direct correlation between a leader's attitudes and organizational performance. Research by Stanford business professors James C. Collins and Jerry I. Porras mentioned previously found that the elements in the success of vision-driven companies were (1) clearly articulated core values and (2) a mission, or reason for being. These elements project themselves into attitudes that in turn shape actions.

It is always easier to be ethical and take the high road when times are going well, but attitudes, which shape vision—the "top line"—are rewarded on the bottom line, even in tough times. In 1982 James Burke, then chief executive of Johnson & Johnson, put together a list of major companies, such as J&J, Coca-Cola, Gerber, IBM, Deere, Kodak, 3M, Xerox, JC Penney, and Pitney Bowes, that paid a lot of attention to ethical standards. Over a forty-year period, from 1950 to 1990, the market value of this group grew at 11.3 percent annually. The growth rate for the Dow Jones industrials as a whole was 6.2 percent a year over the same period. These companies clearly gained from their attitude toward learning. Their return could be measured in terms of ROIR (return on integrity in relationships), as well as ROI.

The success of ROIR over blind ROI is illustrated by Levi Strauss & Co., which halted production in Myanmar and China because of concern about systemic labor inequities, even though doing so cost it $40 million. Levi Strauss attempts to live up to a lofty vision of how to run a modern corporation, a vision that is a combination of traditional liberal idealism with a set of management precepts straight out of the nineties zeitgeist of inclusion and "empowerment." Chairman and CEO Robert D. Haas calls this management approach "responsible commercial success." How financially successful is this responsible organization? The numbers are stunning. After a $1.6 billion leveraged buyout in 1985, record sales and earnings for five of the six years between 1987 and 1993 culminated in a 36 percent rise in profits in 1993, to $492 million on sales of $5.9 billion. And Morgan Stanley & Company estimated that the stock had appreciated 1,300 percent!

Michael Thompson, director of compensation for The Hay Group, suggests that core competencies are what drive performance change. A new leadership path is a core "inner competency" for the learning required to transform the organization into a worth place. Hay research confirms that superior performers do things differently. They work at a higher level of performance. In the learning organization, with a strong shared leadership culture, the communication is clear: Superior performance is achieved when you align your vision and your thinking with others on those few inner-core competencies that differentiate performance.

Wanting to learn to change is the first step on the journey. Archetypal learning can help release a new spirit of enterprise.

It is like a prism that illuminates and throws light where there is a will to change. It avoids stereotypical formulas and off-the-shelf solutions. It enables people in organizations to develop their unique collective voice in order to write their own winning stories. Like all good stories, it starts with "once upon a time" (yesterday)—that is, an assessment of the values they started out with. It comes face-to-face with "slaying the dragon" (today)—that is, the critical issues we must face together—and continues with the vision quest of all we can be (future)—that is, becoming servant-leaders.

Take a moment to visualize what life would be like if you were a visionary leader. Visualize what a learning organization can really achieve. Visualize what a learning community can really become. Visualize what a learning family can become.

To inspire your personal vision of the future, think of geese in flight formation. Their powerful V formation is an archetypal vision of a natural learning organization on a spirit-filled journey. From generation to generation geese have imprinted the thinking and action required for group survival. Let's hope that the human primate has the sense to do the same.

THE PATH OF THE ANCIENTS

"Know Thyself"

It is time to reconnect with our learning traditions. Like the ancients, we can move forward only through learning "Know thyself." It is time to move forward with the ancient Greeks.

Every generation learns to reinvent its own future through the prism of its cultural worldview. The ancient wisdom here is this: So does the modern organization.

"Knowing thyself" and what mental temple we are worshiping at is a new learning journey for each generation. "Knowing thyself" can be achieved, as it was in the past, only by taking time to learn a vision that connects the head, heart, and spirit. Its integrity is lived by taking responsibility for one's actions.

For Socrates, who stated that the unexamined life is not worth living, going aimlessly through life was a waste. In this century Carl Jung meant something similar when he said that to go through life and not to have lived your vocation, myth, or purpose is to have failed life's most important requirement: becoming all that you can be. It really didn't matter what other objectives a person had in mind. The most important task is individuation. In the modern organization it is the learning journey well done; it is achieving transformation.

If we make what we have been calling the four P's—prestige, persona, power, profits—our "god," we are sunk. Those are not the central keys to a life well lived. For Socrates, to miss on self-knowing was to miss the purpose of the whole human journey.

Perhaps the best measuring stick of a life is to judge ourselves by what we have left undone and not really by what we have done. What is it that we still have to do, or to become, in order to be faithful to *ourselves*? If we put off those vital tasks, we may be successful in the eyes of the world, or in business, but we will have missed our core learning responsibility.

To "Know thyself" is the basic psychological building block of life, a sort of spiritual DNA. The biological sciences tell us that while each of us is born with an established DNA identity code we can still do much to work with and influence the process so that our immune systems are working at their optimum. Just as our actual biological cells are constantly changing, so also are our personal DNA codes.

The question is: How is change happening for you? Is it positive, in terms of achieving well-being, or is it negative, in terms of illness? While each of us can be excused for not taking full charge of our actual DNA codes—since nature dictates the ground rules—this reality does not fully apply when it comes to our psychological DNA codes and the change process. We have within us the capacity to take charge and make a difference.

Actually it is more accurate to say that our *attitude* takes charge. It is the navigator for our life. Corinne McLaughlin and Gordon Davidson compare our thoughts to concentrated images held on a piece of movie film. When we shine our light of consciousness through them, the images are projected onto the screen of our lives. The Jewish Book of Proverbs describes the matter this way: "What a man thinks within himself, so is he."

The eye is the window of the soul. It looks out but it also looks in. It especially looks out from within! It's not what goes into someone that defiles that person, said Jesus, but what comes out. It's not what goes into a person's mouth that makes the person unclean, but what comes out.

The computer acronym GIGO (garbage in, garbage out) applies here. If we have garbage in our personal system, that is what we get out of it. Many people and organizations need to do an "inner garbage pickup." We can just dump it, but if we do, we eventually create an environmental and pollution problem. Joanna Macy encourages people to find their own "inner toxic waste," as she calls it, so that they don't contaminate everything and everyone else.

Similarly, when individuals and managers dump their personal, unprocessed psychological garbage onto others—through abuse or negative power and control—a psychological and spiritual pollution problem results. Robert F. Allen and Charlotte Kraft describe this context of our work environment as the "organizational unconscious" (i.e., the corporate culture) that is sick and infected. Our name for this same phenomenon is "the symbolic elephant in the boardroom." Everyone knows the elephant is there; it is just too big to miss. But no one wants to admit to its presence, and no one definitely wants to admit to its waste!

This symbolic elephant in the boardroom is composed of unspoken assumptions in the corporate culture; it's the inner game. In our workshops we ask individuals to list their organizations' unspoken assumptions about money, employees, management, security, change, future, and so on. The feedback usually identifies an incredible "psychological shadow" that, while not visible to the naked eye, is definitely felt by all.

Carl Jung (1875–1961) coined the term *shadow* to refer to that side of ourselves, mostly unconscious, that contains the positive as well as the negative elements of our personalities. The key for directing shadow energy is our consciousness, our awareness of the choices we have. Our attitude is its navigator. Without the ability to choose, we would be at the mercy of the shadow forces within us. Jung said that the encounter with our shadow is a required moral challenge if we are to grow as people. Whether we rise to that essential challenge is something each individual, organization, and community has to come to grips with.

For the ancient Athenians, this challenge preoccupied them in their *philosophia* or "love of wisdom." They had tremendous insight into human nature and knew that "the spirit indeed is willing, but the flesh is weak" and "the best laid schemes o' mice and men" often go awry. Many projects, activities, and hopes start out with the best of intentions and ideals, but if the critical dimension of the shadow of these projects, activities, and hopes is ignored or repressed, they may harbor disastrous, even evil, consequences. There are many examples in history and in organizational life to show this Jekyll-Hyde characteristic of human nature.

The interesting thing about our shadows (individual, organizational, community, national) is that whether they are positive or negative, we tend to recoil at first from facing them. We are reluctant because facing our shadows means dealing with our potential: We have a choice now to become all that we can become. In the case of the positive shadow challenge, this would mean taking active steps to build something of value: either some tangible product, or something less tangible, but just as real, like character. In the case of the negative shadow challenge, this would mean taking active steps to transform or cut off a negative impulse that would harm us or others.

The organizational positive shadow is the potential that can be freed up for employees to accomplish goals. Visionary leaders constellate this positive shadow potential in their organizations when they create a learning organization. It will mean freeing up the spirit of enterprise, acknowledging the great things that can be accomplished, and even they know, as Robert Frost points out, there are still "miles and miles to go." They don't give up but keep on the journey to reach their destination. Their vision sustains them on the journey.

Looking at GIGO from the value path perspective helps us learn to recognize the "garbage" we can put "in from within"—that is, the self-generated inner garbage that builds up because our inner cores may not be healthy or well. This is precisely the garbage that will come out. This thinking explains why ethics reflect our behavioral codes whereas values reflect our inner codes and why the behavioral code is such a major clue to the personal and organizational inner code. We cannot say, for instance, "There goes a value," but we can say, "A person or organization that acts in such and such a manner [behavioral code] is reflecting such and such a value [inner code]."

Thousands of years ago the ancient metaphysician Hermes Trismegistus described this inner-and-outer phenomenon in what has become known as the Law of Correspondences: "As below, so above; as above, so below." It is also what Socrates meant when he said, "There is no disease of the body apart from the mind." Goethe confirmed this as well when he wrote, "What is within—the idea—is also without," and Jung continued this ancient insight by stating that the inner and the outer are the same.

Our task is to make sure our "light" (of consciousness) is as clean and clear as possible. Our eye must not be diseased; otherwise we won't have 20/20 vision. The only way to do that is through the learning of "Know thyself." There is no other way. We may try to skirt this issue, avoid it for a long time, run scared of it, but in the end we must face ourselves. Senator J. William Fulbright remarked one time that we might back off from this task of knowing ourselves because we might be frightened by the possibilities revealed in the self-examination. Courage is always required for the human journey.

The examined life is worth living. It is the only life worth living.

The conclusion for each of us therefore is that in this learning process called life, living is *the* learning program. Educational psychologists even describe learning as change. Change and learning are hence interrelated. The quality of our "studenthood" rests directly on our acquiescence in this process—willingly, as Jung describes it, or as a pig to the slaughter—which in turn rests on our attitude, our disposition, in calibrating our personal DNA value path codes.

Mens Sana in Corpore Sano

Like the ancient Greeks, we must see the wisdom in learning that a healthy mind needs a healthy body. The Roman rhetorician and satirical poet Juvenal summed up the Greek ideal that achieves a balanced life in this sentence: *Orandum est ut sit mens sana in corpore sano* (your prayer must be for a sound mind in a sound body).

The Greeks valued not only learning to strengthen the mind but also athletics to strengthen the body. They connected mind and body. Five hundred years before Christ a little town named Athens took the then-known world by storm by its art and thinking and shaped what was to become our Western world in its mind and spirit. Today we think differently because of Athens. Athenians accomplished this magnificence of soul and spirit even though all around them was a brutal and cruel world. They survived in those tumultuous times because, as classicist Edith Hamilton puts it, "In that black and fierce world a little center of white-hot spiritual energy was at work."

Their love of learning and their search for wisdom made the Athenians free. Other peoples living in countries around Athens were not free. The Athenians were free because they learned to be free interiorly. School for them was leisure because it was a process of freeing them up. A person with interior freedom philosophized—or loved wisdom—and spent time in thinking and finding out about things. The Greeks also played all kinds of games. They loved life, and their time at play showed that. As Hamilton says, "Wretched people, toiling people, do not play." Neither, writes Hamilton, were these Athenians "victims of depression." For the Greeks, mind and spirit met on equal terms.

For today's organizations *mens sana in corpore sano* means seeing that each organization is a living organism that is dependent on the connection between head and body. A healthy mind (corporate thinking) and a healthy body (corporate well-being) make for a healthy "balance sheet." As Hamilton observes,

> "To free up, to let go, to meet the top line," and "to get up to business" might seem strange expressions to the modern ear. The Greeks would have been entirely at ease with these sentiments because for them, freedom meant everything. Because a person was free, a person could create. Freedom allowed thinking. "Fundamental to everything the Greeks achieved was their conviction that good for humanity was possible only if men were free, body, mind, and spirit, and if each man limited his own freedom."

The Greeks believed that self-imposed limits to their freedom were necessary. Freedom was not license to do what you wanted. They obeyed the inner and outer law because they were *willing* to do so. This was not a forced obedience but, rather, as Hamilton says, "the basic condition of freedom for men living together, obedience to kindness and compassion and unselfishness and all the long list of qualities without which life would be intolerable. . . . The limits to action established by law were a mere nothing compared to the limits established by a man's free choice."

The Athenian ideal was captured by their word *sophrosuné*. It is often translated as "self-control," but the real thrust of the word was the spirit behind the two great Delpic sayings "Know thyself" and "Nothing in excess." In practice this meant that the "ideal Greek" would not be arrogant, insolent, exhibiting machismo, or drawing attention to himself. Such a person would not do things in excess but rather would obey the inner laws of harmony and proportion. It is interesting to reflect on the modern problem we have with "workaholism" and the imbalance thus entailed. We have strayed far from the Greek ideal.

Attentiveness to "the golden mean" was critical since the fruits of freedom—energy and a spirit of life—needed appropriate controls for a disciplined spirit. In 1776, when James Madison declared that people have the capacity for self-government, he was being very Athenian-like in his sentiment. Thucydides reports Pericles as saying, "The individual can be trusted. Let him alone." Such a balanced spirit of enterprise, from Athens to America, is what frees up people, pride, and profits.

The archetype of the living organism that we are presenting, just as for the Greeks, requires a healthy mind in a healthy body to survive and grow. Our present organization is suffering from corporate anorexia: The body is ill, and the mind is not responding. If there is a response, it is a technological solution to a relationship issue. Yet, machines have not liberated us except by removing people from the workplace. This approach is an extension of industrial thinking. Organizations find solutions for making profits without seeing the cost to the required contextual wholeness and to the communities they depend on. Diagnosis of the restructured, right-sized, reengineered, total quality, just-in-time, "new improved," "have it your way" workplace only reinforces this verdict. If we are truly honest with ourselves, we have to admit that the contemporary work context—what we call the spirit-oxygen context—is not healthy for many. What companies need to see is that return on integrity in relationships is a better long-term strategy to build people, pride, and profit.

Just as the physical architecture directly affects the way we learn and feel about ourselves, so our mental architecture directly strengthens or weakens what we are building. To "Know thyself," we must also learn to know how important our mental architecture is to our mental health. The ancients built physical architecture as a manifestation of what they valued; places like the Acropolis were sacred. Today we can see this learning journey expressed in the architecture of new republics, such as the Lincoln Memorial and the Capitol Building. These archetypal symbols are a legacy to a time when leadership had the spirit to build them. The Acropolis was, and is, a place where spirit and oxygen flow. It provides an image that connects us to our classical roots. It also provides an image of the architecture that we can carry around in our heads to rebuild today's organization so that spirit and oxygen can flow there as well.

Because we don't have the right archetypal architecture to shape a higher vision, the chemistry of our thinking is affecting the rest of the corporate body. The difference between health and illness is often the meaning attributed to an uncertain situation and how we respond. Our thinking affects the chemical messages the brain sends the body. Robert Frost remarks, "The reason that worry kills more people than work is that more people worry than work." Leadership thinking from the organizational "head" likewise sends messages that strengthen or weaken the corporate "body." Our immune systems are dramatically affected by how we think, by how we feel, and by the quality of our relationships.

In applying an archetypal concept of a healthy mind and a healthy body to the workplace, Martin R. Weisbord, in *Productive Workplaces*, reminds us that productive workplaces enable employees to learn and grow and, at the same time, empower them to improve organizational performance. That's because, as Weisbord points out, this new way of thinking, this new bottom line, is fueled by dignity, meaning, and community in work. The legitimacy of these human factors is being recognized by more and more organizations. Federal Express, Wal-Mart, and Southwest Airlines are good examples of these human value factors at work and with customers. But today's leaders may not necessarily be tomorrow's if they stop learning. Continuous improvement and attentiveness to the task at hand are ongoing requirements. Weisbord is convinced, as we are, that in order to lower costs, develop higher quality, and maintain more satisfied customers, we need to increase dignity, meaning, and community in the workplace. Organizations need to learn that to come of age means to "Know thyself."

For organizations to shift from ROI to ROIR will require that they "move forward with the ancient Greeks." *Mens sana in corpore sano* was truly a demanding standard of excellence for the Greeks. It meant balancing inner and outer, reflection with action, mind with body, and freedom with self-limits. This was the path to wholeness, to integrity. Our view of ROIR (return on integrity in relationships) is very much in the Athenian tradition. It's the need for us to recenter ourselves (metanoia) to return to the path of wholeness if we are to achieve excellence.

The roots of the word *integrity* are illuminating for our purposes here. Integrity contains such images as wholeness, completeness, the uncorrupted state, entirety, health, and soundness. We carry these images over when we talk about being "safe and sound." In organizations, when people say they have their "bases covered," or "all their ducks lined up," or "all their planets in a row," or "all hands on deck," whether they know it or not, they are capturing what the ancients meant by *integrity*. A "return on integrity," then, is a return to our roots of wholeness where both mind and body work in harmony. This requires balance, freedom, and, above all, the pursuit and love of wisdom. And this ideal is accomplished in relationships: to ourselves, to others, and to the world around us. Only then will the fullness and joy of "doing more with more" enable our modern organizations not only to celebrate the people who work there but also, like the ancients, to accomplish something of beauty in their achievements.

The flowering of ancient Greek thinking withered after the fall of Athens. The Greek way of balance, interiority, reflecting, *philosophia* (love of wisdom), and the only security being in "things not seen" eventually disappeared, and in its place, four hundred years later, the efficiency of the Roman way became established. The modern world is very much "Roman" in its ethic. If the Greek way represented the creative life, the Roman way represented the organized life. Hence it is that in modern management books, the "Roman" Catholic Church is listed as one historical example of sound organizational principles.

For the Greeks, independence in thinking and in freedom was sacred; thus, mind and spirit were indispensable. For the Romans, strength was found in unity; thus, will and power were fundamental. If the Greek way led to freedom, the Roman way led to structure. Obedience for the Greeks was the inner demand to search for truth and to love wisdom. This was not an easy journey, for excellence must be "labored for," as Aristotle pointed out. Virtue was also its own reward. Obedience for the Roman was the external deference to authority and disciplined control. Unquestioning obedience—or being a "company person"—was never a part of the Athenian ideal. For the Romans, anyone different was suspect; doing what you were told as a citizen was your job.

If the Greeks thought of human nature as participating in the divine, the Romans thought of it as thoroughly evil. Socrates believed, as did Abraham Maslow in the twentieth century, that we are essentially good with "a spark of the divine light that could be kindled into a flame." The Greeks never admitted the gladiatorial games, as the Romans did later. Socrates was the only Athenian ever put to death for his opinions; the Romans crucified people who disagreed with them. According to Alfred Whitehead, the great philosopher and mathematician, when the Greek Archimedes was killed by a Roman soldier, from a symbolic point of view, the world changed. The Greeks, who were theoretical, abstract, logical, the mediators of ideas, were now to be superseded by the practical, pragmatic Romans. Action and force were to be valued over ideas and concepts. The world indeed had changed. Practicality was to be the order of the day. Minor technical details of engineering, not innovation, as with the Greeks, were to be the promise of the Romans. Unlike the Greeks, who were the dreamers and logicians, the Romans would not give the world new points of view. Whitehead writes, "No Roman lost his life because he was absorbed in the contemplation of a mathematical diagram!"

Modern organizations would do well to reflect on Greek and Roman ways as they begin to set up the learning required to shift mindsets. The entrenched Romanization of our organizations is now learning to face its "shadow side" as it changes to meet the challenges ahead. The "Roman" ways of hierarchy, order, efficiency, structure, command, obedience, uniformity, etc. are giving way to the ancient Greek ways of creativity, spontaneity, self-direction, thinking, imagination, dialogue, and inspiration. We must pause before the magnitude of Greek thinking and the humility the Greeks showed in their search for truth. Balance, wisdom, and visionary leadership are needed more than ever.

Inward Bound

Outward Bound is an inward-bound learning experience.

Today learning organizations are investing in team building using experimental programs such as Outward Bound. The Outward Bound concept evolved from the urgent need to rebuild self-confidence for those who had been torpedoed at sea during the Second World War. Archetypally many of us today also feel as if we have been torpedoed and left to struggle in the constant waves of change.

Thinking fundamentally (inward bound) and acting realistically (outward bound) can be done only by what the Book of Proverbs calls turning our ear to wisdom and applying our heart to understanding. When Solomon was called to be king, he prayed that he would be given *lebh shomea* (a listening heart). Great healing moments in one's personal life and in world history are never really accidents. They are the fruit of *lebh shomea*, of the willingness of the soul to turn inward to the wellspring. The Book of Proverbs recognizes the centrality of the heart in human affairs when it counsels, "Listen, my son, and be wise, and keep your heart on the right path." Further: "As water reflects a face, so a man's heart reflects the man."

The hope we have for the future is not a question of economics or politics but a realignment of all of our thinking. It's a question of attitudes. Transformation always starts from within. Socrates' teaching, "Know thyself," has been echoed by many others throughout the ages. Buddha also encouraged his followers to look within; Jesus counseled that the kingdom of God is within; the Hindu Upanishads remind us that we know the universe by understanding the self; and Muhammad pointed out that by knowing ourselves, we touch eternity.

The question for us now is: Do we have the courage to go inward to take the first step to utilize the critically necessary elements that sustain us all in times of change and adversity? These critical elements are insight, courage, action.

In order to turn around and make the tough decision to go

forward, we must make the even tougher decision to go inward. Our reluctance usually comes from the challenge of facing those sides of ourselves that we would rather keep in the shadows. Carl Jung soberly reminds us that it was the face of our own shadow side that grinned at Western people from the other side of the Iron Curtain. Are we courageous enough to be "inward bound" and look at those sides of ourselves that we would rather leave hidden? History shows that we have not been very successful at this fundamental task. Yet history also shows the disastrous consequences of our *not* doing so. Instead of looking at countries as the enemy, we could learn to look at those "inner countries" within ourselves and our organizations. Turf wars are both internal and external manifestations of this thinking. The competition isn't always outside.

We can take the necessary action to let our organizations breathe, but unless that action has been aligned with the clean and clear process of right thinking—consciousness—we will build organizations designed for failure. For too long now individuals and organizations have taken only the "outward-bound" path to motivate people, pride, and profits. As the ancients knew, it is the inward-bound journey that opens hearts and minds and provides the oxygen and enthusiasm to build great organizations.

The *I Ching*, the ancient Chinese *Book of Changes*, in Hexagram 37, "The Family," emphasizes the central place of relationships in making great changes. "An old Chinese proverb says that if you want to correct the state, you must first correct the family; if you want to correct the family, you must first correct yourself." It starts in the mind. Shifting our thinking demands visionary leaders who have experienced the inward- and outward-bound journeys. *Washington Post* columnist William Raspberry has written: "We don't want ecclesiastics running the government. But we would, I think, welcome a return to government policies that, however secular, proceed from a belief that we are spiritual beings, not merely bundles of appetites." For Socrates, "True politics is first of all a state of soul." This is also true in the organization.

Being inward bound can globalize our mind. We must learn

to use both hemispheres in our learning and decision making. It was after studying the brain cell that Sir Charles Sherrington, a pioneer in neurophysiology, was moved to make a poetic statement: "The human brain is an enchanted loom where millions of flashing shuttles weave a dissolving pattern, always a meaningful pattern, though never an abiding one, a shifting harmony of sub-pattern. It is as if the Milky Way entered upon some cosmic dance." Although we cannot see it, each one of us is the universe. We all can become shining stars. Imagine the natural wisdom unleashed by focusing on understanding the gift of our mind as the prism for decision making. *Imagination does rule our universe.* We have the power to become what we imagine. Dreams are the path to reality.

As we enter the twenty-first century, we have the potential to see once again that the valued compass points of ancient learning are really the connectors for our human story. We are now reconnecting learning from everywhere as we become a global community.

Self-knowledge truly is the beginning of wisdom. Sharing that knowledge is the gift in serving. The fifth pillar in our archetypal journey is mentoring, a learning process that begins in serving others by passing on the valued traditions to the next generation.

PILLAR V

MENTORING

"They be blind leaders of the blind.
And if the blind lead the blind,
both shall fall into the ditch."

MATTHEW 15:14

IMAGINE THAT YOU ARE IN FLORENCE at the peak of the Italian Renaissance. You are in awe of the newfound spirit of learning and mentoring at the heart of the community. Indeed, you are inspired by the number of great thinkers involved in the daily process of visualizing, imagining, creating, learning, and mentoring new ways of seeing and expanding the world of opportunities.

We are the custodians of this inspirational legacy. But how does our thinking compare with such giants? What happened to our spirit of enterprise and passion for learning on the journey?

The great masters of the Renaissance understood the value of mentoring, a transfer of the gift of vision and inspiration and a learning process on the human journey. Benjamin Franklin said it best: "He that can't be counseled can't be helped." In today's organization, mentoring is in the work of the change leaders nurturing the learning team and breathing spirit and life into learning. Mentoring a better way starts from birth. For the fortunate individual it is the imprinted memory of the positive parent-child relationship that shapes self-worth. In the community it is in the action of good governance that encourages building healthy community.

Mentoring requires a shared vision of learning across the organization. Mentoring shifts the collective learning paradigm. It values independence and dependence for personal and organization growth.

The new organization requires a new learning process to develop team-based leadership. The new organization emphasizes the archetype of the living organism. Living organisms require healthy cells, what we, in our corporate work, call vision teams. These cells are the change agents for CELLS or creating effective leadership learning spirit. They are the organizational DNA that communicates ideas and information across the organization in order to transform thinking and create rapid change. Comprised of individuals from across the organization, these vision teams or CELLS are charged with incubating, migrating, and mentoring a 20/20 vision throughout the organization. Through discussion, facilitation, and enthusiasm, a vision team helps nurture a leadership culture and align organizational thinking to support a 20/20 vision that achieves enduring success in a constantly changing world. Like healthy biological cells, they give life and spirit to the organization. They listen and provide feedback to the center.

Changing always means facing the shadow or organizational unconscious. It also requires addressing factors such as corporate well-being, spirit, visioning, and the rerouting of learning away from the strategic to a holistic approach. The holistic approach recognizes that attitude and mindset are the key factors for transformation to a leadership position. Without these elements strategic planning is an oxymoron: It is neither strategic nor planning.

The vision teams that guide the transformation process are not dissimilar to the medieval guilds of artisans who assisted their masters to create the great works from one person's idea and imagination. An industry apprenticeship concept, the guild passed on the secrets and the art of learning of the practice of a specific craft. The guild valued the corporate memory as essential for sustaining organizational thinking. In a sense these were the original adult educators. The learning journey began with indentureship and loyalty to the master, followed by continuous learning of one's craft to become a journeyman. The final stage was to become a master. This recognized that the individual had completed the learning journey and mentoring process and had passed the test. He, too, could now start his own learning organization.

The weakness in the guild mentoring process was its blindness in refusing to accept thinking from outside its protective paradigm. In many ways this form of mentoring separated the workplace into protected jobs and skills and did not regard the organization as aligned to serving its community. New technologies eventually challenged this thinking and made many of these practices irrelevant. In the case of the printing industry these practices were passed on from father to son from the time of William Caxton until the 1970s. Many institutions of higher learning still function and mentor this paradigm and prepare graduates for a reality that no longer exists. With the rediscovery of the learning organization, we need an educational partnership to mentor the knowledge worker.

The Italian Renaissance provides an excellent historical example to measure our thinking about the "new" learning organization. Leonardo da Vinci, for example, observed that things grow, transform themselves, change, and then wither away. Nothing is constant. Da Vinci studied human phenomena in detail, and his observations convinced him rarely to bring his works to completion. His joy was in the process.

In many respects da Vinci's world is not that different from today's. In da Vinci's time Copernicus was discovering that the earth was not the center of the universe, and voyages to the New World were challenging the validity of existing mental maps. Today our universe seems to be changing again; our map is both expanding and contracting. We can't afford to go into the next millennium using nineteenth-century thinking patterns and learning models. Like the people of the Renaissance, we need dialogue to develop a flow of meaning and criticism for the creative tension and sparks that lead to reinventing excellence and leadership. We need a vision.

In Pillar IV we argued for a new way of learning to embrace visionary leadership. We must recognize that learning will take the individual, the organization, and the community on a four-stage journey through *crisis* (or crossroads), *test* (or threshold), *change* (or learning), and *return* (or incorporation).

The crisis (or crossroads) today is that organizational leaders have to go back to school. Our heads have been filled with the practice of management, but our hearts know little of the history or art of the craft. We haven't passed the major test yet. We have passing grades in the IQ skills, but we are failing in the EQ realm. North American management has been mesmerized by the scientific practice of management and has not learned that the art and craft of management can provide the needed balance.

The test (or threshold) that organizations are now facing is: Will they make it? Do they have a future? Many realize that the test here is to "smarten up" to become a learning organization.

Having passed the test and crossed the threshold into a learning organization, we now require the change (or learning) in a new attitude of mind and heart. Business needs to shift from self-absorption to a mental focus more closely aligned to serving the needs of all its interdependent planets—the individual, the organization, and the community.

To create such a change in learning, small mentoring teams like vision teams will need to incubate and mentor a spirit of enterprise at the impact of decision making, so that the return (or incorporation) stage of the journey can be completed. Loyalty, trust, and recognition for a job well done will be key factors in mentoring this new spirit of enterprise.

We have trimmed our sails too soon to ride the current storm of change. Superficial techniques won't be sufficient as the technological avalanche washes away our stumbling institutions. We need new models of mentoring that will liberate our thinking and expand our mental universe, so we can reinvent a yet unseen future of work, wealth, and well-being.

A higher vision requires higher learning. Pillar IV pointed out that all learning is initially an inward journey. Pillar V, mentoring, allows us to move outward and complete a process of organizational transformation.

THE 20/20 LEADERSHIP PATH

REFORMATION OF LEARNING

Our journey has taken us from hunter to farmer to industrialist. Today we need to take a fourth step and transform ourselves into knowledge workers. The term *knowledge worker* does not merely mean somebody who knows how technology works. It also means someone who understands the meaning and application of intellectual and emotional intelligence.

These skills are essential in the new structure of organization, which will be characterized by team-based cells that mentor one another as they interact with the visionary leader at the center. EQ skills will be central to the competencies required to flourish in teams.

REFORMATION OF LEARNING: THE 20/20 PARADIGM

Archetypal Pillar	Vision Team Mentoring	Leadership Lesson
Visioning	How people "see"	Go for the "top line"
Mapping	How people "think"	New clear thinking
Journeying	How people "imagine"	The joy of discovery
Learning	How people "change"	The gift of freedom
Mentoring	How people "grow"	Great expectations
Leading	How people "excel"	Going for the "gold"
Valuing	How people "serve"	"Attitude is everything"

Mentoring focuses our collective energies on a common purpose, a future worth going to. But our culture is obsessed with the pursuit of individualism, a highly dysfunctional journey! It's not worthy as an ideal in the face of adversity and unprecedented change. If we continue to operate on a "me first" paradigm, it will be difficult to mentor teams, alliances, partnering, and other collaborative approaches that will be so central to business success in the coming years. It will take a "reformation of learning" to change our focus and ensure that these collaborative skills spread throughout our culture.

The 20/20 vision is an age of cooperation. To thrive in it, we need to rementor a civilized mind and recapture reverence for our organizations and institutions. We need to reconnect with the great ideas of the Western world for our value compass and, at the same time, be open to the wisdom from the Eastern Hemisphere. Instead of "closing the American mind," we need to open it to new ideas. We need to look at learning as a benefit, not simply a cost.

Domtar Inc., a paper products company, created a learning culture when its former head of human resources, Claude Saillant, initiated a program with forty to forty-five employees from up and down and across the organization to unleash employee ideas and proposals. The model helped the company, previously very traditional and hierarchical, move away from that structure and mentor a team-based future.

Stan Jacobson, general manager of one Domtar division, says the program works only if the employees trust it. "If they don't trust that I'm really giving them the responsibility and the authority, and I don't trust they can make the decisions, this is never going to work." Domtar's mentoring is best summarized by Jacobson's thinking: "People have to see that what we've been saying we're living by. We don't want to have another flavor-of-the-month program."

The program succeeded at releasing new ideas, and it more than earned back its costs. Saillant saw the training not as a cost but as a capital investment. Including employee wages during the sessions, plus an investment of $1.5 million to $2 million, Domtar posted a return of at least $20 million! The secrets behind this profit were key ROIR factors: training, teams, trust.

Mentoring requires that we take learning seriously. It empowers employees' brains to free ideas that employees have often had for years. Suddenly people feel involved and believe that their insights have value. Tom Peters says that we are in an age when all the value comes from brains. Mentoring can be seen as a new form of "production," with wisdom as its product.

Group cultures such as Japan's never lost sight of the collective wisdom of mentoring. This group mentoring didn't start at the organizational door. In fact, it started in the community. Even today, as young people in certain Japanese towns come of age, they assemble and stand in front of the leader to accept the mantle of corporate and community citizenship. Both parties bow, with the leader welcoming them to their obligations.

What rituals and rights of citizenship do you have for coming of age in your community and organization?

Content with Learning

The goal of the visionary leader in the learning organization is to mentor a process of ongoing improvement that results in sustaining both wealth and well-being. This is content with learning. Turning this vision into a reality requires clear, precise, and simple communication so that everyone can see its connection to his or her responsibilities.

Outlined below, in simple language, is what this leadership communication would look and sound like so that you can start to turn the vision into a reality.

CONTENT WITH LEARNING: THE 20/20 PARADIGM

Archetypal Pillar	Mentoring Feature	Learning Benefit
Visioning	Creating hope	Faith in the future
Mapping	Globalizing the mind	Expanding opportunities
Journeying	Call of a higher vision	Personal discovery
Learning	Inner freedom	Wisdom to choose
Mentoring	Sharing experience	Empathy and gratitude
Leading	Insight and courage	Trust
Valuing	Integrity in relationships	Entrusting a future

Organizational value cables, attitudes, and shared values are powerful allies that can rapidly mentor learning and build global vision. Archetypally, cables "hook" the organization and ground its thinking. Intuit Inc., a leading developer of personal finance, small-business accounting, and tax preparation software, has "hooked" its vision to a site on the World Wide Web. Intuit's "Operating Values" site states that its employees not only want to satisfy the customer but want to "WOW" them as well. *WOW* means "creating customer enthusiasm and delight," the site says. "It means giving customers dramatically more value than they expect—whether measured by price, performance, quality, features, or service. We know we're succeeding when we inspire our customers to go out and tell others about our company."

To sustain this value impetus, says Intuit's Scott Cook, the decision making must rest with those closest to the customers. To do this requires an environment of openness, trust, communication, latitude to act. Intuit believes that people "come to work seeking to do great things." Hence Intuit's working environment frees up and fosters employees "to achieve even greater accomplishments."

Visionary leaders are mentors for us all. They are not a product of place or gender; they are those special people from anywhere who are right for any time. Just listen to the words of Konosuke Matsushita, a pioneering leader of Japanese and world industry: "Eighty years have passed since I became an apprentice at the age of nine. I have watched the world change, and through it all, I have accumulated a great deal of experience. No matter how chaotic the world may seem, I am convinced that one can improve his management techniques and make his business prosper."

Great thinking and ideas are timeless. Matsushita's philosophy of business is simple and idealistic, and it gives a new meaning to the word *success*. What visionary leaders have in common is their vision of a people-oriented approach to excellence. For them, human nature embraces both new values of responsibility and the gift of generosity. It is a leadership ethic that mentors fairness, harmony, and gratitude to inspire an ongoing sense of accomplishment—what we call people, pride, and profits. It goes far beyond the quest for profit alone.

Strategic thinking and old methods of management and measurement will not ignite organizational change. Content with learning, then, focuses on people first, valuing the social capital within and outside the walls of our institutions.

North American culture does not easily embrace concepts that don't deliver short-term gain. Failure to mentor long-term gain will only bring long-term pain. Over time, business will be forced to embrace new values and see that the workplace is part of something bigger. It is not only a question of economic production and profits but also a responsibility to sustain community and well-being.

Learning with Content

Learning with content is about mental toughness. It's the contentment that comes from a good mental workout. It comes from recognizing and appreciating our inner resources to get up ready to work. As the economic axis shifts from the Atlantic to the Pacific and intellectual and financial capital is relocated offshore, we need to become mentally tough again simply to maintain what we've built. There's no free ride.

The danger of lack of mental toughness is moral decay when it comes to thinking through the tough problems and acting on ethical solutions. Our lack of respect for older minds and enduring values has weakened our mental toughness. Lest we forget, the freedom we have today is a gift that can be taken away from us.

In a culture obsessed with self and materialism, we lack the mental toughness and reverence for mentoring that are found in other cultures. It is hard to imagine a Western equivalent of what the Japanese call their most gifted people: "living treasures," the contemporary sages who mentor learning to be revered and passed on to future generations as model practices. The Japanese, perhaps because their land was not physically resource-full, became mentally resourceful. They harnessed their own wilderness, a mental frontier, using a self-discipline that valued connectedness for group survival and growth.

Shifting the archetypal American paradigm of the rugged individual to one of the visionary leader demands a new kind kind of mental toughness. A "have it your way" culture simply does not see the need to make the shift. The shift demands too much self-discipline. In a world of declining resources, the frontier of the rugged individual is shrinking.

Becoming mentally tough pushes us to move beyond the fight or flight mindset. Great athletes can be good mentoring models. Joe Frazier, former heavyweight champion, said: "You can either map out a fight plan or a life plan, but when the action starts, it may not go the way you planned, and you're down to your reflexes—which means your training. That's where your road work shows. If you cheated on that in the dark of the morning, well, you're getting found out under the bright lights."

Mentoring is somewhat like a reflex-learning model. You start acting like a leader, and eventually you become one. The archetypal learning process for visionary leadership is similar to Olympic team and astronaut crew training. It provides the visualization to simulate the journey. It enables individuals to go for the gold in their mind. It does, however, require coaching (mentoring) and endorsement (leadership) from the top. This is more believable when communicated from a leader who has already won the gold.

There is no point in just talking about change; we have to be a model of change. Winston Churchill once said that "thinking without action is idleness." He was a decisive leader because he had learned the hard way; he was mentally prepared.

What visionary leaders have in common is the power to communicate imagination. They inspire effort. They endorse mentoring. They dream the dream.

In the same way that aborigines use dreamtime to envision their future, we need to embrace a "corporate dreamtime" when we take time to step out of our roles. Tom Peters once talked about "MBWA," management by walking around. Just as the aborigines go on walkabouts, so we need to take journeys that open our minds to the abundance around us and let higher visions enter our consciousness. These archetypal exercises also give us a chance to tap into our inner resources and listen to the cadence of inspiration and guidance that can be had only by quieting the conscious mind. As individuals we need this meditative rest each and every day; organizations in the new economy cannot sustain their success without it.

Corporate dreamtimes and walkabouts are powerful metaphors for change to happen. They expose the shallowness of such existing metaphors and practices as "how to conduct a meeting," or "let's do lunch"—hardly venues to ignite the imagination or inspire a spirit of enterprise. More often than not they support a negative dreamtime of wishing we were somewhere else. Absenteeism has been replaced by "presentee-ism," a new human resources term to indicate that while the body may be present, the mind is absent.

To mentor the mental toughness and visionary leadership required to create enduring success, we need to connect learning with living. Management case studies are no longer a sufficient method of learning. By connecting learning with corporate living, we can create a seamless learning program that gives balance to organizational living.

Our archetypal image of the emerging 20/20 mental landscape looks something like this:

LEARNING WITH CONTENT: THE 20/20 PARADIGM

Globalization	Community	Organization	Individual
Neorenaissance of ideas via Internet	Open borders, open minds	Visionary leadership	Commonwealth of experiential *learning*
Global value synthesis	Intellectual paradigm shift	Community connectedness	Knowledge worker
Concept R&D economy	Center of knowledge and well-being	ROIR (return on integrity in relationships)	Agent of transformation and change
Trade, not war	Cooperation	Servant-leader	Heart of the matter

Does this learning paradigm make sense to you? If it's confusing, that's great! Because the corporate world of certainty and predictability is over. The unfolding map is global; it can be a pathway to cooperation (trade) or conflict (war). It is also communal (it can be neighborhood or "strangerhood"), organizational (it can be ROI or ROIR), and individual (we can be open to change or refuse to see).

THE PATH OF THE ANCIENTS

Spirit of Enterprise

When you think of a great teacher or mentor who inspired you when you were young, what comes to mind? Don't the memories bring up images of someone you trusted, someone who took time for you, who was passionate about a subject or sport? You can probably see this trusted guide—or mentor—who fired up in you a similar passion and striving for excellence.

The Greeks inspired such passion in their learners.

A beautiful story recounts one young man's excitement about learning. A young man knocks on Socrates' door in the early dawn. Socrates is still half asleep when he answers the door and says, "What's here?" The young man cries out, "O Socrates. Good news, good news!" Of course, Socrates is wondering what could be such good news at such an early hour. The young man continues: "O Socrates, Protagoras has come. I heard it yesterday evening. And I was going to you at once but it was so late—" By this time Socrates is getting curious and wants to know what this Protagoras talk is all about. He asks, "Has he stolen something of yours?" At this the young man bursts out laughing. "Yes, yes, that's just it. He's robbing me of wisdom. He has it, wisdom, and he can give it to me. Oh, come and go with me to him. Start now."

What a wonderful sense of eagerness! What a spirit of enterprise he learned from being mentored, of having Socrates as a teacher.

Isn't this excitement evident also with all great teachers? The students gather around their teacher, their mentor. They want to know more; they want the truth.

Do you get excited about your work or about a project in this way? Are you able to excite a passion for excellence? Can you project a spirit of enterprise?

In Greek mythology, when Odysseus went off to fight the Trojan War, he left Mentor (really the goddess Athena in Mentor's likeness) in charge of his household and to "mentor" his son, Telemachus. Athena, in the guise of the noble Mentor, became the trusted guide, surrogate father, guardian, teacher, and counselor to the young boy, who later was to play a key role in bringing peace between his father Odysseus and the Ithacans.

The notion of "remembering" is also included in the etymology of the word *mentor*. "Mentoring" therefore is passing on the "memory." What are your traditions and corporate memories that need to be passed on? Who shows the way?

Another wonderful way the Athenians mentored a future was their willingness to work together for the good of all. It was considered normal for every Athenian to give time and effort to building and lifting up the common life. Thucydides has Pericles saying that selfish individualism does not override a person's responsibility in the affairs of the community: "We are a free democracy . . . We do not allow absorption in our own affairs to interfere with participation in the city's. We regard the man who holds aloof from public affairs as useless; nevertheless we yield to none in independence of spirit and complete self-reliance."

Public affairs, for the Athenians, was a personal responsibility. It was a treasured memory and a responsibility because when they looked around, they saw a very dark world indeed. Athens was a safe haven in a dangerous world. All around its residents were despotic rulers and slavish subjects, yet Athens was a city of freedom. The Athenians had passion for who they were and the incredible gift of freedom that was their most sacred treasure.

After Athens's defeat by Sparta in the Peloponnesian War, the spirit of enterprise was lost. Fighting had gone on for twenty-seven endless years. The cost? A generation that did not see the greatness or goodness in the commonweal, that lacked a shared vision of partnership in the Athenian democracy—a sacred trust that their ancestors had attained. Socrates believed so much in this sacred trust that he willingly gave his life for his conviction about it even though his friends could have helped him escape.

When we read the Athenian story, it is not difficult to see a parallel to our contemporary youth. As in fourth-century Athens, many of our young people also feel helpless and aimless; they, too, experience a moral crisis in society and believe that the state has failed them terribly. They do not trust our institutions; there is a cynicism and a huge credibility issue. The word *Trust,* for instance, found in some bank names, is sneered at. "How can I put trust in you and the banks when you keep raising fees and telling me that this is so you can stay competitive even though you make incredible profits?"

In fifth-century Athens this had not been so. Mentoring and teaching included a two-year obligatory military course for all who were eighteen. When his training began, the young Athenian went with his family and friends to the temple and took a solemn oath: "I will not bring dishonor upon my weapons nor desert the comrade by my side. I will strive to hand on my fatherland greater and better than I found it. I will not consent to anyone's disobeying or destroying the constitution, but will prevent him, whether I am with others or alone. I will honor the temples and the religion my forefathers established."

The people of fifth-century Athens believed that by completing their army service, these young men had taken a giant step in their education as good citizens. A hundred years later, in the fourth century, when the moral fiber of the state had begun to deteriorate—one scholar says because of greed—Socrates was the mentor and teacher who remained faithful to the ideal. For Socrates the state could be saved only by the inner integrity of the individual, and this was the *only* source of good for the community. Both the individual and the community were interdependent and could not be separated. Only a good individual could be a good citizen, and the state was good only to the extent its citizens were.

The spirit of enterprise therefore rests on the integrity of the individual, and this integrity, or wholeness in mind and body, is a mentored experience. It is a shared memory that is passed on and transmitted. Without this mentored spirit, the joy of being and working is missing. There is no higher vision. For the Celts the shared memory was their oral traditions and mythology. They were truly archetypal learners. As Sarah Ann Osmen writes in *Sacred Places,*

> The very understanding of the spoken word carried with it, consciously or unconsciously, the knowledge that no mythical story could ever successfully be read from a page. The human brain is equipped to accept oral story-telling, with all the human voice's intonation and the visual particularizing that goes with it. The written word could never carry such power or imagination and this is no doubt the reason why the Celtic people refused to have their private mythology transcribed. This is something that modern education has rarely grasped, with its passion for paperwork and examination, both of which negate one of the deepest mechanisms of the visual cortex and old-brain memory systems. Once again, there is evidence that our ancestors had greater knowledge of life than we do.

Watching the faces of people on subways, on buses, in offices, and around cafeterias leaves one with the impression that the joy of work—the spirit of enterprise—is indeed missing. Over the last two hundred years we have gradually lost this joy of working. Enthusiasm—which comes from the Greek word *entheos,* meaning "God-within," "spirit within"—has evaporated. We're not enthusiastic anymore.

Yet enthusiasm is what brings the workplace alive. It is the basis for all profits. It is the emotional and psychological infrastructure for the workplace. It is the essential "stuff" of the *worth* place. We've got to get the joy back into work.

It is very difficult to have enthusiasm when employees are scared, overworked, stressed out, and fundamentally insecure about their jobs. Yet today business leaders are blind to this obvious conclusion. Employees are expected to "produce, or else!" In some organizations, sad to say, this attitude is called participatory management. It is "demanding more for less," instead of freeing up the full potential of employees—not just the *head*-start methods of productivity but the *whole*-start methods, which include both head and heart. In this way organizations can build more for more because "more" employee is utilized.

In our core we are *Homo spiritualis*, individuals who thirst for meaning. When enthusiasm is lacking, an organization faces a crisis of spirit. The ancients experienced this state of affairs as well. Jewish texts often refer to the Israelites as "wandering" in the desert.

We have stated before that a people without vision perish. A people without vision, in modern terminology, is an unconscious people. They are unaware of the *context* of their living. Meaning and purpose are foreign to their considerations. They are reduced to the status of automatons. They are "things" to be manipulated, pawns on an economic scoreboard. They are only people behind the mask. Thomas Moore, in his wonderful book *Care of the Soul: A Guide for Cultivating Depth and Sacredness in Everyday Life,* points out that when you and I don't feel good about our work, we objectify ourselves—just like Narcissus in mythology, who could adore only himself. We allow others then to objectify us and treat us as pawns. When the natural and normal pride that the spirit of enterprise brings to employees is absent, it turns creativity into narcissism, and work becomes simply "getting what I can for the least effort." In doing this, we lose our natural sense of discovery.

The spiritless organization has "objectified" its employees. The impersonal reigns supreme. Excitement about living and working has disappeared. Employees go through the motions; they also go through the emotions. Nothing seems real; work and producing are plastic. In the wonderful children's video *The Never-Ending Story (Part I),* the Great Nothing has taken over the land. Nothing matters. As the mountain states in the movie, "I don't care that I don't care."

The spirit of enterprise in an organization is the exact opposite of this depressive spirit. A spirit-filled organization promotes people, pride, and prophets/profits. Winston Churchill's comment on leadership typifies the leader in such an organization: a person who is able to get people to do what needs to be done so that *they* want to do it. There is respect for employees, and added-valuing of who they are and what they contribute to the organization's success. They live Confucius' remark: "If there are three men walking down the street, there's bound to be one who is my teacher." His version of the Golden Rule is also instructive: "What you do not want done to yourself, do not do to others."

Enlightened management practices build a spirit of enterprise.

In 1494 in a monastery in Italy a monk named Luca Pacioli (1450–1520) sat and worked on an enlightened model of management. From the feathered pen of this scribe came the formula for double-entry accounting.

The foundational values of our modern financial cathedrals can be traced back to a similar sanctum sanctorum (holy of holies). Modern banking was aided by the Knights Templar warrior monks, who acted as trusted keepers of the realm's wealth. Formed as a small band of knights around 1118 to protect pilgrims visiting Palestine after the First Crusade, the order grew large and rich over the next two hundred years. These knights eventually became bankers for a large part of Europe and in the process amassed great wealth. However, because of envy by secular and ecclesiastical authorities, and because their aggressive warrior-monk stance fighting the Muslims was no longer in vogue, the order was suppressed in 1312 by Clement V and its property assigned to the rival Knights Hospitalers, although most of it was in fact seized by Philip IV of France and by King Edward II, who disbanded the order in England. In 1314 the last grand master and other leaders were burned as heretics, and supposedly the order came to an end. However, today the Knights Templars are members of the York Rite of the Masonic system.

Luca Pacioli and the Knights Templars tell us that business education foundational values have a spiritual source. But somewhere along the way we lost touch with our past and forgot that work was a labor of love. When Newton and Descartes effectively chopped off our ancient body of knowledge and presented us with a head on a platter full of certainty, it was then a small step to shift from a flow of meaning to a flow of production and dead matter.

The philosophy of materialism has not delivered the promise hungered for by the human spirit. Jungian analyst Marion Woodman says that in worshiping matter (i.e., "things"), we in effect serve the dark side of the goddess, or Great Mother—*Mater,* or "matter" in English. Philip Wylie in *A Generation of Vipers* brilliantly calls this act of adoration momism. In our culture especially, many male executives are totally in the service of the Great Mother, or corporation. Their whole lives are absorbed by her, and little time is left over for family and the ordinariness of life. We have an inborn need for spirit. Be careful, advised Jung, to know which spirit you're worshiping because you will worship one, be that food, sex, money, power, momism, or the real spirit of life and enterprise. If we are smart enough to keep one eye on the past and one eye on the future, we will seed and harvest yesterday's values of freedom, loyalty, and faith to propel us into a future worth going to. Work will be a process of discovery.

As the reclusive French postimpressionist novelist Marcel Proust writes in commenting on our need for a compelling new outlook on life and death that brings us hope and a shift in mood, "The real voyage of discovery consists not in seeking new landscapes, but in having new eyes."

The visionary leader's new eyes will be ones that mentor the value, integrity, and necessity of an inner and outer spirit of enterprise. This shared memory, as it is transmitted and lived by everyone, will bring the joy of being and working back into the workplace. This higher vision will indeed create a worth place.

Reformation of Work

We have to recover the spirit of work.

We have lost the connection of work and love, that good work is a labor of love. We need to rebuild that sense of craftsmanship embodied by workers of other ages, who joined heart, head, and loyalty in their labor of love. When people work at what they love, they experience work not as a boring chore but as something filled with energy and spirit.

Konosuke Matsushita, the octogenarian and one of this century's most accomplished visionary leaders, outlines a model blueprint for an enlightened management ethic in *Not for Bread Alone: A Philosophy of Financial Success and Personal Achievement*.

Starting as an apprentice at age nine—the traditional mentoring path—Matsushita developed wisdom over an eighty-year span of work. His humble beginnings taught him that strong leadership was founded on a day-to-day basis in providing guiding principles and values to encourage everyone in the company. He set out the following code of corporate governance in July 1933:

MATSUSHITA'S ENLIGHTENED MANAGEMENT ETHIC

Principle I	Spirit of service through industry
Principle II	Spirit of fairness
Principle III	Spirit of harmony and cooperation
Principle IV	Spirit of striving for progress
Principle V	Spirit of courtesy and humility

In August 1937 he added two more points:

Principle VI	Spirit of accord with natural laws
Principle VII	Spirit of gratitude

Matsushita's seven principles of governance have guided his global companies from their humble beginnings since that time and remain the founding values for tens of thousands of employees.

The Work of Reformation

We must therefore begin the work of reformation to mentor the values and vision with one eye on the past and the other firmly on the future. The flowering of the human spirit must come alive again in our organizations. It can happen. It *is* happening in some organizations.

In transformed organizations the emphasis has radically shifted. The spirit of enterprise has replaced the greed of taking. These organizations have given up what W. Edwards Deming called the deadly diseases that bog down an organization in mediocrity: the lack of constancy or purpose, the short-term profit mentality, the mobility of management, and the running of a company on visible figures alone. The work of reformation seeks to align individuals, organizations, and the community in a single vision of work, wealth, and well-being.

Transforming organizations that do the work of reformation mentor a spirit of enterprise in their workplaces. Rubbermaid, Coke, Procter & Gamble, and 3M are consistently among the top ten companies on *Fortune*'s Corporate Reputations Survey. Organizations with a spirit of enterprise, while obviously taking quarterly financial results into account, look beyond them and emphasize that such factors as the quality of management, products, and services are more important. John Ginnetti, an executive vice-president of Hartford Life Insurance, says, "Management creates the identity of an organization. It builds reputation by providing focus, direction, and incentive."

Transforming organizations also mentor higher visions, particularly when it comes to ethics. In 1988 the Business Roundtable and the Ethics Resources Center in Washington, D.C., completed a study of companies that had been in existence and public for at least thirty years, had codified sets of ethics, and had excellent records in practicing what they preached. The results? A 10.2 percent growth in profits, compounded since

1953, or 1.5 times the growth of the U.S. gross national product for the same period! Even though the U.S. GNP in 1988 was 11.7 times greater than in 1953, the net income of the ethical companies was 24.5 times greater! What about shareholder returns? A shareholder who invested $30,000 in 1973 in a composite of the Dow Jones industrial average realized a value of $276,000. However, a shareholder who invested $30,000 in the ethical companies realized a value of $1,878,221—or, almost seven times more!

The Dayton Hudson Corporation, a family-owned retail business established in Minneapolis in 1902, has a strong community ethic. In 1932 George Draper, the founder, wanted a new assumption for his company. It was to predicate success on the company's being useful to and serving society. The DH constitution reads: "The business of business is serving society, not just making money. Profit is our reward for serving society well. Indeed, profit is the means and the measure of our service—but not an end in itself."

Merck Frosst, Canada's largest innovator and manufacturer of prescription drugs, is another remarkable example of the work of reformation going on in corporations. Judged by the *Financial Post* as one of the best companies to work for, it is the industry leader, as is its parent, U.S.–based Merck & Company, Inc. Merck Frosst not only "talks the talk" but "walks the walk." A few years back it decided to recall a product with an errant tablet. Even though the tablet posed no medical threat to the health of potential buyers, the company ordered a full recall in spite of the cost and possible embarrassment. "The Merck Frosst way of doing things," would allow no other option. The director of public affairs Al MacDonald, a twenty-five-year Merck Frosst veteran, said, "We have a corporate memory that allows us to overlay innovation onto what has worked in the past, to improve upon it." Experience and innovation are central to "the Merck Frosst way of doing things." So is volunteerism. The well-being of community counts.

If we could mentor just seven things to build visionary leadership to embark on our voyage of discovery, they would include:

- Faith in a higher vision
- Loyalty to community
- Freedom to create
- Trust to innovate
- Competence to succeed
- Spirit to propel
- Leadership to serve

Winston Churchill once said that there comes a special moment in our lives when we are figuratively tapped on the shoulder and offered a very special thing to do, unique to us and fitted to our personal talents. He went on to say what a tragedy it would be to find ourselves unprepared or unqualified for the work that would be that, our finest hour.

For the ancients *kairos* was special time. It was very different from *tempus,* or clock time. We believe that *kairos* time has arrived. Yesterday the Latin poet Horace would have urged us: "Carpe diem." Today we say, "This is the moment for us to act." How does *kairos* fit with the new corporation? It relates to being constantly prepared to change. A proverb says, "Whom the gods want to destroy they send forty years of success."

Peter Drucker says that the years ahead will see rapid changes. Technology and markets, consumer behavior, finance, political realities, economic policies will make existing theories of business obsolete. In ten years what we think is valid today may not work without major modifications. Those companies that have started the change process to become learning organizations will realize that it will not be possible to sustain this thinking without investing in a spirit of enterprise.

Thomas Watson of IBM embodied the belief in people when he said, "I believe the real difference between success and failure in a corporation can very often be traced to the question of how well the organization brings out the great energies and talents of its people . . . any great organization . . . owes its resiliency not to its form of organization or administrative skills, but to the power of what we call beliefs and the appeal these beliefs have for its people."

Watson could easily have said that success is very often traced to the fact and quality of the mentoring of a shared memory that an organization has. Such an organization indeed mentors a spirit of enterprise. Such an organization lives in the spirit of the following Chinese proverb:

> If you want one year of prosperity,
>   grow grain,
> If you want ten years of prosperity,
>   grow trees,
> If you want one hundred years of prosperity,
>   grow people.

Mentoring people is growing people. People who are growing and transforming are the true core of prosperity. We are now ready to proceed to the sixth archetypal pillar, leading.

PILLAR VI

LEADING

*"And when we think we lead
we are most led."*

LORD BYRON (1788–1824)

IMAGINE RIDING A STORM in the mid-Pacific in an open outrigger canoe. Steering this mental experience to a safe destination requires an intense focus. Imagine the total team effort to achieve the shared goal of survival.

Your voyage of discovery to reinvent work, wealth, and well-being in your organization will require faith in your own leadership abilities.

Leader*ship*. Think of it as an archetypal concept. The vessel. Your thinking. Your crew's destiny. How are you going to ride the wave? How are you going to steer (lead), not row (manage)?

Today many organizations are rowing against the tide, not steering with the new current. They are still managing, not "leadering."

Confident crews (organizations) have seen the new vision (leadership) and have all hands on deck (vision teams and other similar mentoring teams); they are steering (turning vision into reality) on the never-ending learning journey. Crew members with a poor captain are working the bilge pumps to try to keep their ship steady and afloat. A corporate SOS (save our souls) is going unheard. The captain is still steering, but many of the crew have abandoned ship or accepted their fate.

* * *

The *right* stuff. A visionary leader turning vision into reality, using both imagination and innovation.

J. P. Bryan of Torch Energy Advisors, Inc., Houston, Texas, is an individual worth listening to. He leads in oil, an industry that is global in nature. In a recent speech he talked not about business but about the importance of leadership in conducting business. J.P. has his compass pointing in the right direction.

He believes that North America in general, and Canadian and American business specifically, are in desperate need of leadership. "Great leadership would be preferable, but almost any leadership would be better than management which is a hollow substitute."

In his view, visionary leadership would encourage creativity, innovation, imagination, and talent across the organization. Instead what we have had for more than fifty years has been a managed system of controls, memos, meetings, and thinking by committee. Author and consultant Warren Bennis reminds us that the difference between leaders and managers is that leaders master the context, managers surrender to it. It's an attitude at the heart of the organization.

Managers still have a role to play in the organization, but we need more leaders. The supply has been limited because business schools have for the most part taught management rather than leadership. Business graduates who later "managed" organizations ended up creating bureaucratic mindsets and structures. Their business success was measured by how well they created the right management system. The organization became an image of their thinking or a figment of their imagination. Then the managed god of quantification became the supreme veneration and the numbers the votive offerings. The beatitudes of corporate learning were accounting, strategy, and control.

Shifting the paradigm to visionary leadership will create enormous differences in the way we see the organization and the way we do business. Instead of only ratifying the "bottom" line, we'll be learning what a "top" line can do for us.

P. K. Sung, recently retired CEO of Samsung General Chemical, Seoul, Korea, is a member of the Intuition Network and has formed Creatia Management (a combination of *utopia* and *creativity*) to integrate what he calls quantum management or wave paradigm thinking. He's going for the top line as he builds his visionary leadership dream for organizations. He believes that such a leadership philosophy incorporates the "natural laws of the universe."

According to J. P. Bryan, leadership is not about going to meetings, writing and reading long memos, reviewing budgets, studying stock option programs, serving on diverse campaigns and chambers of commerce, and not worrying about the end product or service. What it is all about, in our view, is as follows.

20/20 VISION OF VISIONARY LEADER

Both	*And*
"Top line"	"Bottom line"
People	Things
Spontaneous	Organized
Ideas	Results
Path	Goal
Heart	Mind
Vision	Common Sense

"The suggestion that you need to be managed should be an insult," says Bryan. Peter Block argues that no one should be paid for planning, organizing, directing, or controlling anyone. Ask yourself: Do you think that you need to be managed? Does this enhance your self-worth? Does this improve your performance? We realize that some people like the safety net of being managed, but we're emphasizing leadership and taking charge of your own life. Bryan asked in his speech, "Are you so insecure that you need to control others' conduct to the extent that you depress their initiative and their creativity?"

What are the characteristics, for Bryan, of a visionary leader?

- The leader must be a good listener.
- The leader should encourage criticism but not disrespect.

- The leader should celebrate employees' efforts.
- The leader must do what is right rather than what is popular.
- The leader must be courageous and a risk taker.
- The leader must be open to change.
- The leader must change to be open.
- The leader must exhibit humility and empathy.
- The leader serves and defends.
- The leader must aspire to do better.
- A leader must be accountable to a "higher authority"—namely, God.

Aristotle reminds us that we cannot learn without pain. This is not the neurotic pain of avoidance or refusal to change. This is the effort expended in excellence. In the eighth century B.C. Hesiod wrote, "Before the gates of Excellence the high gods have placed sweat." A people in transformation work at it and get the job done. It can be their finest hour. The visionary leader frees them and leads them on a path to do this.

THE 20/20 LEADERSHIP PATH

THE LEADERSHIP VALUE PATH

Visionary leadership can act as a model to transmit a spirit of enterprise back into the corporation. It serves as a channel that lets the spirit flow through the hearts and minds of an organization.

Today *leadership* may be better described by the term *leadering*. The old concept of leadership often implied an aggressive, hierarchical posture, focused on chains of commands rather than empowerment. Transformation requires receptivity, not aggressiveness.

The receptive force is rich with potential; the aggressive force (too much thinking, planning) kills receptivity. The *I Ching* says receptivity gives us the wisdom to be strong yet yielding. While some situations may require aggressive leadership, it is not an effective daily working style.

Visionary leadership is "servanting-leadering." It allows us to respond, not blindly to react, to situations. An example of the responsive leader is the one who takes time to listen to the corporate voice and chooses the required response. He or she does the right thing. All too often we experience the reactive approach. Thinking is done impulsively. Reactive styles just focus on the present; they have no eye on the past or the future.

Research by Charles Hampden-Turner and Alfons Trompenaars that studied the values and thinking of fifteen thousand managers from around the world found that some had a tendency for sequential thinking, so that they saw yesterday, today, tomorrow, as distinctly unconnected, whereas other managers had a strong tendency toward synchronous thinking, perceiving a direct relationship and connectedness with yesterday, today, tomorrow.

Receptivity and perspective are essential insights for leadership in a world that is changing so rapidly. The visionary leader connects both sequential thinking and synchronous thinking. Our transformational journey requires no less. This connectedness provides a mental bridge to the future.

The leadership value path requires this holistic thinking to understand and inspire an openness and receptivity that integrate new ideas from everywhere.

Can our thinking go beyond culture? It must if we are to shift the paradigm. Holistic, congruent thinking is relevant for enduring success anywhere. The visionary leader understands the importance of mapping and mining IQ and EQ capital.

Since the future success of organizations hinges on how well they develop ROIR (return on integrity in relationships), leaders will need to recognize that feelings and intuitions in relationships are important organizational data but also potential hurdles in the decision-making process. The new data in the

NEW CLEAR THINKING FOR THE NEW ORGANIZATION

Design for success, not failure.
Use both-and thinking, e.g., both technical and creative, both past and future.
Endorse and learn a learning ethic.
Invest in generational learning to sustain the vision.
Foster new ways to look at the business from the outside in.
Encourage dialogue to integrate thinking.
Mentor a shared purpose to develop team spirit.
Liberate minds to break mental bondage.
Celebrate leaders as servants and stewards.
Incubate mental skunk works for innovation.
Work with the corporate culture if you need to change it.
Reframe issues for optimal perspective.
Respond rather than just react (IQ + EQ).
Loop the loops, aligning individual, organization, community circles.

---

decision-making process will include not only IQ, the intelligent deliberation of the subject at hand but also the EQ factor, the responsiveness for how the change process is working. In the global brain economy, visionary leaders value the *whole* person as their most important advantage.

Visionary leaders throw away job descriptions and knock down physical and mental barriers to achieve organizational transformation. In the new organization, pride is in becoming *a team member of an organization with a charter of values.*

What would this charter of values require to succeed?

A VISIONARY LEADER'S CHARTER OF VALUES

Faith in a higher vision
Mastery in competence
Courage in shared vision
Trust in growing ideas
Spirit in enterprise

> Service in leading
> Integrity in relationships
> Prophet in profit
> Wisdom in thinking
> Humility in purpose

Faith in a higher vision gives the organization the insight and courage to take action to change. It builds organizational character to sustain the individual, the organization, and the community in the good times and in the bad times.

It's time to ask yourself now: Are you a noun or a verb?

If you're a noun, you're a manager; if you're a verb, you're going to lead. You inhabit a grammatical universe, and words last longer than institutions. So choose them carefully. You are what you think. Ron Fellows, director of the Applewood Center, a site worth visiting on the World Wide Web, made an interesting comment to us: "Descartes, who as much as anyone is responsible for our fragmented view of the world, had a dream about walking in the wind and having the left side of his body bent and folded. From the perspective of present-day brain-body theory, his dream predicted the consequences of his 'I think, therefore I am' concept."

From the Jungian perspective, the left side is the rational, discursive side. Being bent and folded is a clear archetypal image of what happened to Descartes by his rational imbalance. It's interesting to ponder that his thinking has shaped our worldviews. We have mentioned the importance of connecting to the organizational unconscious in order to start the change process. In René's case we should have checked out his dream long ago. It's time to wake up! If he had only listened to his dream, he would have realized that the spirit (wind) was trying to tell him something. He could have stood upright.

We are coming to realize, says Peter Drucker, that business theory is not a law of nature. The only thing that can effectively turn around our present economic system and satisfy our need for community is to turn around our thinking to reformulate the meaning of business and then to realign our organizations both on an old and on a new set of assumptions. This requires us to stop saying, "We know," and begin saying, "Let's listen for a change." When we think we lead, we are most led. Leadership truly is character.

20/20 VISION OF LEADERSHIP THINKING

Both	And
Right brain	Left brain
Creative	Rational
Intuitive	Pragmatic
Innovative	Productive
Imaginative	Concrete
Vision	Strategy
Prophet	Profit

In the past we could decide to act and change our organizations and, like Admiral Nelson at the Battle of Trafalgar, turn our blind eye into a competitive advantage. He said, "I see no ships." Today that blindness might not secure advantage. The technological winds of change don't favor a change process that steers from a mental blind side. Today we need leader*ship* in the vanguard.

Today's visionary business thinkers have rejected the "by-the-numbers approach" to enterprise and are seeking a new paradigm for interpreting success. This new paradigm represents a new pattern of behavior that seeks harmony rather than dominance. GE's Jack Welch, an exponent of visionary thinking, says it's time to go beyond training seminars to a fundamental rethinking of how management works.

The new field of organizational transformation (OT) is concerned with holistic transformation. It includes leadership communication, mentoring team building, and opening up to the more profound issues in myth, ritual, and spirit. A case example for OT is Jim Channon, formerly a lieutenant colonel in the U.S. Army Task Force Delta, whose personal transformation led him to construct an image of himself as a shaman.

Says Channon: "Three things are missing from almost every organization I've been through. A sincere desire to love each other in a brotherly way, an ability to incorporate spiritual values in their work, and an ability to do something physical together." Just as we have connected the path of the ancients with the necessary thinking required for tomorrow, so Channon connects the values of tribal cultures for tomorrow's organizations. "Just because those guys can't make toasters doesn't mean that singing together, dancing together, and telling stories around a fire isn't a damn good thing to do."

These sentiments may seem threatening and alien, even pointless. But if visionary thinking that is building the new paradigm by treating people with dignity, valuing integrity in relationships, and working like a spirited team qualifies as the new ideal, we're all for it.

To accomplish this objective, nothing less than new minds will do. The tides of change are upon us. The time to develop a new mind is now, and learning archetypally is how to do it. The table below provides such archetypal images for reflection.

ARCHETYPAL IMAGES FOR THE VISIONARY LEADER

Archetypal Icon	Archetypal Metaphor
PILLAR I: *Visioning* decision window	New clear thinking
PILLAR II: Global mind *map*	Expanding universe
PILLAR III: Compass for the *journey*	Voyage of discovery
PILLAR IV: Open *learning* door	Temple of knowledge
PILLAR V: The *mentoring* circles	Sustaining traditions
PILLAR VI: *Leadership* value path	Principle of duty
PILLAR VII: *Valued* spirit of enterprise	Tending the flame

Steering, Not Rowing

What are these tides of change we face together? They can be like quicksands of the mind or, as Shakespeare writes in *Julius Caesar*:

> There is a tide in the affairs of men,
> Which, taken at the flood, leads on to fortune;
> Omitted, all the voyage of their life
> Is bound in shallows and in miseries.
> On such a full sea are we now afloat;
> And we must take the current when it serves,
> Or lose our ventures.

The old "rowing" concept of leadership was easy. It was focused; we knew our boundaries and what we could control. The new "steering" archetypal concept is more diffuse and certainly visionary. We believe that American management is too focused on science and not focused enough on the art of transformation—even though people are asking for a new vision of hope. For them the old thinking is starting to sound like the clanging gong. It is the sound that's left when the wisdom's gone. Nearly two thousand years ago Paul of Tarsus described this very well: "For the time will come when men will not put up with sound doctrine. Instead, to suit their own desires, they will gather around them a great number of teachers to say what their itching ears want to hear. They will turn their ears away from the truth and turn aside to what the crowd wants to hear."

But some organizations are trying to fine-tune their ability to steer instead of row. General Motors has been learning to shift its paradigm from an industrial to a customer organization. Recognizing the importance of relationships as a key factor for success, GM is working in partnership with the United Auto Workers' union around core values and competencies known as the quality network. This network has a core value of customer satisfaction achieved through people, teamwork, and continuous improvement. The chart below represents GM's paradigm shift from sum = ROI to relationship = ROIR.

SHIFTING THE PARADIGM: GM'S QUALITY NETWORK

Relationship	Commitment
People	Inviting the people of GM to be full partners in the business
	Recognizing people as its greatest asset
	Demonstrating its commitment to people
	Treating people with respect
	Never compromising integrity
Teamwork	Building through teamwork and joint action
	Taking responsibility for leadership
	Making communications work
	Trusting one another
	Demanding consistency in the application of the value system
Continuous Improvement	Making continuous improvement the goal of every individual
	Putting quality in everything each does
	Eliminating every form of waste
	Using technology as a tool
	Accepting change as an opportunity
	Establishing a learning environment at all levels

Leaders like you can also begin the process of "steering, not rowing" by working to acquire these four competencies, which Warren Bennis says a leader must possess.

- *Management of attention:* your ability to draw others to yourself because you have a vision, a dream, a set of intentions, an agenda, an ability to communicate an extraordinary focus of commitment
- *Management of meaning:* your ability to communicate your vision and align work together

- *Management of trust:* your ability to develop the main determinant of trust: reliability or constancy
- *Management of self:* your ability to know your skills and deploy them effectively; your capacity to concentrate on the intention, the task, and the decision

The visionary leadership path builds on the best of the rational and the intuitive. Its strength is in providing the archetypal thinking to focus holistically. The new focus on the "top line"—the 20/20 vision—aligns thinking and connects strategy to guide organizational transformation. The visionary leader connects both ancient wisdom and learning, as a principle of duty, to achieve enduring success.

Principles of Duty

Some cultures already connect ancient wisdom and learning. They see the family as an integral image for organizational design.

Organizations are a culture; they are irrational and can become comfortable with what's wrong, not with what's right. Their attitudes and values can limit future potential. Konosuke Matsushita, reflecting on the question of organizational development, states:

> I know the analogy probably sounds outrageous, but I wonder if there is not a certain parallel between childbearing and employee education. I am talking about the crucial importance in both of conviction. If we want to bring up our children properly, we need to have clear ideas of the basic goals in a life of integrity and humanity, and how to be a good member of the family and community. Everyone has a different world view and outlook on life; one is not necessarily right and the others wrong. The important thing, whatever our outlook, is never to vacillate in our attitudes toward the basic issues.
>
> People in top management also need firm, well-formed views on society, business, and life if they are to exert a solid influence

on those under their supervision. When senior executives are consistent in their thinking and behavior, their subordinates will trust them and follow their examples with a sense of security. But corporate management requires a little more than conviction and consistent attitudes. It needs what I call a sense of purpose.

Why are Matsushita's wisdom and learning lacking in Western business logic? Indeed, it often seems that we find the wisdom of the ancients to be irrelevant. Because we are disconnected from our classical roots, we have become focused on freedom as rights. As we saw in Pillar IV, fifth-century Athenians knew that freedom could not exist without both an inner discipline and self-limits and an outer duty to the common good.

Ask yourself: With so much change and conflict in our world, how can we depend on the competitive model to solve our relationship obligations?

If our organizations stopped being blinded by simplistic free market thinking and the focus on individual self-interest and began to design themselves to serve both individual and community interests as a principle of duty, we would surprise ourselves by how smart, loyal, and trusting our customers would be.

David Selbourne in *The Principle of Duty* states: "Intellectual hyper-specialization of responses to the circumstances of human existence and behavior has been accompanied by moral confusion in the face of that which cannot be reduced to quantities and statistical tables. To address a 'principle of duty' to such a world is to speak a foreign moral language." Selbourne's conviction is that without a principle of duty, the mere politics of rights forms ethical myopia and carries the seed of our own destruction.

A visionary leader gladly accepts his or her civic responsibility and recognizes an obligation to grow people, pride, and profits, not simply to take from the community. *Time* magazine has written that "visionaries are possessed creatures, men and women in the thrall of belief so powerful that they ignore all else—even reason—to ensure that reality catches up with their dreams. But always behind the action is an idea, a passionate sense of what is eternal in human nature and also of what is coming but as yet unseen, just over the horizon." Visionary leaders steering at the helm can reroute us.

THE PATH OF THE ANCIENTS

Idol Worship

With the ancient role of classical criticism missing from contemporary discourse, we can no longer hear wisdom. Like Narcissus, we want to listen only to Echo. In hearing ourselves think, we really hear only what we want to hear. In so doing, we avoid a critical analysis—whereby the mind can judge, discriminate, determine the subtleties, and discern—and we fail to hear the many voices crying for our attention.

The word *criticism* is related to *crisis,* and as we've seen, crisis or crossroads is the first stage on our transformational journey. If we miss recognizing the crisis we're facing or the crossroads we're at, because we're pulled by the seductive winds and thinking of distraction or consumerism, we are indeed unable to assess our situation critically. We will not hear the truth. Warren Bennis says that real leaders know the importance of having someone around who will tell the truth.

Allan Bloom puts it exquisitely: "What a people bows before tells us what it is." Sadly, we and our ancestors have experienced much confusion about what we should bow before.

In and around the seventh century B.C.E., the Jews began to tell the story of when God created the heavens and the earth. We usually read at the start of the Book of Genesis, "In the beginning . . . ," which, to Western ears, suggests a more or less definite moment in the past. The Hebrew for this, however, is more truly translated as "when," indicating an indefinite time in the past. To the Jewish mind, the story was important not because of its chronological emphasis but rather because of the overarching role of God in their story as a chosen people.

As the story developed over time, Jews learned how God was

truly a visionary leader who led his people safely out of Egypt, away from slavery, to trek on a journey to a land flowing with milk and honey. They learned that on this journey their ancestors had received the value code, the Ten Commandments. History shows that the Israelites broke Commandment one—"You shall have no other gods before me"—time and time again, turning to golden calves and other idols whenever they lost their faith in the God of Israel. Courage often failed them on their journey, they strayed from their visionary leadership calling, and they often paid a heavy price. It is instructive to ponder for a moment on this Jewish experience because it points out the following: Visionary leaders may be "doing all the right things" and trying to keep our eyes on the purpose of the journey, but we also have to cooperate. A visionary leader keeps the sights clear; we must honor that discernment, act on it, and keep the faith.

Idol worship is our struggle as well. Especially in this age of consumerism, we moderns often break the First Commandment. Says Richard Smoley: "Looking at American public festivities, an intelligent alien might conclude that we adore a trinity consisting of the Easter Bunny, Santa Claus, and Frosty the Snowman." And like the ancients, we pay the price. We are choking on our own acquisitiveness; we are weighted down by our possessions; we are desperately searching for meaning in places other than "things." Writer Alan M. Marcus comments that people who have some begin to want more, and people who have more want more again. What starts out as a reasonable quest for an improved life turns into greed, and acquisitiveness becomes an end in itself.

Alan Durning's report from the World Watch Institute in Washington offers a very brutal assessment of our North American lifestyle. We have more than enough, says Durning, and have been accumulating "stuff" now for more than forty years. In our spirit of acquisitiveness we, one fifth of the world's population, get turned on because something is new, or bigger, nicer, or better. We are insatiable in wanting diversion, excitement and entertainment. Despite things and conveniences, we still don't spend enough time with our families, or building relationships with our neighbors, or doing work in the community, or even learning new things. We watch television. And we're not any happier. Is "consumer confidence" really a holistic measuring stick from a bigger perspective? Should we not be talking about gross national cost (GNC) in achieving gross national product (GNP)?

Over the last three hundred years, following Jean-Jacques Rousseau's *The Social Contract,* we have made the shift in our contract from worshiping *God* to worshiping *self*. We now believe in idols, not the real thing. We have turned around the understanding of what nature is and elevated our own sense of importance.

From the time of Aristotle personal fulfillment was found *in* and *through* nature. Today we don't believe that nature can tell us anything; we must "conquer" it, "subdue" it, "dominate" it. We have extended this same thinking to our personal, family, and work relationships. We are now paying the price, what Bloom calls our "suffering from a three-hundred-year-long identity crisis." With no teleological or vocational end purpose to life, we have to "invent" who we are all the time. We don't trust our *reason*ableness. We are only what we feel. We worship the idol of self, not the true God. We are divorced from nature. We think we can treat nature and life as we like. Common sense, on the other hand, tells us that when we need balance, we should go outside and let nature fill the vacuum.

Carl Jung was correct: We need to worship the real God or we pay an awful price. Rather than look within the nature of things for what ails us, we go within ourselves. The psychology and worship of self and individualism have produced addicted organizations and communities. The UN's World Health Organization describes an addiction as a compulsivity around a person, place, or substance that eventually has life-threatening consequences. Are our relationships giving us health? Do the relationships in our organizations create "life-threatening consequences"? How safe and healthy are our communities? To return to health and well-being, we need to return to the essential nature of things, to a respect of the natural order and away from idol—and idle—worship.

What we need today are teachable leaders, skilled in "leadering." We need artists of living who will help us discover meaning and higher purpose. In an organization that is a worth place, employees do what they have to do because they *want* to in relation to the goals and purpose of their organization. In other words, leadership in these organizations encompasses a higher-purpose vision about which employees feel passionate. Organizational psychologist Jack Hawley says, "The Spirit agenda consists of ancient issues coming home, mooring at the docket of management, cosmic queries, the curriculum of humankind's eternal search to be part of something greater, the calendar of the soul, the hunger for purpose and meaning and identity."

Leadership Skills for Technical Managers (LSTM), a five-day workshop developed by the Center for Creative Leadership in North Carolina, highlights the contrast between good managers and great managers. According to Doug Bowie, former president of the Niagara Institute, these programs reveal that good managers are fine when it comes to working with content, but in managerial situations that draw on one's expertise in the art of influencing relationships to accomplish goals, they are lacking. On the other hand, great managers had leadership ability that, for him, included the capacity to make meaning, to find purpose and learn, and the ability to manage ambiguity.

If managers are the "hands-on," day-to-day practitioners of organizational *content*, leaders are the "visionaries" who capture the subtleties of the *context*. Managers are pragmatists, rule makers, and appliers; leaders breathe spirit into the process of organizational success.

The ancients distinguished between two realities: *nomos* (or the law, rules, and regulations) and *epikeia* (the spirit). We have come to know these realities as the "spirit" of the law and the "letter" of the law. Managers are *"nomos-*dependent"; leaders are *"epikeia-*freed." *Nomos* without *epikeia* leads to a dispirited organization; *epikeia* without *nomos* leads to an aimless organization. *Nomos* tempers *epikeia; epikeia* inspirits *nomos.*

The danger today, after decades of *nomos-*organizational living, is that we will cast caution to the wind *(epikeia)* and collapse into disarray. Kenneth Olsen, founder of computer maker Digital Equipment Corporation (DEC), highlights this tension between the letter *(nomos)* and the spirit *(epikeia)* of the law when he says that the invention of the spreadsheet program is one of the worst things that happened to business. Why? Because, he says, "too often, the spreadsheet becomes the goal. Understanding the business, the problems, the staff, the products, the customer, the economy, and all the other factors that contribute to a company's fate can get lost in the spreadsheet." What does he include in "those other factors"? Understanding relationship dynamics. Olsen continues, "Wrongly founded assumptions about what should happen replace accurate assessments of what is happening. . . . And that inaccurate picture of reality breeds bad managerial decisions."

Idol worship would keep us addicted to the god of quantification. GE's Jack Welch even goes so far as to say, "The budget is the bane of corporate America. It should never have existed. . . . Making a budget is an exercise in minimalization." Why? Because "you're always trying to get the lowest out of people, because everyone is negotiating to get a lower number." The leadership value path moves us beyond this kind of myopia to a vision of wholeness.

In today's "reign of quantity," says Ernest McClain, professor of music at Brooklin College, "it's never possible to have enough nuclear weapons, or enough billions in the bank. In ancient times, the smallest numbers are the most prestigious ones. The most important number to the ancients is one, unity. Any unity is a point of reference." In contrast, we focus on big numbers. We want more of everything even though experience tells us that "more" doesn't create happiness.

To keep a healthy "balance sheet" is indeed a truly human act, but a very difficult one. Organizational idol worship gives in to rigidity and says, "This is the only way things can be done," and leaves its polar opposite—organizational growth—to go unchecked. We have now paid the price: inflation, the fruits and agonies of greed, the recession, and the corporate anorexia of downsizing. Aristotle was correct: *In medio stat virtus* (Moderation is the mean).

The Learning Circle

Visionary leadership required for today is not so much about the things we do as it is about the place leaders come from with whatever they do. Václav Havel has remarked that there is only one way to strive for decency, reason, responsibility, sincerity, civility, and tolerance, and that is decently, reasonably, responsibly, sincerely, civilly, and tolerantly. These trusted values and ancient wisdom provide the value anchors for individual, organizational, and community balance in a world of flux.

Leadership in the borderless world recognizes that applied knowledge is going to be the determining factor for the generation of wealth and well-being. The global economy requires us to download our old thinking because it provides only a narrow way of seeing things. Our brain and its patterns helped us see and build the community into the nation-state, but now we must expand our vision from new eyes and ears of information technology and integrate the paradox of the local and the global.

The visionary leader, yesterday, today, and tomorrow, like Spartacus, will always fight for the dignity and well-being of people. Period. This is the transformed leader who has learned "Know thyself" and has a personal value point reference.

If we're going to reinvent the future, we should step outside our paradigm into the learning circle of life to listen to voices that never lost sight of a shared vision. The learning circle is a circle of life from the dawn of learning. In the circle of life we are dependent on the earth and are its stewards. All life is connected and interdependent, and our earth can be trusted. It provides its own compass. This compass is the circle of life, what we now call the learning circle.

In the learning circle, the leader stops standing at the top of the old organizational pyramid and becomes the facilitator of a community of learners. This position is rotational and depends on the needs of the organization. The leader works from the center. The leader and the learners are interdependent for each other's growth and well-being.

In this learning circle, east is knowledge, south is life, west is the power of change, and true north is wisdom. Within the learning circle is great energy to empower ROIR. The learning circle symbolizes the visionary power to imprint the organizational images needed to fuel transformation. It is a temenos, or sacred container, that makes this transformation possible.

In a larger sense the four directions of the learning circle represent images that enable the organization to change. The learning circle, with the leader guiding the way, starts the change process from true north, which is wisdom. This is the recognition that we need to let go and acknowledge a higher vision. We then move east, which is knowledge. This is knowing that we can let go and trust the journey. We then move south, which is life. This is accepting the abundance of life. Finally, we move west, which is the power to change. We have now developed the creative energy to build our future. At this point the compass once more points north to align our thinking and purpose to realize that we're not alone but vitally interconnected.

An interesting contemporary example of "rotational learning" is found in the Rotational Exchange Program developed by three U.S. security agencies—the CIA (Central Intelligence Agency), DIA (Defense Intelligence Agency), and NSA (National Security Agency). To foster the career development of intelligence officers, the program provides rotational learning opportunities within the intelligence community (IC). It's interesting to note that the DIA's most comprehensive reorganization since the end of the Cold War has been described as a cultural change that deals with what it calls the spiritual aspects of the organization rather than merely shift office symbols. These examples are further evidence of how the establishment is changing its thinking at the core.

In a learning circle, corporate memory is developed. Connectivity keeps everyone, so to speak, in the loop. Each rotational exchange provides a leadership outreach. Everyone is connected; everyone is in the circle, albeit a large one, and memory is fostered. Sir Thomas Browne (1605–1682), English physician and writer, wrote, "There is no man alone, because every man is a Microcosm, and carries the whole World about him."

Leadership organizations connect to the integrity of their own corporate story. They treasure their shared memory to foster commitment. Whenever new people come into their circle, they are taught to honor this history. They build a sense of belonging. A core set of purpose, values, and competencies drive their energies and unleash the spirit of enterprise.

An integral archaeology of the corporate story would discover the links to the trusted value anchors from the past that bring that past alive—not to tell people what happened or to explain the past but to let the past live so it can explain us and make a better future possible and we can become all that we can be. By valuing its corporate memory, Merck Frosst can build on what has worked in the past and overlay innovation onto their successes for the future.

For the ancients, corporate memory was sustained through oral tradition. For us moderns, corporate memory is oral and written. Many organizations are searching for ways to manage the volume of information and research that adds up to written corporate memory. What Marble Associates, Inc. of Waltham, Massachusetts, calls the Corporate Memory Infrastructure (CMI), consists of methodologies and enabling technologies that let employees access information resources by content and attribute. In this way information is leveraged and disseminated across organizational boundaries. The learning circle can remain unbroken.

We cannot forget our past, our roots, our history, our story. Naim Kattan says, "Our memory of the past must be faithful to the future if it is to act as stimulus for the present." Shelbourne writes that community is shared or related memory, language, belief, values, custom, and knowledge. But people need to be connected. Right now many people don't understand their past. Their worldview has been shaped largely by a media prism.

Northrop Frye reminds us that a civilization without memory becomes senile. This insight holds true also both for the individual and the organization. What counts now in leading is what has always counted: putting people first. The fruit of that experience is authentic commitment.

Revaluing the Future

For too long now we have permitted a society in which any group that so wishes can claim it is an exception to the common rule of living in community. We need to begin to create a future in which we pursue a higher vision of the common ideals of community governance. Longtime adversaries Plato and Aristotle could disagree about the nature of the good because their concern for the common good linked them. They knew that they needed each other in order to understand their mutual search for truth. Allan Bloom remarks, "They were absolutely one soul as they looked at the problem." They had integrity in their thinking. It was connected to the world they lived in.

John Steinbeck (1902–1968), in conversing with a political correspondent, remarked one time, "There used to be a thing or a commodity we put great store by. It was called the People. Find out where the People have gone."

Visionary leaders need to ensure that their thinking has the same integrity and is connected to the world they are living in. Archetypally that means "looping the loops" of the individual, the organization, and the community so that all three are aligned to a common purpose of work, wealth, and well-being. The three loops are the loci of change. In the next section we show how visionary leaders can align these three loops so they are all pointing true north.

Transformation happens one person at a time. Unless others shift their thinking, you're traveling alone. All of us must move quickly to a mindset that puts people first and stops seeing them only as "things" or costs to the organization. The new ethic of leading says that relationships matter. Return on investment (ROI) must have a metanoia. The transformative fruit of that metanoia will be return on integrity in relationships (ROIR).

Humans were organized long before organizational charts became a reality. The concept of what Antony Jay calls the corporate man is a very recent animal. In a *Harvard Business Review* article called "Managing Without Managers," Ricardo Semler, president of Semco S/A, Brazil's largest marine and food-processing machinery manufacturer, says that in his organization "we try to respect the hunter that dominated the first 99.9% of the history of our species." According to Semler, "After the hunt, primitive people shared their kill. Today's mammoth meal is profits." He accents this idea even more pointedly when he later writes, "If executives are embarrassed by what they make, they probably aren't earning it."

To put people first, the visionary leader creates the context for people to do what they need to do to accomplish organizational goals, not so much because the leader demands that as because the leader's inspirational spirit propels these people. A basic motivational principle is that people do what hooks them, emotionally, intellectually, organizationally. The visionary leader knows this and inspires their emotional, intellectual, and organizational energy with the spirit of enterprise. At the root of all leadership integrity is the leader's personal transformation.

Civic pride—pride in belonging—is the mark of community. Our grasping for profits at the cost of loyalty, trust, and relationships has killed much of this pride, an essential quality that allows all of us to hold our heads up high. Georges Bernanos (1888–1948), French novelist and political writer, writes, "It's a fine thing to rise above pride, but you must have pride in order to do so." We have to get back to the basics. Building personal and organizational pride is one of them.

This requires a temenos, a sacred repository or container of values. The organization, as a community of learners, is such a temenos. For transformation to occur, the "raw material" (people) must be transformed into "gold" (knowledge). Too much heat (chaos, uncertainty, shadow decisions), and the vessel cracks; not enough heat (attention to people, learning, higher purpose), and there is no transformation. The leader must attend to the flame (burning desire for growth) so that the organization becomes more than the sum of its parts. This leads to one people, one purpose.

* * *

The theologian and ecologist Matthew Fox points out that without the prophetic voice, and left only to the mercy of the rational profit voice, we are in an extremely vulnerable position. "Left-brain-itis is a lethal disease that today has quite literally the power to destroy all the earth." What we need today are *prophets in the boardroom*—people who announce balance, not in the sense of "profit" only, but in the sense of "prophet," or justice and relationships.

The German poet Rainer Maria Rilke writes, "You must give birth to your images. They are the future waiting to be born . . . fear not the strangeness you feel. The future must enter into you long before it happens. . . . Just wait for the birth . . . for the hour of new clarity." When the Kinney Shoe Corporation began to integrate men's and women's work and communication styles into the organization and strengthen the power of its new images, it realized it had also strengthened its competitive advantage. By living our commitments to new life-giving images, we show that we have the vision to stick with it to achieve real long-term gain.

As people we are image makers as well as toolmakers. Let us hope that our future images are not just idols and false profits, but ones filled with hope and spirit. Since we have made our world what it is today because of a series of acts of the imagination, we can, with insight, courage, and action, reimagine a better future for tomorrow. Business plays an incredible role in this act of reimagining the world because of its contribution to the organizational life that is the hallmark of this century.

In Yeats's "The Second Coming," he writes, "Things fall apart; the centre cannot hold." Many are concerned today and asking themselves if the center will in fact hold. One business editor wonders, "If the Centre Cannot Hold, Will We Invent a New Centre?" One of the stated purposes of the United Nations reads: "To be a center for harmonizing the actions of nations in the attainment of . . . common ends."

Through self-knowledge, confidence, and action, the visionary leader knows that the center will indeed hold and that the Delphic "Know thyself" is more imperative today than ever.

This is not just a conscious knowing, but a deeply intuitive, inner knowing that comes from transformative reflection. Pierre Teilhard de Chardin captures this special knowing and confidence about the center in these beautiful words:

> And so, for the first time in my life perhaps . . . I took the lamp and, leaving the zone of everyday occupations and relationships where everything seems clear, I went down into my inmost self, to the deep abyss whence I feel dimly that my power of action emanates. But as I moved further and further away from the conventional certainties by which social life is superficially illuminated, I became aware that I was losing contact with myself. At each step of the descent a new person was disclosed within me of whose name I was no longer sure, and who no longer obeyed me. And when I had to stop my exploration because the path faded from beneath my steps, I found a bottomless abyss at my feet, and out of it came—arising I know not from where—the current which I dare to call *my* life.

We now have six archetypal pillars of learning for our new organization. The seventh pillar will validate them so that the center holds.

PILLAR VII

VALUING

*"The value of life
lies not in the length of days
but in the use you make of them;
he has lived for a long time
who has little lived.
Whether you have lived enough
depends not on the number
of your years but on your will."*

MONTAIGNE (1533–1592)

IMAGINE VALUES, eternal pillars, edifices that don't crumble, values that anchor us in fast-changing times. Values are what hold the center together, what keep organizations, communities, families, and individuals intact when all else around them seems to be shifting.

Throughout *The Seven Pillars of Visionary Leadership*, we have highlighted the perilous state of our value code and emphasized that strong values are essential if we are to flourish in the next millennium. In fact, our leadership value path *is* a path of "value," a path to flourish. It provides the keys to open pathways to learning.

To follow the value path, we need to cultivate three elements of our values: *ethos, pathos,* and *logos.* Ethos is our way of life, how we are to live and be civil in community with one another. Pathos refers to our way of valuing, how we feel and express empathy with one another. And logos indicates our way of developing understanding and our ability to think decisively.

All three of these are affected by our declining ability to relate. If we are to attain visionary leadership and get ourselves out of this quagmire, we need to stop destroying and start nurturing our relationships—at home, at work, and in our communities. We will need to lay down our inner weapons so that we don't have the outer ones in reality. We're not advocating being naive. We need to be prepared for conflict, but we should focus our energies on our similarities, not on our differences. We should remind ourselves that who and where we are largely an accident of birth. This insight should give us the humility to realize that "the other" is not always the enemy but in fact could just be a "shadow" of ourselves. Since World War II we have been living out this shadow projection internationally. It's time to see things more clearly. There are no borders on a sphere; by the same token, there are no flowcharts in relationships. If we start seeing and opening our minds to the abundance around us, we can start "doing more with more," to grow our future and move away from the paralysis that comes from "doing more with less."

We need to connect the best of our values to reinvent the meaning of work, wealth, and well-being. When we value ourselves and one another, we will value our labor. We will be able to transform our workplaces into worth places that provide meaning and purpose. Without our valuing the whole human journey, its past, its present, and its future, the center cannot hold.

The human experience is ethical and valuable because it is celebrated, not quantified, controlled, or repressed. The dead reckoning we face is serious because good people are beginning to tune out. They are no longer listening. If enough good people stop listening and believing in a future worth going to, and tell their children there's no hope, we are indeed in grave danger. For whom does the bell toll then?

In the past we were faced with similar dead reckonings that challenged our commitment to be steadfast in our values. At the time of the Vikings communities were gripped in a dark age. Western civilization just scraped through. If it hadn't been for the integrity of the monks, who acted as keepers of knowledge, we all would have been dragged into the abyss.

Today we are threatened with a new kind of Viking, a roaming mindset that disregards our community values. We no longer have the gift of being able to rely on monks to save us. It will be our individual integrity that stands up and is counted.

Bad things happen when good people don't get involved. Many leaders have mission statements nailed to the wall, but do they live by them? We cannot afford to entrust our future to the blindness of quantification. It's time for real leaders to "get up off their bottom line" and be counted in a different way. It's time to make sure that the seventh pillar, valuing, finds its place in the architecture of the new organization.

THE 20/20 LEADERSHIP VALUE PATH

The "visionary" 20/20 leadership value path is shared organizational learning. It is a transformational journey that requires insight, courage, and action to succeed. By reconnecting with our ancient valued path—the historical value roots that have sustained us throughout the centuries—we can better understand and anticipate our collective future reality.

Before we begin our journey, we need to prepare ourselves mentally by putting on the armor of visionary leadership. Our helmet is insight. Our shield is courage. Our lance is action. We will need them on the journey ahead.

We will also need the ability to *value* on the journey, for at every step along the way there is much to value. The ability to value, respect, and hold dear in fact is a key component of 20/20 visionary thinking.

Before you embark on the leadership value path, you might want to ask yourself the following questions to make sure you are ready for the journey. How do you value these qualities? If the answer is "not much," what can you do to increase your respect for them?

THE LEADERSHIP VALUE PATH

I. Visioning	Spirit of enthusiasm	How do you value enduring success?
II. Mapping	Spirit of direction	How do you value a higher vision?
III. Journeying	Spirit of discovery	How do you value true north?
IV. Learning	Spirit of transformation	How do you value a temple of learning?
V. Mentoring	Spirit of sharing	How do you value learning to change?
VI. Leading	Spirit of service	How do you value the transformational journey?
VI. Valuing	Spirit of community	How do you value enthusiasm at work?

THE VALUE OF INSIGHT

We need to examine very seriously what we are actually accomplishing by breaking the value code of loyalty between worker and organization that we have understood for generations. Are we adequately guarding the dignity of work in the drastic changes that are occurring all around us? The economic loss alone of the historical value code of loyalty for American business is estimated to be between $60 and $70 billion dollars annually!

Thomas Bausch, professor and former dean of the College of Business Administration at Marquette University, points out that as meaning and fulfillment of work decline, the need for these qualities in our organizations is on the upswing.

If business organizations are to succeed in this new economy, employees will need to experience meaning and fulfillment in their work in order to give that "extra" that provides added-value and added valuing. According to Bausch, "Models of leadership consistent with the dignity of the person and work are demanded." This is what the leadership value path is all about. It is also called servant leadership.

The late Robert K. Greenleaf, founder of the Center for Applied Ethics in Indianapolis, developed his servant leadership ideas while working as an executive at AT&T. The key servant leadership question is: "As a manager [or teacher, parent, etc.] of those whom I serve, am I helping them grow as persons?" Greenleaf would argue that today's layoffs, for instance, are not unethical since choice is the centerpiece of ethics, and there is no real choosing for many companies if they want to survive. What *is* the ethical problem are the huge egos of managers of yesteryear, who built such large organizations, often as monuments to their own fame and glory—what we have been calling hubris and idol worship. Those kinds of organizations did not meet stockholder, worker, consumer, or society needs, and today employees are left paying the price for these historical management ego trips.

The leadership value path is a process to change that thinking. Archetypally the new insights of what we value looks like this.

Old Thinking—ROI	*New Clear Thinking—ROIR*
Hierarchy: everything in its place	Visionary leadership
Closed system: departmental turf	Vision teams
Nineteenth-century concept of competition	Archetypal learning circles
Employees as automatons	Community vision
Responsiveness decision chain very slow	Value space
Management as bureaucracy	Both mind and heart
Stability and predictability	Work, wealth, well-being
Lifetime commitment	Seamless decision making
Organizational man	Continuous journey

Throughout our journey we have focused on the need to shift thinking and develop a learning paradigm for the new organization. The new temple of learning is something that people can learn to believe in. What a people bows before tells us much about them. What they believe in fuels their actions.

A visionary leader has the insight to live by a value charter. Such a charter creates a covenant of beliefs grounded and rooted in trusted values. Beliefs in turn are acted out in behavior and expressed in a shared code of conduct. The actions of the leader and the organization are accountable. The charter is like a corporate Magna Carta; it keeps the leader honest and the people committed.

THE VALUE CHARTER

Seven Archetypal Beliefs	Seven Archetypal Values
We believe in 20/20 visioning	We value abundance
We believe in mapping our future	We value direction
We believe in journeying together	We value discovery
We believe in learning to change	We value knowledge
We believe in mentoring excellence	We value wisdom
We believe in leadering a value path	We value commitment
We believe in valuing the spirit of enterprise	We value community

The Value of Courage

Visionary leadership—indeed the entire process of organizational transformation—requires great courage. It takes even greater courage to pursue this process in tough economic times.

The new economy has eliminated millions of jobs. People have lost their livelihoods and, for some, their senses of hope and self-esteem. The bonds of trust, loyalty, commitment, and shared motivation, the values that built community, have been badly severed. Without these bonds we are building a workplace that is disconnected from the needs of community well-being.

We must have the courage to face the truth that management,

as it is now practiced, is not equipped to make the next transition. And we need the courage to change.

Insight	Courage	Action
Keep good people, not fire them.	Make the tough people decisions.	Put people first.
Vision, not strategy, leads.	Recognize vision is spirit.	Lead the way.
Let people empower themselves.	Create the environment.	Get out of the way.
Greatness is a shared event.	Become part of the whole.	Lead by being led.
Organizations embody spirit.	"Know thyself."	Let the light shine.
Learning = change.	Be open to change.	Change to be open.

The Value of Action

We are *valuable* people. We are people of values. To miss acknowledging and nurturing this necessary spirituality of the workplace is to ask employees to work in an environment without oxygen. Spirituality is who we are, not what we have, or some religious affiliation. We cannot avoid our spirituality any more than we can escape ourselves.

The leadership value path acknowledges spirituality in the workplace because it acknowledges a very fundamental reality: Employees need to breathe! Employees who breathe take in breaths of air; breath, as we have seen, is *ruah,* or spirit.

Only the spirit of enterprise brings employees alive.

Eduard C. Lindeman, one of this century's early adult educators, knew that dialogue led to new thinking, a change of attitudes, and the opening of the mind. He wrote, "We do not 'think through' problems; we act through. Thinking carries us only so far, then action must follow or we become lost in the wilderness of verbalism."

Visionary leaders not only have the insight but also value action and have the courage to act.

INSPIRATIONAL PLAN OF ACTION

The Visionary Leader Points the Way.

Visioning
Recognize a change situation exists, and do something about it.
Mapping
Analyze issues inside and outside, and identify change points.
Journeying
Listen to the voice and heart of the organization, where they've been and where they want to go.

The Vision Team Lights the Path.

Learning
Free up your intellectual and social capital for discovery.
Mentoring
Implement both-and learning opportunities.

20/20 Vision Aligns the Leader.

Leading
Inspire a spirit of enterprise, and get out of the way.
Valuing
Make sure the center holds and point the compass true north.

THE PATH OF THE ANCIENTS

Archetypal learning requires an openness to accepting ancient wisdom. It values meditation and reflection as part of the personal change process. Developing a deeper understanding and perspective of the value of ancient wisdom is an essential rite of passage. The path of the ancients points us in the right direction for personal discovery.

An Ancient Perspective: The Value of the Seven Pillars of Visionary Leadership

PILLAR I: The Ancient Value of Visioning

Organizations on the leadership value path recognize that vision is the cornerstone from which their values for the future also flow. This cornerstone is their heart and soul. Archetypally, when they value the cornerstone, they make a commitment to a leadership covenant. If, however, a vision of uncertainty becomes our cornerstone, we are forced to concentrate on the "bottom line" instead of the "top line," on a vision of where we've been instead of who we are and where we're going. A vision focused on finance, not on people, encourages managers to learn short-term command and control behavior (i.e., making the numbers) while ignoring the higher aspects of developing a sustainable future. Managers in such companies take their vision from each day's stock prices and overlook the long-term profit benefits of valuing a wider vision.

Do we have visionary economists? Do we have visionary accountants? The logic of these disciplines inherently promotes an economy of the mind, not steps to an ecology of abundance. Auditing the physical and financial capital of what has been is more important for them than valuing the abundance of social and human capital that they critically need to invest in to sustain a future. A spiritual and psychological cornerstone sustained the ancients and every other people throughout the ages. Only a vision let the ancients envision and sculpt something as magnificent and powerful as Stonehenge, Solomon's Temple, Jericho, the Parthenon, Hadrian's Wall, St. Peter's, or Chartres Cathedral. America itself was founded on a belief, on a vision. Its edifices and institutions were built on visions far more expansive than the typical three-month or three-year corporate strategy.

What will be left of *our* visionary cornerstones? Will future generations stand in amazement of what we worshiped: the industrial architecture in New York, Toronto, Los Angeles, Chicago? How will they define where our center is? Will our downtown and suburban concrete visions inspire the same passion and inner vision that Israel's Wailing Wall evokes? What are we valuing with our concrete visions? Does working on the sixty-fourth floor in a downtown office building create a sense of value, of wonder, of passion? Do we go home at the end of the day feeling more valued because of our work?

Yesterday's sacred monuments still serve today's needs. Poet Robert Bly remarks, "We think rocks don't talk, but that's because it takes them a hundred years to complete a sentence." The ancients remind us that visionary time is real time.

THE VALUE OF ANCIENT VISIONING

Question:

What ancient vision, myth, or ritual as archetypal learning is relevant to you today?

20/20 LVP Meaning:

Crisis is a time of getting to "know thyself" so that real growth can happen.

Visionary Top Line Learning:

A people without vision perishes. Plain and simple.

PILLAR II: *The Ancient Value of Mapping*

A vision map helped the ancients persevere on their journey. Just as it sustained Job through his trials and the Israelites on their journey to the Promised Land, so we must have the courage to listen to the inner voice to stay the visionary course. We need to reflect on what we are valuing and what maps to use to make sense of our human and corporate journeys.

In valuing the compass map, we secure a future. The compass

points us to this future. The compass gives direction for leadership. Archetypally, valuing the compass is preparing for discovery.

As the Israelites wandered through the desert, they often got distracted, went off course, and forgot their map. But the community of sojourners did not forget. Someone, somewhere in the tribe valued the map to get them back on course. Their journey was to the Promised Land. The value of the map reminded them that the promise was true. They did have a destination.

Ask yourself: What kind of value compass are you handing to your children? Your employees? Your community? What is the canon that you adhere to and are willing to pass on? Who are the great teachers today? The CEOs? The pastors? The politicians? The professors? The media?

We have to earn our futures. They cannot be handed to us. This takes learning. We can stumble into the future and, by that token, be at its mercy, or we can keep an eye on the wisdom of the past and on our integral vision of the future and learn to earn that future.

We become what we worship; we become what we value; we become what we learn.

As our organizations embark on the learning journey, they have to value their map so that the pillars on which they are building their new temple of learning are made of substance, not sand.

PILLAR III: *The Ancient Value of Journeying*

For the ancients, in valuing their journey, there was a deep sense of appreciation for what life offered. The Latin *diurnum* means "daily portion"; we get the word *journey* from it. Journey and one's daily allotment go hand in hand. An attitude of reverence and gratitude for what each day brings is part of this ancient valuing of journeying.

Life did not have the conveniences we so easily take for granted. Yet the ancients had an inner thankfulness and joy in discovery. The psalmist says that he will praise the name of God

THE VALUE OF ANCIENT MAPPING

Question:

What ancient vision, myth, ritual as archetypal learning is relevant to you today?

20/20 LVP Meaning:

We carry the universe in our head; it tells us what we can and cannot do.

Visionary Top Line Learning:

Maps have great power to shape our imagination in what we can achieve.

---

with a song and thanksgiving. This will be better than sacrificing any ox, which, for the ancients, was a prized possession indeed. By this the psalmist means that an internal or spiritual sense of the journey with their higher vision was becoming more fundamental. Their outer journey through the wilderness was real, but the true journey was the inner journey of discovery made possible by a higher vision and a compass-map.

The urgency of the journey for the ancients was apparent when Jesus, for instance, told his disciples to get on their way and not worry about carrying a bag, or food, or money, an extra tunic, sandals, or a staff. The important thing was to get on the journey. In the first century A.D., in the Acts of the Apostles, Barnabas recounts how Saul of Tarsus (later St. Paul) saw the Lord while on his journey. It is when we are *on* the journey that great things happen.

For the ancients, *discovery happens while one is on the journey.* This insight is a good measuring stick for our organizations. Are we willing to risk the journey? Do we reward those who have a spirit of discovery? "Nothing ventured, nothing gained" is an old maxim. But it is still true. Thucydides was correct in saying that courage is the secret of freedom. Antoine de St.-Exupéry, author of *The Little Prince,* said that he knew of only one freedom, and that was the freedom of the mind.

What's our level of courage? Are we willing to risk taking the journey? The ancient sense of valuing the journey gives us the confidence that we can expect great things, but we have to *be* on the journey. If the Hebrews' journey took them from bondage to a land flowing with milk and honey, we can, with Henry Wadsworth Longfellow, trust that thought will take us from slavery into freedom. Freedom is real when we become conscious of it. A slave, says Ezra Pound, is someone who waits for another to free one. Journeying makes freedom happen. Journeying is the joy of discovery. The ancients knew that intimately; we have to believe it also.

THE VALUE OF ANCIENT JOURNEYING

Question:

What ancient vision, myth, ritual as archetypal learning is relevant to you today?

20/20 LVP Meaning:

Inward bound is instrumental in getting in touch with ourselves.

Visionary Top Line Learning:

Journey is a voyage of personal discovery through the belly of the whale that transforms us as individuals in the process.

PILLAR IV: The Ancient Value of Learning

Our learning journey will be marked by attainments of excellence, just as in the past the great books of the mind served as spiritual and intellectual way stations or points of arrival and departure. In reading the great books, one meets the great teachers. They leave their spiritual imprint on the pages of history.

In *The Western Canon: The Books and School of the Ages,* Harold Bloom tells us that he believes the Western canon—what he calls "the image of the individual thinking"—is in danger of falling apart, of the center not holding. He is saying that value connectors throughout history (our valued compass) are not understood or honored in today's society.

Once upon a time learning to honor valor, duty, sacrifice, heroics were seen, accepted, and lived as integral to the human journey. These value points helped make us strong. One becomes part of this historical great human journey today by mastering the same qualities and living the eminent values founded on the cornerstone of a great and worthy vision. We ignore them at our peril.

For Francis Bacon (1561–1626), the English essayist and philosopher, the value of learning surpassed everything else in nature. He expressed this value by naming it pleasure and delight of knowledge and learning. Bacon believed one could experience what he called satiety, or enough, in all pleasures except learning. Learning stretches us to go for more. In *The Hitopadesa* a collection of Hindu writings around A.D. 500, it is written: "Learning is superior to beauty; learning is better than hidden treasure; learning is a companion on a journey to a strange country; learning is strength inexhaustible."

Learning is a journey into the unknown. The ancients knew that, but they were willing to proceed anyway. Strange things could happen, but one could never be the same after. Learning was a experience of change and freedom.

PILLAR V: *The Ancient Value of Mentoring*

How do we recapture the vision of discovery when so many today seem to be sleepwalking? Who is there to show us the way? Who are our guides?

We must open our eyes and the eyes of others to the excitement of the journey. We must, like the ancients, become searchers of knowledge. We must open ourselves up to the education of the mind *(educare* = "to lead out").

The ancients valued mentoring through sharing their experiences. As a result, they learned empathy and gratitude. They were very aware that sharing experiences helped people grow; their oral traditions and stories were the backbone of their

---

THE VALUE OF ANCIENT LEARNING

Question:

What ancient vision, myth, ritual as archetypal learning is relevant to you today?

20/20 LVP Meaning:

Learning is a calling and a leadership responsibility. We will be judged by our actions.

Visionary Top Line Learning:

Great ideas shape the world which we pass on and inherit—for better or for worse.

---

tribes. A sense of great expectations fostered a magnificent spirit of wonder and initiative. Shakespeare was correct when he said that we know what we are but not what we can become. The ancient Roman Publius Syrus said that we really don't know what we can do until we try. The ancients were willing to try.

Thomas Hobbes reminds us that knowledge is power. The ancients knew the value of what Hobbes meant. To name something, for the ancients, meant that a person had power over that reality. A wise teacher, or mentor, would skillfully guide a novice in the rites of passage. For instance, because a name revealed the identity and character of a person, God refused to name himself to Moses. Instead, the Book of Exodus tells us that God responded to Moses' request for a name in a very ambiguous way: "I am what I am." It is sometimes translated as "I am who I will be." Not a very satisfying answer!

But there is a very important valuing process going on here: God, in mentoring Moses, is leading him out *(educare)*, not by giving him the answers but rather, as Moses later discovered, by guiding him on a journey of self-discovery. God, as mentor, taught Moses that character is earned, not glibly given, and, as such, can never be taken away. Benjamin Franklin said something similar when he remarked that the proof of gold is fire.

Fire is the transformative agent. Mentors sustain us as we are crafted in the crucible of life's lessons.

The learning organization knows that true education is not content regurgitation but rather a process more akin to Plato's insight of the cave. Plato's cave portrayed individuals chained in the darkness; they couldn't see one another. If they could break free of their chains and escape from the cave, they could see reality as it really was. For Plato, the shadowy world of the cave is just the world of appearances. Escaping from the cave symbolized a person's transition into the "real world."

Today leadership organizations with a vision are making that transition and mentoring a way; they know the power of knowledge. They are learning organizations. A vision more bold and dynamic than resignation has energized them. They now have a compass. They walk out into the sunlight with a spirit of hope and enterprise. Their knowledge people are inspired with a sense of purpose and a higher vision.

Employees in any organization with an integral vision and a value compass have a real feeling of support, purpose, challenge, excitement, and belonging. They are valued for *who* they are and *what* they can do, both being and having.

THE VALUE OF ANCIENT MENTORING

Question:

What ancient vision, myth, ritual as archetypal learning is relevant to you today?

20/20 LVP Meaning:

Mentoring is the service of giving, not taking; it is visionary and servant leadership.

Visionary Top Line Learning:

It ensures a future from generation to generation and is essential to transformation and transition planning.

PILLAR VI: *The Ancient Value of Leading*

The visionary leader is the keeper of the value compass. Visionary leadership will rebuild the new temple of learning to integrate vision, values, and spirit with the individual, the organization, and the community.

Over the centuries the ancients stood at cultural and religious crossroads many times. But they never made a future unless they had a higher vision worth trusting and following, a compass of values giving them direction on the journey, and a love of learning, of building a temple—inner and outer—that expressed this love.

At our crossroads today we need to build a new temple, an organization based on a higher vision and strong values. To do so, the visionary leader must value the pillars—the pillars of learning, the pillars of strength.

Abraham Lincoln remarked that if we could first know where we are and where we are tending, we could better judge what to do and how to do it. A similar value of leading is found in Thomas A. Edison's words "There's a better way to do it . . . find it."

The value of leading is found in the commitment the ancients brought to the journey. Great leaders then, and now, inspire excellence. Marshall Field & Company portray this excellence in great leadering in the following words: "To do the right thing, at the right time, in the right way; to do some things better than they were ever done before; to eliminate errors; to know both sides of the question; to be courteous; to be an example; to work for the love of work; to anticipate requirements; to develop resources; to recognize no impediments; to master circumstances; to act from reason rather than rule; to be satisfied with nothing short of perfection."

PILLAR VII: *The Ancient Value of Valuing*

As we enter the third millennium, there is an openness to learn beyond borders and find solutions from places we've never con-

THE VALUE OF ANCIENT LEADERSHIP

Question:

What ancient vision, myth, ritual as archetypal learning is relevant to you today?

2020 LVP Meaning:

Leadership is founded on service to the state, the organization, and others.

Visionary Top Line Learning:

Visionary leadership is the rediscovery of an old ethic of servant leadership.

---

sidered before. The Dalai Lama lost his physical temple, but he still has great influence. His inner temple has pillars founded on an integral vision. In this time of insecurity he offers us some very insightful advice:

> We have a good brain . . . allowing us to judge what is right and what is wrong, not only in terms of today's concerns, but considering ten, twenty, or even a hundred years in the future. Without any precognition, we can use our normal common sense to determine if something is a right or wrong method; we can decide that if we do such and such, it will lead to such and such an effect. . . . We must safeguard our mental capacity for judgement. For that, we cannot take out insurance; the insurance company is within: self-discipline, self-awareness. . . . But first we must change within ourselves.

We have a chance now to redesign our image of what a life well spent can mean. We can be more inclusive, embracing both prophets and profits, both vision and practical common sense. The evidence is in: High-performing organizations *are* spirit-driven. Drucker observes that a postcapitalist society requires a unifying force and a leadership group that can focus local, particular, separate traditions onto a common and shared commitment to values, a common concept of excellence, and mutual respect.

Valuing the pillars is faith in a future. The pillars are the architecture that make a strong future. They are the bricks and mortar for the learning organization. Archetypally, valuing the pillars is an investment in a future.

The ancient value of valuing comes through loudly and clearly in the Sermon on the Mount. Jesus uses many metaphors, parables, and examples to help his listeners grasp the critical importance of valuing. In underscoring how God values human beings, he reminds his audience that they must not worry. Even the birds of the air are looked after. What people have to value is the "kingdom within"—that is, the inner life. Nothing else is as important to Jesus as valuing: God, or the higher vision, first of all, and others secondly. Vision and service.

We become what our vision values. James Allen, in his beautiful little book *As a Man Thinketh*, reminds us that we will realize the vision of our hearts, be it base or beautiful or a mixture of both. Columbus, for instance, cherished a vision of another world and discovered it; Copernicus fostered the vision of a mul-

---

THE VALUE OF ANCIENT VALUING

Question:

What ancient vision, myth, ritual as archetypal learning is relevant to you today?

20/20 LVP Meaning:

The "bottom line" ROI is founded on the sacred geometry of the "top line" ROIR.

Visionary Top Line Learning:

"In God We Trust," the symbol of the eye, and the pyramid are not on the U.S. bank note for nothing. They are a legacy from the thinking of the Founding Fathers. Valuing is what we are worshiping; it is time to get back on track.

tiplicity of worlds and a wider universe and revealed it; Buddha beheld the vision of a spiritual world of stainless beauty and perfect peace, and he entered into it. Allen writes: "For you will always gravitate toward that which you, secretly, most love. Into your hands will be placed the exact results of your own thoughts. You will receive that which you earn; no more, no less. Whatever your present environment may be, you will fall, remain, or rise with your thoughts—your vision, your ideal. You will become as small as your controlling desire; as great as your dominant aspiration."

What are your dominant aspirations? What do you value the most? How does your leadership value path measure up to the task?

The path of the ancients is common sense today. It is an event waiting to happen. The ancients have gone before us on their journey; they can light the path to our unfoldment.

In these pages we have introduced many organizations and individuals that are using visionary thinking to embark on new learning journeys in search of new organizations. These courageous, visionary leaders are the real agents of change. Their skill in crafting a vision, endorsing a vision, and building a share of mind around that vision will help all of us through our transformation.

APPENDIX

PERSONAL ASSESSMENT PROFILE

INDIVIDUAL

Instructions: Listed below are 49 statements that explore your preparedness for the leadership value path. There are no right or wrong answers. Just give your honest perception of yourself in relation to the 49 items. Use the following scale to make your judgment for each item.

1 = To a very little extent
2 = To a little extent
3 = To some extent
4 = To a great extent
5 = To a very great extent

I agree that I ...   My rating

#	Statement	My rating
1	Have a clear vision of where I'm going.	
2	Always find new and creative ways to do things.	
3	Celebrate people's accomplishments.	
4	Get excited about learning something new each day.	
5	Value experience and know-how.	
6	Demonstrate obvious leadership qualities.	
7	Nourish and value winners.	
8	Look for new opportunities every day.	
9	Am in touch with the depth of my convictions to manage change.	
10	Follow through on my well-thought-out plans.	
11	Love learning.	
12	Invest time and money in self-development.	
13	Aim to be an inspiration, both to myself and to others.	
14	Honour and value my contributions.	
15	Have a good future because of what I see as possible.	
16	Develop effective personal goals.	
17	Effectively meet challenges as they occur.	
18	Value innovation highly.	
19	Foster a genuine sense of community wherever I am.	
20	Am continually building a champion mindset in myself.	
21	Have character and ethics in my daily living.	

22	Definitely go beyond tunnel vision in planning my future.	
23	Know what to do to make effective personal changes.	
24	Am well along the way to a balanced lifestyle.	
25	Am learning effective ways to provide for my future.	
26	Am making a worthy effort to leave my mark in life.	
27	Inspire myself and others to live a holistic lifestyle.	
28	Value risk-taking and innovative ideas.	
29	See me as "leading edge" in my thinking.	
30	Have a clear focus on what my priorities are.	
31	Am currently making the appropriate changes in my life.	
32	Am excited about new learning and new thinking.	
33	Am a good role model.	
34	Am a natural leader who inspires trust, originality, and challenge.	
35	Nurture commitment through motivation and community.	
36	Invent exciting ways to meet the future.	
37	Am effective in thinking through how to handle difficult situations.	
38	Am building a future worth going to.	
39	Love new ways of learning how to stay current.	
40	Not only want to do things right, but also do the right things.	
41	Nurture a real spirit of enterprise in all I do.	
42	Constantly search out countless opportunities to improve myself.	
43	Honestly do think "out of the box."	
44	Have a very realistic mental picture of where I'm going.	
45	Am exceptionally strong in building morale and commitment.	
46	Always figure out how to turn adversity into opportunity.	
47	Motivate those around me to believe fully in themselves.	
48	Bring out the best in myself and others.	
49	Practice what I preach.	

Manual Scoring Instructions:

VISIONING: Add your score from items 1, 8, 15, 22, 29, 36, 43
MAPPING: Add your score from items 2, 9, 16, 23, 30, 37, 44
JOURNEYING: Add your score from items 3, 10, 17, 24, 31, 38, 45
LEARNING: Add your score from items 4, 11, 18, 25, 32, 39, 46
MENTORING: Add your score from items 5, 12, 19, 26, 33, 40, 47
LEADING: Add your score from items 6, 13, 20, 27, 34, 41, 48
VALUING: Add your score from items 7, 14, 21, 28, 35, 42, 49

To plot your LVP Personal Assessment Profile, place each score with a dot (•) on the appropriate pillar below. Join all seven dots with a line.

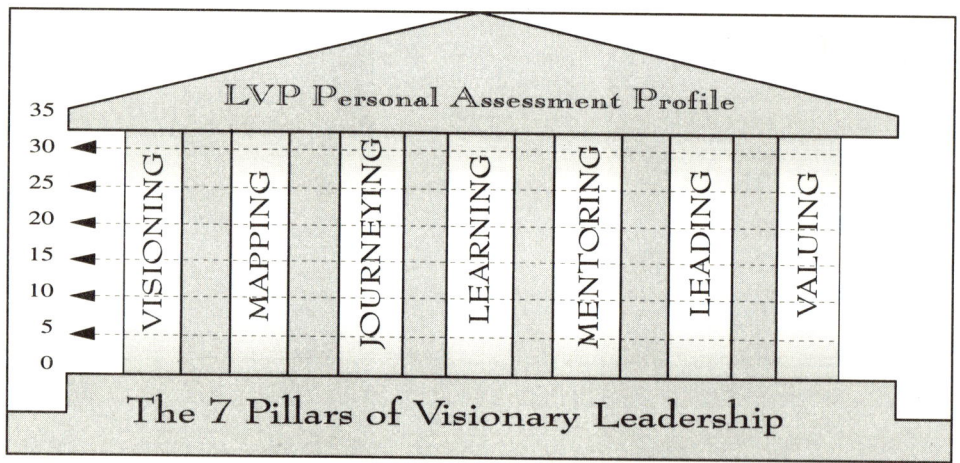

Interpretation:

Range	Description
0 - 5	Personal leadership value path showing **considerable** weakness.
6 - 10	Personal leadership value path showing **definite** weakness.
11 - 15	Personal leadership value path showing **some** weakness.
16 - 20	Personal leadership value path showing **balance**.
21 - 25	Personal leadership value path showing **some** strength.
26 - 30	Personal leadership value path showing **definite** strength.
31 - 35	Personal leadership value path showing **considerable** strength.

APPENDIX

ORGANIZATION ASSESSMENT PROFILE

ORGANIZATION

Instructions: Listed below are 49 statements that explore your organization's preparedness for the leadership value path. There are no right or wrong answers. Just give your honest perception of your organization in relation to the 49 items. Use the following scale to make your judgment for each item.

1 = To a very little extent
2 = To a little extent
3 = To some extent
4 = To a great extent
5 = To a very great extent

The organization I work for ...

		My rating
1	Has a clear vision of where it's going.	
2	Always finds new and creative ways to do things.	
3	Celebrates people's accomplishments.	
4	Fosters excitement about learning something new each day.	
5	Values experience and know-how.	
6	Demonstrates obvious leadership qualities.	
7	Nourishes and values winners.	
8	Creates an environment filled with new opportunities every day.	
9	Has the depth in its convictions to genuinely manage change.	
10	Follows through on its well-thought-out plans.	
11	Is a learning organization.	
12	Invests time and money in people development.	
13	Builds champions.	
14	Honours employees and their contributions.	
15	Has a good future because of its living corporate vision.	
16	Develops shared organizational goals.	
17	Effectively meets challenges as they occur.	
18	Values innovation highly.	
19	Fosters a genuine sense of community.	
20	Brings out the best in people.	
21	Practices what it preaches.	

22	Definitely goes beyond just corporate tunnel vision.
23	Knows what to do to make effective changes.
24	Is well along the way to organizational health.
25	Is effectively learning how to change structures and systems.
26	Cultivates and nurtures wisdom.
27	Promotes economic growth, prosperity, and well-being.
28	Value risk-taking and innovative ideas.
29	Clearly has "leading edge" thinking.
30	Has a clear focus on what its priorities are.
31	Is making changes in the right way.
32	Promotes new learning and new thinking.
33	Develops good role models.
34	Has leaders who inspire trust, originality, and challenge.
35	Nurtures commitment through motivation and community.
36	Invents exciting ways to meet the future.
37	Thinks through the proverbial "rock and hard place" situations.
38	Is building a future worth going to.
39	Is constantly learning new ways to improve itself.
40	Not only wants to do things right, but also does the right things.
41	Nurtures a real spirit of enterprise in the work environment.
42	Believes in what it's doing.
43	Thinks "out of the box."
44	Works well at crafting new organizational roadmaps.
45	Is a real community, both in spirit and in action.
46	Allows employees to learn from their mistakes.
47	Applies knowledge constructively to what it already knows.
48	Inspires employees to meet their goals.
49	Practices what it preaches.

APPENDIX

Manual Scoring Instructions:

VISIONING: Add your score from items 1, 8, 15, 22, 29, 36, 43
MAPPING: Add your score from items 2, 9, 16, 23, 30, 37, 44
JOURNEYING: Add your score from items 3, 10, 17, 24, 31, 38, 45
LEARNING: Add your score from items 4, 11, 18, 25, 32, 39, 46
MENTORING: Add your score from items 5, 12, 19, 26, 33, 40, 47
LEADING: Add your score from items 6, 13, 20, 27, 34, 41, 48
VALUING: Add your score from items 7, 14, 21, 28, 35, 42, 49

To plot your LVP Organization Assessment Profile, place each score with a dot (•) on the appropriate pillar below. Join all seven dots with a line.

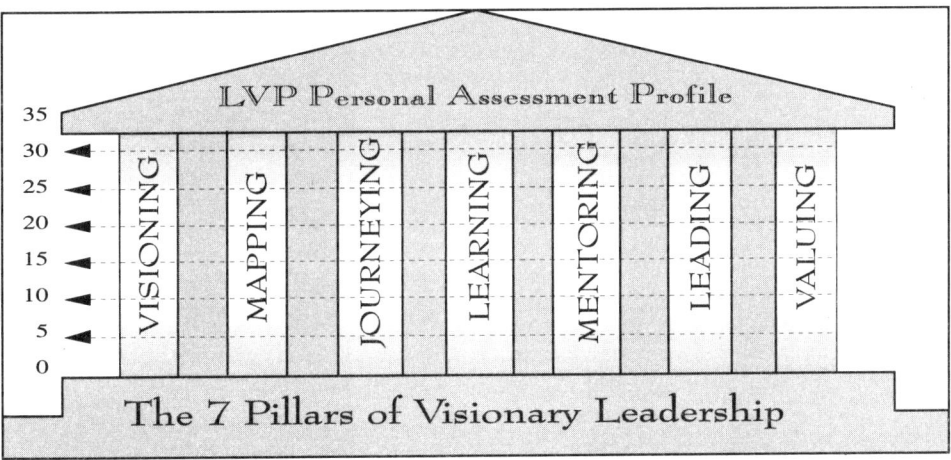

Interpretation:
- 0 - 5   Personal leadership value path showing **considerable** weakness.
- 6 - 10   Personal leadership value path showing **definite** weakness.
- 11 - 15 Personal leadership value path showing **some** weakness.
- 16 - 20 Personal leadership value path showing **balance.**
- 21 - 25 Personal leadership value path showing **some** strength.
- 26 - 30 Personal leadership value path showing **definite** strength.
- 31 - 35 Personal leadership value path showing **considerable** strength.

MINDSCAPE VALUE ASSESSMENT PROFILE

MINDSCAPE

Instructions: Listed below are 42 statements that explore your preparedness for the new thinking required to build the leadership value path. There are no right or wrong answers. Just give your honest perception of yourself in relation to the 42 items. Use the following scale to make your judgment for each item.

1 = To a very little extent
2 = To a little extent
3 = To some extent
4 = To a great extent
5 = To a very great extent

In building a future worth going to (defined as work, wealth, and well-being), I realize the following ...

PILLAR I: VISIONING

My rating

Dead Reckoning:
| 1 | We are definitely at a social and economic crossroads. | |

New Directions:
| 2 | We urgently need *both* top-line *and* bottom-line thinking. | |

Added Valuing:
| 3 | *Added valuing* means putting people first. | |

Danger Ahead:
| 4 | There is a need for *both* explicit *and* tacit learning. | |

Sensus Fidelium:
| 5 | We must listen to the "inner voice" in our decision-making. | |

Valuing the Spirit:
| 6 | Vision is spirit-driven | |

APPENDIX

PILLAR II: MAPPING

My rating

Parting of the Mindsets:

| 7 | We must connect *both* rational *and* intuitive mental maps. | |

Breaking Mental Maps:

| 8 | Open borders need open minds. | |

Valuing Net Worth:

| 9 | Business is more than a box of contracts. | |

People of the Way:

| 10 | Organizations either work together or wither together. | |

Wilderness Journey:

| 11 | New thinking requires vision guides. | |

Preparing for the Journey:

| 12 | The future requires leadership on a value path as the compass. | |

PILLAR III: JOURNEYING

My rating

Revolution of the Imagination:

| 13 | Abundance starts in the imagination. | |

Seeing the Vision:

| 14 | The new horizon requires thinking that does more with more. | |

Value Path to 20/20 Vision:

| 15 | Leadership requires igniting a spirit of enterprise. | |

The New Journey:

| 16 | Outward bound starts with an inward journey. | |

A Pilgrim's Progress:

| 17 | We must be open for new learning. | |

Tribal Tensions:

| 18 | Organizations are learning circles with a radius of trust. | |

PILLAR IV: LEARNING

My rating

Assessment of Opportunity:

| 19 | Mastery requires continuous learning. | |

Measuring the cost:

| 20 | Soft is hard. | |

Harvesting the *bene*-fit:

| 21 | Vision-driven organizations have clearly articulated values and reap greater rewards. | |

Know Thyself:

| 22 | There is wisdom in connecting learning with trusted traditions. | |

Mens Sana in Corpore Sano:

| 23 | Organizations are living organisms where mind and spirit meet on equal terms. | |

Inward Bound:

| 24 | Imagination does rule the world. | |

PILLAR V: MENTORING

My rating

Reformation of Learning:

| 25 | Mentoring a better way starts at birth. | |

Content with Learning:

| 26 | Mentoring requires that we take learning seriously. | |

Learning with Content:

| 27 | Great thinking and ideas are timeless. | |

Spirit of Enterprise:

| 28 | A spirit-filled organization promotes people, pride, and profits/prophets. | |

Reformation of Work:

| 29 | We need to reconnect with a leadership ethic of work, wealth, and well-being. | |

The Work of Reformation:

| 30 | The new work of reformation means to start growing people. | |

PILLAR VI: LEADING

My rating

The Leadership Value Path:

| 31 | Visionary leadership is servant leadership. | |

Steering Not Rowing:

| 32 | We must align our thinking and connect our strategy to a 20/20 vision. | |

Principle of Duty:

| 33 | Business has a civic reponsibility to grow people, pride, and profits/prophets. | |

Idol Worship:

| 34 | Steadfastness on the true priorities is a must. | |

The Past Is Prologue:

| 35 | Servant leadership sustains the flame by building on corporate memory. | |

Revaluing the Future:

| 36 | The new leadership ethic means that genuine relationships build one people, one purpose. | |

PILLAR VII: VALUING

My rating

The Value of Insight:

| 37 | Insight unlocks the future. | |

The Value of Courage:

| 38 | Courage is needed to make the tough people decisions. | |

The Value of Action:

| 39 | Visionary leaders inspire a spirit of enterprise and let their people grow. | |

Valuing the Cornerstone:

| 40 | Mental architecture is as important as the physical architecture. | |

Valuing the Compass:

| 41 | The leadership value path is a strategy for a common purpose. | |

Valuing the Pillars:

| 42 | The 7 *Pillars:* the learning structure to sustain transformation. | |

Manual Scoring Instructions:

VISIONING: Add your score from items 1, 8, 15, 22, 29, 36
MAPPING: Add your score from items 2, 9, 16, 23, 30, 37
JOURNEYING: Add your score from items 3, 10, 17, 24, 31, 38
LEARNING: Add your score from items 4, 11, 18, 25, 32, 39
MENTORING: Add your score from items 5, 12, 19, 26, 33, 40
LEADING: Add your score from items 6, 13, 20, 27, 34, 41
VALUING: Add your score from items 7, 14, 21, 28, 35, 42

To plot your LVP Mindscape Assessment Profile, place each score with a dot (•) on the appropriate pillar below. Join all seven dots with a line.

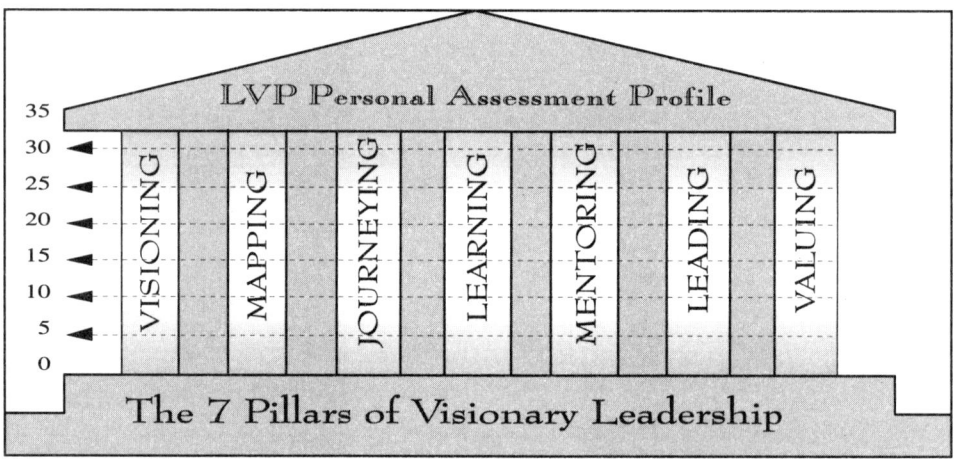

Interpretation:
- 0 - 4   Personal leadership value path showing ***considerable*** weakness.
- 5 - 9   Personal leadership value path showing ***definite*** weakness.
- 10 - 14   Personal leadership value path showing ***some*** weakness.
- 15 - 18   Personal leadership value path showing ***balance.***
- 19 - 22   Personal leadership value path showing ***some*** strength.
- 23 - 26   Personal leadership value path showing ***definite*** strength.
- 27 - 30   Personal leadership value path showing ***considerable*** strength.

DISCUSSION QUESTIONS
TO BEGIN BUILDING
THE 7 PILLARS LEADERSHIP VALUE PATH

Essential Questions to Consider
When Developing a
VISION

- How is your organization endorsing a vision for the 21st century?
- How is your organization connecting its vision to the future horizon?
- How is your organization freeing up a vision of enterprise?
- How is your organization connecting vision to build community?
- How is your organization developing a vision connected to strategy?
- How is your organization sustaining its vision for the future?

Essential Questions to Consider
When Developing a Mental
MAP

- How is your organization developing a mental map for the 21st century?
- How is your organization making innovative decisions based on that map?
- How is your organization developing a strategy for a borderless map?
- How is your organization connecting its past with its future?
- How is your organization planning for the future?
- How is your organization setting its compass?

Essential Questions to Consider on the
JOURNEY
to the 21st Century

- How is your organization moving to a global business reality?
- How is your organization working with "one vision, one purpose"?
- How is your organization developing great expectations on the way?
- How is your organization making the journey worthwhile?
- How is your organization becoming all it can be?
- How is your organization learning beyond borders?

Essential Questions for the
LEARNING
Organization

- How is your organization becoming a "smart" community?
- How is your organization learning to change?

- How is your organization harnessing social and intellectual capital?
- How is your organization championing a learning attitude?
- How is your organization growing as a thriving community?
- How is your organization changing to learn?

Essential Questions for
MENTORING
Success

- How is your organization developing the foresight for change?
- How is your organization equipping its people for change?
- How is your organization empowering its people to make decisions?
- How is your organization modelling a spirit of enterprise?
- How is your organization championing knowledge workers?
- How is your organization "stepping out of the box"?

Essential Questions for
LEADING
the Way

- How is your organization building a leadership value path?
- How is your organization optimising its efforts?
- How is your organization serving by leading?
- How is your organization celebrating entrepreneurs?
- How is your organization trusting *both* the past *and* the future?
- How is your organization benefitting from inspiring a high vision?

Essential Questions for
VALUING
a Future Worth Going To

- How is your organization entrusting its future?
- How is your organization celebrating its people?
- How is your organization inspiring a sense of pride?
- How is your organization building a stronger bottom line?
- How is your organization investing in relationships?
- How is your organization valuing its achievements?

NOTES

Note to reader: The following endnotes are in the order in which they appeared in the text. Additional material can be found on the World Wide Web (WWW) and its many servers. One we have found exceptional is by Digital Equipment Corporation. The site is: http://www.altavista.digital.com/

INTRODUCTION

Peter Salovey, as quoted in Nancy Gibbs, "The EQ Factor," *Time* (October 2, 1995), 60, 62–66, 68. WWW site: http://www.pathfinder.com/@@@1CIdZEDJQAAQOc3/time/magazine/.domestic/1995/951002/951002.cover.html.

Rosabeth Moss Kanter, "Thriving Locally in the Global Economy," *Harvard Business Review* (September–October 1995), 151–160.

Nancy Gibbs, "The EQ Factor," *Time* (October 2, 1995), 60, 62–66, 68. WWW site: http://www.pathfinder.com/@@@1CIdZEDJQAAQOc3/time/magazine/.

James M. Sanford, as quoted in Bernard Wysocki, Jr., "The Danger of Stretching Too Far," *Toronto Globe and Mail*, August 15, 1995, A15.

Daniel Goleman, *Emotional Intelligence* (New York: Bantam, 1995). See also: Daniel Goleman, "Kinder, Gentler Smarts Pay Off," *Toronto Globe and Mail*, September 26, 1995, B16; Daniel Goleman, "Treating the Ailing Spirit," *New York Times Book Review*, March 5, 1995, 12–13; Daniel Goleman, "Not about Sex, but Power," *Toronto Globe and Mail*, October 26, 1991, D10; Daniel Goleman, "Grins, Grimaces Enhance Feelings, Some Psychologists Say," ibid., July 22, 1989, D4; Daniel Goleman, "How the Mind Can Make It Up," ibid., June 1, 1994, A17; Daniel Goleman, "Teaching Kids Alternatives to Violence," ibid., August 27, 1993, A15; Lynn Smith, "Forget IQ, Emotional Intelligence Called Key," *Toronto Star*, November 17, 1995, E3.

Peter Kizilos, "Fixing Fatal Flaws," *Training*, vol. 28, no. 9 (September 1991), 66–70; George Pearson, "New Look in Development of Tomorrow's Executive," *Canadian HR Reporter*, vol. 7, no. 21 (December 5, 1994), 13–14; Lee Smith, "Burned-Out Bosses," *Fortune*, vol. 130, no. 2 (July 25, 1994), 44–46, 50, 52.

World Bank, "Priorities and Strategies for Education. A World Bank Review." WWW site: http://www.worldbank.org/html/extpb/PrioritiesEducation.html.

Peter F. Drucker, *Post-Capitalist Society* (New York: HarperBusiness, 1993).

John A. Byrne, *The Whiz Kids* (New York: Currency Doubleday, 1993), 8. Also, Jennifer Wells, "The Boys Who Knew Too Much," *Globe and Mail Report on Business Magazine*, vol. 10, no. 5 (November 1993), 37–38.

Peter Drucker, *The Practice of Management* (New York: Harper & Row, 1954).

William G. Ouchi. *Theory Z: How American Business Can Meet the Japanese Challenge* (New York: Avon, 1981).

Michael Hammer and James Champy, *Reengineering the Corporation: A Manifesto for a Business Revolution* (New York: HarperBusiness, 1993).

Peter M. Senge, *The Fifth Discipline: The Art and Practice of the Learning Organization* (New York: Currency Doubleday, 1990).

Margot Gibb-Clark, "Survivors Also Suffer in Downsizing: Expert," *Toronto Globe and Mail*, May 23, 1995, B5.

Bernard Wysocki, Jr., "The Danger of Stretching Too Far," *Toronto Globe and Mail*, August 15, 1995, A15.

Edward E. Lawler, as quoted in Chris Lee, Ron Zemke, "The Search for Spirit in the Workplace," *Training*, vol. 30, no. 6 (June 1993), 28.

For information on Pierre Teilhard de Chardin, see the following WWW site: http://maple.lemoyne.edu/~bucko/Teilhard.html.

PILLAR I: VISIONING

Anna VerSteeg, as quoted in Lawrence Surtees, "Northern Telecom: The Morning After," *Toronto Globe and Mail*, July 5, 1993, B1, 4.

Thomas J. Usher, as quoted in Jonathan P. Hicks, "Usher's Style at U.S. Steel Brings 'Breath of Fresh Air'," *Toronto Globe and Mail*, April 6, 1992, B4.

Rita Gunther McGrath and Ian C. MacMillan, "Discovery-Driven Planning," *Harvard Business Review* (July–August 1995), 44–46, 49–54.

Tom Peters, "Taking Stock for 2001," *Acumen* (January/February 1995), 15–19.

Henry David Thoreau, *Nature/Walking: Selection of Works by Emerson and Thoreau* (Boston: Beacon Press, 1971), 71.

Rosabeth Moss Kanter, "Thriving Locally in the Global Economy," *Harvard Business Review*, September–October 1995, 151–160.

James C. Collins and Jerry I. Porras, *Built to Last: Successful Habits of Visionary Companies* (San Francisco: HarperBusiness, 1995).

Karen Boylston, as quoted in Nancy Gibbs, "The EQ Factor," *Time* (October 2, 1995). WWW site: http://www.pathfinder.com/@@@ 1CIdZEDJQAAQOc3/time/magazine/domestic/1995/951002/951002.cover.html.

Research from Michigan State University and the Department of Management and Organizations at the University of Iowa, in John E. Hunter, Frank L. Schmidt, and Michael K. Judiesch, "Individual Differences in Output Variability as a Function of Job Complexity," *Journal of Applied Psychology*, vol. 75, no. 1 (1990), 28–42.

William Elliott, "A Coversation with Dr. Elisabeth Kübler-Ross," *The*

Quest, vol. 7, no. 3 (August 1994), 18–25, 84–87; Ken Mark, "Managing the Aftermath of Downsizing," *Canadian HR Reporter* (March 12, 1993), 10–11.

For a discussion on our four Ps, see the PPFF model in Marion Woodman, "From Concrete to Consciousness: The Emergence of the Feminine," in *Betwixt & Between: Patterns of Masculine and Feminine Initiation,* ed. Louise Carus Mahdi, Steven Foster, and Meredith Little (La Salle, IL: Open Court, 1987), 201–222.

Ralph Waldo Emerson, as quoted in Ronald B. Adler and Neil Towne, *Looking Out/Looking In: Interpersonal Communication.* 7th Edition (Toronto: Harcourt Brace Jovanovich College Publishers, 1993), 205.

For Bernard Lonergan, see Donald Jones, "Philosopher/Priest Hailed for His Deep Insights," *Toronto Star Saturday Magazine,* July 14, 1990, M4.

Royal Bank of Canada, as quoted in "The Civilized Workplace," *Royal Bank Letter,* vol. 73, no. 2, March/April 1992, 1–4.

For Lewis Platt, see Rahul Jacob, "Corporate Reputations," *Fortune,* vol. 131, no. 4 (March 6, 1995), 64.

John Ginnetti, as quoted in Rahul Jacob, "Corporate Reputations," *Fortune,* vol. 131, no. 4 (March 6, 1995), 54.

Brent Schlender, "Why Andy Grove Can't Stop," *Fortune,* vol. 132, no. 1 (July 10, 1995), 88–92, 94, 98. See WWW site: http://www.pathfinder.com/@@v5XDYLDOVAMAQF0a/fortune/magazine/1995/950710/infotech/grove/grove.html.

Gospel of John, 3.

For Corporate Ten Commandments, see Marshall Loeb, "Ten Commandments for Managing Creative People," *Fortune,* vol. 131, no. 1 (January 16, 1995), 135–36.

Pillar II: Mapping

Peter Block, Stewardship: *Choosing Service Over Self-Interest* (San Francisco: Berrett-Koehler Publishers, 1993), 101.

For the Lotus Development Corporation and Novell Inc., see Geoffrey Rowan, "On a Different Plane," *Toronto Globe and Mail,* October 13, 1992, B1, 17.

"Lotus Chief Quits after IBM Marriage," *Toronto Star,* October 12, 1995, D7.

Sir Sunny Ramphal, former secretary-general of the Commonwealth, speaking at a presentation, Empire Club, Royal York Hotel, Toronto, Ontario. See also his book *One World to Share: Selected Speeches of the Commonwealth Secretary-General* (London: Hutchinson Benham, 1979).

David Robert, *Waging Business Warfare: Lessons from the Military Masters in Achieving Corporate Superiority* (New York: Scribner, 1987).

John Naisbitt, "Global Paradox," *Success* (March 1994), 1A–8A.

Gregory Clark, "The Essence of Japanese Culture," in *The Dawns of Tradition,* co-ed. Teiji Itoh (president of Kogakuin University) (Tokyo: Nissan Motor Company Ltd., 1983).

T. S. Eliot, "The Love Song of J. Alfred Prufrock," in T. S. Eliot, *The*

Complete Poems and Plays: 1909–1950 (New York: Harcourt, Brace & World, Inc., 1971).

Adam Smith, *An Inquiry into the Nature and Causes of the Wealth of Nations* (1776); David Crane, "They're Calling for a Kinder Capitalism," *Toronto Star,* May 28, 1995, D2. For an interesting discussion on "Father, Son, And Adam Smith," see Jeff Pooley, "God and Greed," WWW site: http://hcs.harvard.edu/~perspy/mar95/xcap.html.

For Jack Welch on trust and respect, see Alan M. Webber, "What's So New about the New Economy?" *Harvard Business Review* (January–February 1993), 41.

Eberhard E. H. Weber, "Forging a New Economy," WWW site: http://csf.colorado.edu/ecolecon/authors/Weber.Eberhard/forging.

For Taco Inc. and EQW, see Thomas A. Stewart, "How a Little Company Won Big by Betting on Brainpower," *Fortune,* vol. 132, no. 5 (September 4, 1995), 121–122.

Adrian J. Slywotzky, *Value Migration: Strategies to Preempt the Markets of Tomorrow* (Boston: Harvard Business School Press, 1996).

Paul Leinberger and Bruce Tucker, *The New Individualists: The Generation after the Organization Man* (New York: HarperCollins, 1991).

Charles Handy, "Trust and the Virtual Organization," *Harvard Business Review* (May–June 1995), 41.

Robert Frost, "Mending Wall," in *The Poetry of Robert Frost,* ed. Edward Connery Lathem (New York: Holt, Rinehart and Winston, 1969), 33–34.

Andrew Stark, "What's the Matter with Business Ethics?" *Harvard Business Review,* vol. 71, no. 3 (May–June 1993), 38–40, 43–44, 46, 48.

Andrew S. Grove, "A High-Tech CEO Updates His Views on Managing and Careers," *Fortune,* vol. 132, no. 6 (September 18, 1995), 229–230.

Ann Silver Allee, "Will There Be a Future With Meaning?: A Contribution from Jungian Psychology." Public lecture sponsored by McGill School of Social Work, February 1970.

Allan Bloom, *The Closing of the American Mind* (New York: Simon and Schuster, 1987), 227. Also C. G. Jung, *The Development of the Personality,* WWW site: http://miso.wwa.com/~nebcargo/Jung/jung45.html.

Robert Wright, "The Evolution of Despair," *Time,* vol. 146, no. 9, (August 28, 1995). WWW site: http://www.pathfinder.com/@@TZ8KeKBlQwIAQP4g/time/magazine/domestic/1995/950828/950828.cover.html.

For the internal game, see Eileen C. Shapiro, *Fad Surfing in the Boardroom* (Reading, Mass.: Addison-Wesley Publishers Ltd., 1995).

William J. Morin, *Silent Sabotage: Rescuing Our Careers, Our Companies, and Our Lives from the Creeping Paralysis of Anger and Bitterness* (New York: AMACOM Books, 1995).

Richard Leviton, "Designing Your Own Pilgrimage: What You Need to Bring," *The Quest,* vol. 7, no. 4 (Winter 1994), 24–29.

PILLAR III: JOURNEYING

For King Tamatoa, see James A. Michener, *Hawaii* (New York: Fawcett Crest, 1959), 89.

E. H. Schein, *Career Dynamics: Matching Individual and Organizational Needs* (Reading, Mass.: Addison-Wesley, 1978).

D. C. Feldman, "A Socialization Process That Helps New Recruits Succeed," *Personnel*, vol. 57 (1980), 11–23.

Michael Higgins, "Remembering Merton the Ideal Pilgrim," *Toronto Star Saturday Magazine*, December 24, 1995, M24.

Robert Frost, "The Road Not Taken," in *The Poetry of Robert Frost*, ed., Edward Connery Lathem (New York: Holt, Rinehart and Winston, 1969), 105.

J. E. Cirlo, *A Dictionary of Symbols*, 2d ed. (London: Routledge & Kegan Paul, 1978), 164, 165.

St. Augustine, *Confessions*, I, 1. See WWW site: file://iclnet93.iclnet.org/pub/resources/text/history/augustine/conbk01.txt.

David Rutherford, "Worshipping at the Altar of False Images," *Toronto Star*, May 13, 1992, A19. Also Michael Salter, "Shopper's Heaven," *Toronto Globe and Mail Report on Business* Magazine (June 1989), 62–69; Isabel Wilkerson, "Sky's the Limit for Shoppers," *Toronto Globe and Mail*, December 21, 1993, B1, 8.

Judy Steed, "The Radical Banker, Part 1," *Toronto Star*, November 19, 1995, D1, 5; "A Company of Earners, Part 2," *Toronto Star*, November 20, 1995, B1, 7.

For Wayne Calloway, see Stratford Sherman, "How Tomorrow's Leaders Are Learning Their Stuff," *Fortune*, vol. 132, no. 11 (November 27, 1995), 90–93, 95, 100, 102. WWW site: http://pathfinder.com/@@2evVIAHdtAMAQD1R/fortune/magazine/1995/951127/manag.leaders.html.

For Dan Branda, see Bill Gillies, "Looking for Leaders," WWW site: http://www.waysmag.com/CyberPlex/Ways/Ways5/features.leaders.html.

"Thought Summit," *Sloan Management Review*, vol. 36, no. 3, (Spring 1995). WWW site: gopher://gopher.enews.com:2100/00/magazines/alphabetic/su/smr/Current%20Issue/040195.1.

Michael Valpy, "When Crying Misery, Consider the Context," *Toronto Globe and Mail*, May 20, 1993, A2; John Geddes, "Canada is World's Best Place to Live," *Financial Post*, April 16, 1992, 7. See also John Meyer, "Growth Is Not Prosperity," *Toronto Globe and Mail*, December 12, 1995, B16.

For Henry Mintzberg, see Ann Gibbon, "Niches," *Toronto Globe and Mail*, June 27, 1995, B14.

James C. Collins and Jerry I. Porras, *Built to Last: Successful Habits of Visionary Companies* (San Francisco: HarperBusiness, 1995).

For Francis Fukuyama, see James Ogilvy, "The Economics of Trust," *Harvard Business Review* (November–December 1995) 46–47.

Al Gore, *Earth in the Balance: Ecology and the Human Spirit* (Boston: Houghton Mifflin, 1992), 171.

For Paul, Romans 5:1–11.

Thomas Merton, *No Man Is an Island* (New York: Image Books, 1967 [1955]), 194.

Ezekiel, 37.

Rosanne Bonanno, "FedEx's 'People-First' Philosophy Key to Innovative Leadership Program," *Canadian HR Reporter*, vol. 7, no. 4 (February 28, 1994), 7, 15.

Jennifer J. Laabs, "Hewlett-Packard's Core Values Drive HR Strategy," *Personnel Journal* (December 1993), 38–40, 42, 44, 46, 48.

Stratford Sherman, "Leaders Learn to Heed the Voice Within," *Fortune*, vol. 130, no. 4 (August 22, 1994), 92–94, 96, 98, 100.

For James Collins, see Statford Sherman, "How Tomorrow's Leaders Are Learning Their Stuff," *Fortune*, vol. 132, no. 11 (November 27, 1995), 90–93, 95, 100, 102. WWW site: http://pathfinder.com/@@2evVIAHdtAMAQD1R/fortune/magazine/1995/951127/manag.leaders.html.

Bernie Siegel, *Love, Medicine and Miracles* (New York: Harper & Row, 1986), 76–77.

The I Ching Book of Changes, 3d. ed., Richard Wilhelm translation rendered into English by Cary F. Baynes, foreword by C. G. Jung (Princeton, N. J.: Princeton University Press, 1967).

Gary Lamphier, "CEO of the Year," *Financial Times of Canada,* February 4, 1995, 8–9.

T. S. Eliot, "The Waste Land," in T. S. Eliot, *The Complete Poems and Plays: 1909–1950* (New York: Harcourt, Brace & World, Inc.), 1971.

T. S. Eliot, "The Hollow Men," in T. S. Eliot, ibid.

For Francis Fukuyama, see James Ogilvy, "The Economics of Trust," *Harvard Business Review* (November–December 1995), 46–47.

For Hewlett-Packard's stock value of 7,885 percent, and Aspen Institute, see Stratford Sherman, "How Tomorrow's Leaders Are Learning Their Stuff," *Fortune*, vol. 132, no. 11 (November 27, 1995), 90–93, 95, 100, 102. WWW site: http://pathfinder.com/@@2evVIAHdtAMAQD1R/fortune/magazine/1995/951127/manag.leaders.html.

Philip Dorrell, "Bankruptcy as a Metaphor for Depression," WWW site: http://www.xmission.com/~gastown/dorrell/consc.htm.

For realignment of corporate journey, see William F. Ryan, *Culture, Spirituality, and Economic Development* (Ottawa: IDRC, August 1995). Also, International Development Research Centre (IDRC). WWW site: http://www2.infoseek.com/NS/Titles?qt=International + Development + Research + Centre.

"The Duty of Civility," *Royal Bank Letter* (May–June 1995), 1–4.

Bill Bradley, "Civil Society and the Rebirth of Our National Community," *Responsive Community* (Spring 1995). WWW site: gopher://gopher.enews.com:2100/00/ren-room/religion/responsive_c/Current%20Issue/040195.2.

For David Mathews, see Nancy Kruh, "The We Decade: Rebirth of Community" series, *The Dallas Morning News,* March 5–12, 1995. WWW site: http://www.pic.net/tdmn/intro.html.

For communities and neighborhoods, see Susan Campbell, "A Sense of the Whole: The Essence of Community," WWW site: http://vision-nest.com/vn/cbw/Authors.html.

For Gary Hamel, see Merv Walker, "The Stretch to Create Tomorrow: A Conversation with Gary Hamel," *Ways Magazine,* vol. 7 (September 1995). See WWW site: http://www.waysmag.com/CyberPlex/Ways/Ways7/inthamel.htm.

Thomas Moore, *Care of the Soul: A Guide for Cultivating Depth and Sacredness in Everyday Life* (New York: HarperCollins, 1992), 187.

Bahá'í International Community's Office of Public Information, "The Prosperity of Humankind," WWW site: http://sunsite.unc.edu/Bahai/Texts/The-Prosperity-Of-Humankind.html.

For Milton Friedman, see Frank Rose, "A New Age for Business?," *Fortune,* vol. 122, no. 9 (October 8, 1990), 156–160, 162, 164; John Richfield, "Free-Market Ideas Will Triumph, Father of Monetarism Predicts," *Toronto Star,* August 3, 1992, C5. Harvard economist John Kenneth Galbraith once said, during President Reagan's tenure, that Reaganomics is the theory that "if you feed the horse enough oats, something will pass through for the sparrows." In Marcus Gee, "Voltaire on Stilts Strolls through History," *Toronto Globe and Mail,* September 10, 1994, C26. Also Douglas Goold, "Capitalism's Conscience in the '90s," *Toronto Globe and Mail,* June 21, 1993, B4.

Peter F. Drucker, *Post-Capitalist Society* (New York: HarperBusiness, 1993), 101–110.

PILLAR IV: LEARNING

Susan George and Fabrizio Sabelli, Faith *And Credit: The World Bank's Secular Empire* (London: Penguin, 1994), 73ff.

For Cliff Hakim, see: Tom Brown, "Life without Job Security," *Industry Week,* vol. 243, no. 15, (August 15, 1994), 24–26, 30–32. Also, Luis S. Richman, "Getting Past Economic Insecurity," *Fortune,* vol. 131, Number 7 (April 17, 1995), 162; *Training & Development,* vol. 49, no. 3 (March 1995), 81.

Peter F. Drucker, *Post-Capitalist Society* (New York: HarperBusiness, 1993), 13.

Adam Smith (pseudonym for G. J. W. Goodman), "Japan Inc. Is Still in Business," *New York Times Book Review,* March 19, 1995, 6. Book review of Eamonn Fingleton, *Why Japan Is Still on Track to Overtake the U.S. by the Year 2000* (Boston: Houghton Mifflin, 1995). Also, Eamonn Fingleton, "Jobs for Life: Why Japan Won't Give Them Up," *Fortune,* vol. 131, no. 5 (March 20, 1995), 119–120, 122–123, 125, and Eamonn Fingleton, "Fine, Thank You," The Atlantic, vol. 271, no. 5 (May 1993), 24, 35–39.

Tony Buzan with Barry Buzan, *The Mind Map Book: Radiant Thinking: The Major Evolution in Human Thought* (London: BBC Books, 1993).

Bill Marvel, "We Decade: The Roots of Renewal," in "The We Decade: Rebirth of Community" series, *The Dallas Morning News,* March 5–12, 1995, WWW site: http://www.pic.net/tdmn/roots.html.

On best practices, see "Financial Results Are Linked to Job Practices, Study Finds," *Toronto Star,* June 6, 1995, D4.

Thomas A. Stewart, and Research Associate David C. Kaufman, "Getting Real About Brainpower," *Fortune,* vol. 132, no. 11 (November 27, 1995), 201–203. WWW site: http://pathfinder.com/@@tdwaHwHdtAMAQEJR/fortune/magazine/1995/951127/leadedge.brain.html.

Carol A. Twigg, "Toward a National Learning Infrastructure, Part 3: Navigating the Transition," Educom Review (November–December 1995), WWW site: http://sunsite.unc.edu/horizon/gems/gemtwig3.html.

For David Noer, see Lee Smith, "Burned-Out Bosses," *Fortune,* vol. 130, no. 2 (July 25, 1994), 44.

"Layoffs Creating New Work Rules," *Toronto Star,* December 26, 1992, D2.

Michael Porter, *The Competitive Advantage of Nations* (New York: The Free Press, 1990).

Charles Hampton-Turner and Alfons Trompenaars, *The Seven Cultures of Capitalism: Value Systems for Creating Wealth in the United States, Japan, Germany, France, Britain, Sweden, and the Netherlands* (London: Piatkus, 1995).

Edward T. Hal, *Beyond Culture* (New York: Anchor, 1981), 1.

Chris Lee, "The Vision Thing," *Training,* vol. 30, no. 2 (February 1993), 27.

Kenneth Labich, "The New Crisis in Business Ethics," in *Business Ethics 95/96,* ed. John E. Richardson (Sluice Dock, Guilford, Connecticut: Dushkin Publishing Group, 1995), 130–132. Originally published in *Fortune* (April 20, 1992), 167–168, 172, 176.

G. Pascal Zachary, "Exporting Rights: Levi Tries to Make Sure Contract Plants in Asia Treat Workers Well," ibid., 171–173.

"Managing by Values," ibid., 196–200. Originally published in *Business Week* (August 1, 1994), 46–52.

Claudine Kapel, "The Colour of Motivation," *Human Resources Professional,* vol. 11, no. 9 (November 1994), 13–16. Also, Tricia McCallum, "Competency Gathers Momentum," *Human Resources Professional,* vol. 10, no. 10 (November 1993), 17–19; Heather D. Whyte, "Tailoring Salary to Performance," *Financial Post,* April 10, 1993, 10.

For idea of thoughts and movie film, see Corinne McLaughlin and Gordon Davidson. *Spiritual Politics, Changing the World From the Inside Out* (New York: Ballantine Books, 1994), 143.

Proverbs 23:7.

For Joanna Macy, see Alan Atkinson, "Guardians of the Future: An Interview with Joanna Macy," *In Context,* Spring 1991; quoted in Corinne McLaughlin and Gordon Davidson, op. cit., 179, 434.

Robert F. Allen and Charlotte Kraft, *The Organizational Unconscious: How to Create the Corporate Culture You Want and Need* (Englewood Cliffs, N.J.: Prentice-Hall, 1982).

For Hermes Trismegistus and Socrates, see Corinne McLaughlin and Gordon Davidson, op. cit., 24, 25.

Edith Hamilton, *The Greek Way* (New York: W.W. Norton & Company, 1930), 16ff.

Edith Hamilton, *The Echo of Greece* (New York: W.W. Hamilton & Company, 1957), 20b–21ff.

Alfred Whitehead, "On Mathematical Method," in *Gateway to the Great Books* vol. 9 (Toronto: Encyclopaedia Britannica, 1963), 66–67.

Robert Frost, quoted in Michael Kesterton, "Social Studies," *Toronto Globe and Mail,* July 7, 1992, A15.

Martin R. Weisbord, *Productive Workplaces* (San Francisco: Jossey-Bass Publishers, 1988).

For *lebh shomea,* see 1 Kings 3:9.

Proverbs, 3:1 (4:23); 27:19.

Carl Jung, *Man and His Symbols* (New York: Doubleday, 1964), 85.

The I Ching or Book of Changes. The Richard Wilhelm Translation rendered into English by Cary F. Baynes, foreword by C. G. Jung. 3d ed. (Princeton, New Jersey: Princeton University Press, 1967).

William Raspberry, "The Desire for a Life That Makes Sense," *Washington Post,* December 10, 1993.

Socrates, quoted in Corinne McLaughlin and Gordon Davidson, op. cit., 129.

Sir Charles Sherrington, quoted in Buzan, op. cit., 26–27.

PILLAR V: MENTORING

For Richard Barrett, see Michael McAteer, "Banking on Spirituality," *Toronto Star,* April 15, 1995, J14.

For Benjamin Franklin, see "Growing People," Office of the Assistant Secretary of the Army (Financial Management and Comptroller), Comptroller Proponency Office, Attn: SAFM-PO, Room 3D622, 109 Army Pentagon, Washington, D.C. 20310-0109. WWW site: http://134.11.192.15/profdev/mentor/mentor.htm.

For Hubert Saint-Onge, see Thomas A. Stewart, "Intellectual Capital," *Fortune,* vol. 130, no. 7 (October 3, 1994), 68–71, 74.

For Stan Jacobson, see Janet McFarland, "How Domtar Workers Added $20 Million to Profit," *Toronto Globe and Mail,* (October 20, 1995), B9.

Intuit Inc., see WWW site: http://www.careermosaic.com/cm/intuit/intuit3.html.

Konosuke Matsushita, *Not for Bread: A Philosophy of Financial Success and Personal Achievement* (New York: Berkley Books, 1984), back cover.

For Tom Peters, see Brian Stanfield, "Learning a Living," *Edges,* vol. 6, no. 1 (Winter 1994), 3–4.

Joe Frazier, as quoted in Ronald B. Marks, William V. Clymer. *Personal Selling: An Interactive Approach* (Englewood Cliffs, N.J.: Prentice Hall, 1992), 200.

For presenteeism, see Chris Knight, "How Do You Measure an Absence?" *Canadian HR Reporter,* vol. 8, no. 8 (April 24, 1995), 1, 2; W.A. Kahn, "To Be Fully There: Psychological Presence at Work," *Human Relations,* vol. 45, no. 4, (1992); "Looking Present When You're Absent," *Data-*

mation, vol. 41, no. 3 (February 15, 1995), 84; Jeremy Rifkin, "After Work," *UTNE Reader* (May–June 1995), 66–67.

For Socrates and Protagoras, see Edith Hamilton, *The Greek Way* (New York: W.W. Norton & Company, 1930), 45ff.

For Thucydides, see Edith Hamilton, *The Echo of Greece* (New York: W.W. Hamilton & Company, 1957), 30–31.

For Athens' defeat by Sparta, see Edith Hamilton, ibid., 29–33.

For the Athenian oath, see Edith Hamilton, ibid., 52, 53.

For Celtic people, see Sarah Ann Osmen, *Sacred Places* (New York: St. Martin's Press, 1990), 88–89.

Thomas Moore, op. cit., 10.

For Confucius, see Robert Williamson, "Kwok's Connections Open Doors to Asia," *Toronto Globe and Mail,* April 6, 1992, B4.

Marion Woodman, "From Concrete to Consciousness: The Emergence of the Feminine," *Betwixt & Between: Patterns of Masculine and Feminine Initiation,* ed. Louise Carus Mahdi, Steven Foster and Meredith Little. La Salle, Illinois: Open Court, 1987), 203.

For Marcel Proust, see Peter C. Newman, "New Age Dreams in Hard Times," *Maclean's* (October 10, 1994), 38.

For W. Edwards Deming, see "Niches," *Toronto Globe and Mail,* February 1, 1994, B24.

For John Ginnetti, see Rahul Jacob, "Corporate Reputations," *Fortune,* vol. 131, no. 4 (March 6, 1995), 54–57, 60, 64.

For the Business Roundtable and the Ethics Resources Center in Washington, D.C., see David Pyette, "Worth Repeating," *Toronto Globe and Mail,* November 23, 1991, B2.

For Dayton-Hudson Corporation, see James O'Toole, *Vanguard Management* (New York: Berkley Books, 1985), 176.

For Merck Frosst, see "Cultivating Quality: Corporate Cultures That Drive Business Excellence—Five Case Studies," WWW site: http://www.waysmag.com/CyberPlex/Ways/Ways6/feature.quality.html.

"Carpe diem!"—Horace (Quinton Horatius Flaccus, 65–8 BC); Carpe diem (kar′ pa di′ em) (Lat.). Seize the present day. Enjoy yourself while you have the chance. *"Dum vivimus, vivamus."*—Carpe diem, quam minimum credula postero.—Horace. *Odes* I, xi, 8. Seize the present, trust tomorrow e'en as little as you may. Ivor H. Evans, *Brewer's Dictionary of Phrase and Fable.* centenary ed., rev. (New York: Harper & Row, Publishers, 1981), 200.

For Thomas Watson, Jr., founder of IBM, see Thomas J. Peters and Robert H. Waterman, Jr., *In Search of Excellence* (New York: Warner Books, 1982), 280.

Assistant Secretary of the Army (Financial Management & Comptroller), "Growing People," Washington, D.C.: Comptroller Proponency Office, WWW site: http://134.11.192.15/profdev/mentor/mentor.htm.

PILLAR VI: LEADING

For J. P. Bryan, of Torch Energy Advisors Inc., Houston, Texas, see Scott Feschuk, "Gulf Canada Does a John Travolta," *Toronto Globe and Mail,* December 1, 1995, B8.

Warren Bennis, On Becoming a Leader (Reading, MA: Addison-Wesley, 1989), 44.

For P.K. Sung, recently retired CEO of Samsung General Chemical, Seoul, Korea, see "Former Samsung CEO Injects New Science Learnings Into Modern Management Technique," WWW site: http://www.newleadersnet.org/nln/news/profilef.html.

Peter Block, *Stewardship: Choosing Service Over Self-Interest* (San Francisco: Berrett-Koehler Publishers, 1993), 66.

Hesiod (father of Greek didactic poetry), *Works and Days, in The Great Thoughts,* compiled George Seldes (New York: Ballantine Books, 1985), 183.

Ronald Fellows, Discussion Group, AppleWood Center for Spiritual Studies "By the Fire" *Listserver,* 13:22:39 (November 27, 1995). Quoted with permission.

For Jack Welch, see Ronald Henkoff and Reporter Associates Cindy Kano and Rajiv M. Rao, "New Management Secrets From Japan—Really," *Fortune,* vol. 132, no. 11 (November 27, 1995), 135–136, 140, 144, 146. See WWW site: http://pathfinder.com/@@p6UAIwHdtAMAQERR / fortune / magazine / 1995 / 951127 /man.japan.html. Also, for Jim Channon, see Frank Rose, "A New Age for Business?" *Fortune,* vol. 122, no. 9 (October 8, 1990), 156–160, 162, 164.

William Shakespeare, *Julius Caesar,* IV, 3.

Paul of Tarsus, 2 Timothy 4:3.

Russell Ackoff, "The Second Industrial Revolution," April 20, 1972, Wharton School of Finance and Commerce, University of Pennsylvania, 11. For a discussion of Russell Ackoff's ideas, see Charlene Marmer Solomon, "HR Facilitates the Learning Organization Concept," *Personnel Journal,* WWW site: http://www.hrhq.com/archive/2670.html; also, "Problems Facing Humanity," WWW site: http://www.pacificrim.net/~wginwrep/WorldGame/doright.html.

GM's "The Quality Network," personal communication.

Konosuke Matsushita, *Not for Bread: A Philosophy of Financial Success and Personal Achievement* (New York: Berkeley Books, 1984), 36.

David Selbourne, *The Principle of Duty: An Essay on the Foundations of the Civic Order* (London, Toronto: Sinclair-Stevenson, 1994), 12.

Allan Bloom, *The Closing of the American Mind* (New York: Simon and Schuster, 1987), 204.

Warren Bennis, "Managing," in "Fifth Column," ed. John Raymond, *Toronto Globe and Mail,* December 11, 1991, B3.

Cover story, *Time,* November 1987. Thanks for reference to Bennis, op. cit., 170.

Richard Smoley, "The Religion of No-Religion," *Gnosis Magazine,* no. 35 (Spring 1995), 15.

For Alan M. Marcus (writer), see letter to editor, "The Dark Side of Prosperity," *Toronto Globe and Mail,* November 30, 1988, A7.

For David Thoreau, see Jan Cienski, "Consumerism: Beginning of the End?" *Toronto Globe and Mail,* February 18, 1992, A20.

For Alan Durning's report from the WorldWatch Institute in Washington, D.C., see Karen Hall, "Just How Much Is Enough?" *Toronto Star,* August 3, 1992, A13.

Jack Hawley, *Reawakening the Spirit in Work* (New York: Simon & Schuster [Fireside Books], 1993), 11.

Cynthia Davenport, "Technical Managers Find Leadership Not Built on Scientific Solutions," *Canadian HR Reporter,* vol. 7, no. 19 (November 7, 1994), 11–12.

For Kenneth Olsen and the spreadsheet, see The Entrepreneur's Page, "Against the Spread," *Toronto Globe and Mail,* January 17, 1994, B4.

Marshall Loeb, "Jack Welch Lets Fly on Budgets, Bonuses, and Buddy Boards," *Fortune,* vol. 131, no. 10 (May 29, 1995), 145–147.

For Ernest McClain, see "Music's Discipline of the Means: An Interview With Ernest McClain," *Parabola,* vol. XVI, no. 4 (November 1991), 85–91.

For Rotational Exchange Program, see "The Intelligence Community Agency Reinvention Activities," WWW site: http://www.loyola.edu/politics/hula/npr93act.html.

Sir Thomas Browne (1605–1682), English physician, writer, in *The Great Thoughts,* compiled George Seldes (New York: Ballantine Books, 1985), 52.

Minh Huynh, Laird Popkin, and Matthew Stecker, "Constructing a Corporate Memory Infrastructure from Internet Discovery Technologies," Marble Associates, Inc., WWW site: http://www.ncsa.uiuc.edu/SDG/IT94/Proceedings/CorInfSys/huynh/cmi.html.

Naim Kattan, *Language & Society,* Fall 1987, in *The Dictionary of Canadian Quotations,* ed. John Robert Columbo (Toronto: Stoddart, 1991), 330. Thanks for reference to Neil Bissoondath, *Selling Illusions: Canada and the Cult of Multiculturalism* (Toronto: Penguin Books, 1994), 28.

"Northrop Frye Talks about the Role of the Humanities," *University of Toronto* (Fall 1985), 6–7.

Allan Bloom, *The Closing of the American Mind* (New York: Simon and Schuster, 1987), 382.

For John Steinbeck (1902–1968), a political correspondent conversing with Steinbeck, *Travels with Charley: In Search of America,* quoted in *The Columbia Dictionary of Quotations* (New York: Columbia University Press, 1993). Listed under "People" in Microsoft Bookshelf CD-ROM.

Ricardo Semler, "Managing without Managers," *Harvard Business Review* (September–October 1989), 76–84.

For Georges Bernanos (1888–1948), French novelist and political writer, *The Diary of a Country Priest,* in *The Columbia Dictionary of Quotations* (New York: Columbia University Press, 1993). Listed under "People" in Microsoft Bookshelf CD-ROM.

Matthew Fox, *Original Blessing: A Primer in Creation Spirituality Presented in*

Four Paths, Twenty-Six Themes, and Two Questions (Santa Fe, N. M.: Bear & Company, 1983), 14.

Rainer Maria Rilke, *Letters to a Young Poet*, letter #3.

William Butler Yeats, "The Second Coming," 1922. WWW site: http://www.en.utexas.edu/~benjamin/316kfall/316kunit4/studentprojects/kiplingyeats/yeats.html.

William Thorsell, "If the Centre Cannot Hold, Will We Invent a New Centre?" *Toronto Globe and Mail,* February 11, 1995, D1, 5.

"The Purposes of the United Nations," WWW site: http://www.un.org/Overview/Charter/chapter1.html.

Pierre Teilhard de Chardin, *The Divine Milieu: An Essay on the Interior Life* (New York: Harper Torchbooks [Cathedral Library], Harper & Row, 1957), 76–77.

PILLAR VII: VALUING

Thomas Bausch, "The Servant–Leader: Guarding the Dignity of Work," *Catholic World,* vol. 237, no. 420 (July–August 1994), 170–175.

Robert K. Greenleaf, "The Servant as Leader," *Servant Leadership* (New York/Mahwah: Paulist Press, 1977). "In the 1970s, a Quaker businessman named Robert Greenleaf began espousing 'a new ethic' when he wrote an essay called *The Servant as Leader.* It was based on an idea he borrowed from Mr. Hesse's *Journey to the East,* the notion that those who serve are best equipped to lead," in "We Decade: Seeking the Soul of Business," in "The We Decade: Rebirth of Community" series, *The Dallas Morning News,* March 5–12, 1995. WWW site: http://www.pic.net/tdmn/spirit.html.

Eduard C. Lindeman *The Meaning of Adult Education* (Montreal: Harvest House, 1961 [1926]), 121–123.

For Robert Bly, see Ronald Fellows, Discussion Group, AppleWood Center for Spiritual Studies "By the Fire," Listserver, 19:43:59 (October 30, 1995). Quoted with permission.

Harold Bloom, *The Western Canon: The Books and School of the Ages* (New York: Harcourt Brace & Company, 1994), 35.

Francis Bacon (1561–1626), English essayist and philosopher, in *The Great Thoughts,* compiled by George Seldes (New York: Ballantine Books, 1985), 27.

For Publius Syrus, see *The Best of Success: A Treasury of Success Ideas,* compiled Wynn Davis (Lombard, Ill.: Great Quotations Publishing Company, 1980), 257.

For Moses' response, see Book of Exodus, 3:14.

The Hitopadesa, a collection of Hindu writings around A.D. 500, in *The Great Thoughts,* op. cit., 187.

For Thomas A. Edison, see *The Great Thoughts,* ibid., 105.

For Marshall Field & Company, see *The Great Thoughts,* ibid., 103.

Dalai Lama, *A Policy of Kindness* (Ithica, N. Y.: Snow Lion Publications, 1990 [1993]), 50.

James Allen, *As a Man Thinketh,* WWW site: http://wiretap.spies.com/ftp.items/Library/Classic/thinketh.txt.

INDEX

absenteeism, 112
abundance, 1, 3, 6, 9
abyss, 152
acceptance, 14
accidents, 59
accounting, 126; double-entry, 118
acquisitiveness, 45, 139
Acropolis, 95
action, xix
addiction, 140
adult education, 156
adversity, 19, 106
agents of change, 170
aggressiveness, 128
Allen, James, 169
alliances, 27
alternatives, 1
amen, 18
American Crisis, The, 51, 51
American business culture, 70, 134, 137
American Management Association, xv
ancestors, tribal, 13
ancient wisdom, xiv, 136
ancient echoes, 47
anger, 14
annihilation, 22
Applewood Centre, 131
apprenticeship concept, 103ff.
archetypal exercises, 111; learning, 74ff.; images, 133
archetype, 75ff.
Archimedes, 98
architecture, 39, 72, 73, 168
Argonauts, 44
Aristotle, 66, 97, 128, 140, 142
arrogance, xii, 65
As a Man Thinketh, 169
Aspen Institute, 66
aspiration, 23, 44; dominant, 169
assets, employees as, 82
assumptions, 90, 132
Athenian democracy, 115; ideal, 97
Athens, 115
attentiveness, 94, 96
attitude, xiii, 3, 108
attitudinal readjustment, 16

Augustine, 45
authenticity, 16
automatons, 117
awareness, xvii, 36

Bacon, Francis, 163
Bahá'í International Community's Office of Public Information, 71
balance, 97; balance sheet, 142
bankruptcy, spiritual, 46; and depression, 66ff.
bargaining, 14
Barrett, Matthew, 45
baselines, economic efficiency, xv
Battle of Grünwald, 26
Bausch, Thomas, 153
beachcombers, mental, 5
being and *having*, 166
belief, 2, 15, 62
belonging, xiv
Bennis, Warren, 126, 135–36, 138
Berlin Wall, 34, 53
Bernanos, George, 147
best practices, 81
binary-mind, 2
blindness, xviii, 3, 104, 132, 152
Block, Peter, 23, 127
Bloom, Allan, 36, 138, 140, 146
Bloom, Harold, 163
blunders, 18
Bly, Robert, 159
book of changes, xviii
bordered thinking, 6, 26
borderless economy, 143; world, 23
borders, xi, 19, 23; open, xviii, 3; mental, xvii
both-and thinking, 1
bottom line, xvi, 2, 34, 61; bottom-line thinking, 6
boundaries, 134
box of contracts, 33
Boylston, Karen, 9
brain, 24, 101, 143
breath, 20, 154
bridge, pragmatic business, xvii
Bryan, J.P., 126, 127

INDEX

Buddha, 169
budget, 142
Burke, James, 86
business plans, intergenerational 19
business: metaphor for consciousness, 66, 132
Business Process Reengineering (BPR), xv
Business Roundtable and the Ethics Resources Center, 121
Buzan, Tony, 80
Byrne, John A., xvi

California gold rush, 44
capabilities, human, 1
capital, intellectual, 6, 17, 32
capital, human, xii capitalism, 46, 71
Care of the Soul, 70
career development, 144
"Carpe diem," 123
catalyst, 32
Caxton, William, 104
cells, 103
Celts, 116
center, 58, 165; eternal quest for, 42; spiritual, 8
Center for Creative Leadership, xii, 10
Center for Applied Ethics, 154
certainty, 28, 29, 113
challenges, 42
change, 1; barrier to, 24; storms of, 4
change agents, 74
changes, book of, xviii
Channon, Jim, 132
chaos, 147
character, 132
charter of values, 130–131
Charybdis, 35, 37
chemistry of our thinking, 95
childbearing and employee education, 136–37
chimneys, 23
Chinese proverbs, 15, 45, 124
choice, 36, 154
Church of the Shopper, 45
Churchill, Winston, 27, 111, 118, 123
circle of life, 7
Cirlot, J.E., 44
citizenship, democratic, 69; rights of, 108
civic responsibility, 134
civility, 31, 32, 69, 143
civilization, 31
clarion call, 49, 53
Clark, Gregory, 29
classical roots, 54, 137
coaching, 111
cocoon, 31

"coffee spoons" (T.S. Eliot), 30
Cogito ergo sum, 27, 131
cogs, xvi
Cold War, 144
Collins, James C., Porras Jerry I., 8, 51, 60, 86
Columbus, 169
command, 23, 27, 37
commitment, 11, 27, 38, 79, 145, 151, 158
common good, 137; purpose, 106; sense, 81, 140, 168, 170
commonweal, 115
Commonwealth of Nations, 27
communication, 108
communities, emerging galaxy of workplace, xvii; knowledge, 7; community of communities, xi; community, crucible of, 4; community worth, 3; community of learners, 143, 147
comparative advantage, 7, 32, 66
compass, xiv, xvii, 28, 101, 166; organizational, xvii
compassion, 94
competence, xvii, inner-core, 78ff.; leader, 135ff.
Competencies (makers), 7
Competing for the Future, 69
competitive edge, 57; model, 137
competitiveness, 32
complexity, low, medium, high, 10
compulsivity, 140
concepts (thinkers), 7
Confessions, 45
confidence, 31
conflict, 64, 113
Confucius, 118
congruence, 4
connected mind, 93; connectedness, 4, 7, 14, 110, 129
connections (traders), 7
connectivity, 144
consciousness, xvii, 36
consumerism, 138
continuous learning, 47, 104; improvement, 96
control, xiv, 16, 126
conversion, 55
cooperation, 64; age of, 107
Copernican revolution, inner, 86
Copernicus, 104, 169
cornerstone, 158
corporate anorexia, 142; culture, 50; governance, 120; killing fields, 28; memory, 20; Reputations Survey, 18; SOS, 125; story, 145; Ten

Commandments, 21; window dressing, 62
counterintuitive, 48, 63
courage, xvii, xix, 42, 92, 139
covenant, old, 8
craftmanship, 120
creative tension, 69, 104
creative tension, 69
creativity, 7, 69, 73; serious, 34
credibility, 56, 115
criticism, 104; and crisis, 138
crossroads, mental, 6
crossroads, xi, 13, 14, 17, 27, 44, 57, 61, 62, 84, 166
Crusades, 118
culture, American business, 70
curriculum, new, 72
cynicism, 39, 115

da Vinci, Leonardo, 104
daily portion, 161
Dalai Lama, 168
Dayton Hudson Corporation, 122
de Chardin, Pierre Teilhard, 149
dead reckoning, xiii, 3, 5, 27, 151
decency, 143
decision making, 3 Declaration of Independence, 51
Declaration of Interdependence, 6, 7
dedication, 43
deeds, 8
defensiveness, 66
delayed gratification, 53
delight, 164
Deming, W. Edwards, 121
denial, 14
dependence, 64
depression, 14, 93; in workplace, 48; and bankruptcy, 66
Descartes, René, xv, 27, 36, 119, dream, 131
desert fathers, 43
desire, controlling, 169
destination, 160
destiny, 44, 52, 76, 125
dialogue, 33, 38
dignity, 65, 96, 153
dilemmas, 70
discovery, 160, 162; voyage of, xiv
diurnum, 161
DNA, organizational, 103
DNA value code, 93
doing "more with more," 6, 9, 97
Domtar Inc., 107
Dorrell, Philip, 66

double-entry accounting, 118
Dow Jones, 87, 123
downsizing, 2, 142
Draper, George, 122
drawbridges, mental, 27
dreams, 1, 137
dreamtime, corporate, 111
Drucker, Peter, 71, 78, 79, 123, 131
dry bones, 55, 62, 71
Durning, Alan, 139

eagerness, 113
ears, 6
Easter Bunny, 139
Echo, 138
ecology of abundance, 159
economy, global, xi; knowledge, 19, 23, 32
educational institutions, 54ff.
efficiency, xiv-xv, 2, 31
effort, 11, 111
ego, 13, 154
Einstein, Albert, 6
either-or thinking, 2
Eliot, T.S., 30, 64
Emerson, Ralph Waldo, 15
emotional intelligence, xii, 53, 106
emotions, 117
empathy, xii, 151, 165; strategic, 9, 37, 39
empires of the mind, 27
endeavor, human, xx
endurance, 42, 43, 52, 53
enduring success, 136
energy, xiv, 7
enfant terrible, 25
engineering, 98
enterprise, spirit of, 4
enthusiasm, 34, 116, 103
epikeia, 141
epiphany, 8
EQ, xii, 105, 129
Erikson, Erik, 77
ethic, enlightened management, 120
ethical myopia, 137
ethics, 71, 154; codified set of, 121
ethos, 150–51
Etzioni, Amitai, 81
Eurydice, 43
evolution, tribal economic, 5
excellence, 109, 113, 117, 128
excitement, 117
exercises, archetypal, 111
exhaustion, xiv
expanding-pot approach, 3
expectations, 12, 19
experiential learning, 58

INDEX

facilitation, 103
failure, xii
fairness, 109
fairy tales, 45
faith, 33; leaps of, 4
faithfulness, 13, 18
fame, 16
family, corporate, xvi; system, xvi
fate, 35
Federal Express, 56–57
feedback, 360-degree, 68
feelings, 14
Fellows, Ron, 131
financials, 19
Fishery Products International Ltd., 63
Fitzgerald, F. Scott, 52
fixed-pie approach, 2
flowcharts, 151
focus, long-term, 2
Ford Foundation, 69
foresight, 72
forgiveness, 56
founder, 21
four Ps, 15, 89
Fox, Matthew, 148
Franklin, Benjamin, 102, 165
fraternity, 69
Frazier, Joe, 111
freedom, 64; and rights, 137
Friedman, Milton, 71
Frost, Robert, 34, 44, 91, 96
Frosty the Snowman, 139
Fry, Art, 21
Frye, Northrop, 145
Fukuyama, Francis, 52, 65
Fulbright, Senator J. William, 92
fulfillment, xvii
future, 4; reinvent, 1

game, internal, 38
garbage, inner, 90, 92
garden, 29
generational planning, 19
generations, 153
generativity, 77
generosity, 109
genesis, new xi
George, Susan, 76
GIGO, 90, 92
Ginnetti, John, 19
globalization, xviii, 5, 60
goals, short-term, xviii
Goethe, 92
gold, 111, 147
Golden Fleece, 44
Golden Rule, 118

Gore, Al, 52
governance, 146
grammatical universe, 131
gratitude, 109, 165
great expectations, 165
great leaders, 167
great books, 163
Great Mother, 119
greed, 115, 121, 142
Greek vs. Roman way, 97ff., esp. 98
Greek ideal, 93
Greeks, 15
Greenleaf, Robert K., 154
gross national cost (GNC), 140
gross national product (GNP), 140
Grove, Andy, 19
growth, 49
guides, inspirational, 74
guilds, medieval, 103

H-P Way, 18
Haas, Robert D., 87
Hakim, Cliff, 77
Hall, Edward, 85
hamartia, 68
Hamel, Gary, 69
Hamilton, Edith, 93
hands, 12
Handy, Charles, 33
Hannibal, 28
harambee, 30
hard stuff, 66
Hartford Life Insurance, 19
Havel, Václav, 143
Hawley, Jack, 141
head, 37, 58
head, 37; *head* sight, 17; head space, 62; *head*-start methods, 117
heart, 12, 13, 17, 34, 37, 58
hemispheres, 24, 29, 78, 79, 101
Hercules, 44
heroes, 8, 42
heroines, 42
Hesiod, 128
Hewlett-Packard, 18, 57, 66
hierarchy, xii, 3
Higgins, Michael, 43
high performers, 10
higher vision, 166
history, 5, 26
Hobbes, Thomas, 50, 165
Hoffer, Eric, 73
holism, 17
Holy Grail, xiv, 5, 45
"home page" (Internet), 28
home, 58; spiritual, 7

Homo spiritualis, 117
hope, xix, 53
Horace, 123
horizon, 62
hot buttons, 74
hubris, 13, 20, 68
human capital, xii; condition, 26; nature, 137
human side of enterprise, 49
humanities, 54
humility, xvii
hunches, 4
hurdles, 15

I Ching: The Book of Changes, 61, 100, 129
iceberg, organizational, 38, 85
identity, corporate, 18; crisis, 140
ideological dragon, 79
idol worship, 15, 139, 142, 154
idolatry, 65
illusions, 17
imagination, 1, 4, 73, 101; revolution of the, 1
impact, 16
Inc., 62
incorporation, 62, 105
Indentureship, 103
individualism, 20, 24, 30, 70, 106
individuation, 35
industrial mindset, declining, xi
industrial-era road map, 23
inflation, 142
infrastructure, xv, 7, 37, 116
inheritance, xviii
inner-core competencies, 78ff.
innovation, 4, 73, 78, 98, 122
inscape, 54
in sight, 17
inspiration, xix
institutes of leadership and imagination, 77
integrity, xii, xix, 96, 116, 145
Intel Corp., 19
intellectual capital, 6, 17, 32
intelligence, emotional, xii; organizing, 17
interdependence, 3
intergenerational management, 19
international marketplace, 24; markets, 26
Internet, xiv, 76, 81
interpersonal skills, xii
introversion, 54, 58
Intuit Inc., 109
IQ, xii, 105, 129
isolation, 4
issues, 23

Jacobson, Stan, 107
Jay, Antony, 146
Jericho, 34, 53
job descriptions, 130
Johnson & Johnson, 86–87
journey, corporate, xviii, xix; human, xvii; leadership, xvi, 1; night sea, xiv; wilderness, 23
Julius Caesar, 134
Jung, Carl, 35, 75, 89, 100, 140
Juvenal, 93

kairos, 123
Kanter, Rosabeth Moss, xi, 7
Kenya, 30
Kettering Foundation, 69
Khan, Genghis, 28
Kikuyu tribesmen, 30
Knights Templar, 118
knowledge, communities, 7; economy, 19, 23, 32; as power, 46; 106
Kübler-Ross, Elisabeth, 14

ladder, corporate, 8
lamp, 149
Lander, holy, 5
landmark, 30
Law of Correspondences, 92
Lawler, Edward E., xvi
layoffs, 48, 154
leaders, characteristics of visionary, 127–128; vs. managers, 126; teachable, 141
leadering, 125, 128, 141
leadership, arrogant, 2; edge, 13, 19; journey, xvi; value code, 10; valuing, xvi; visionary, xvi, xix
LEAP (Leadership Evaluation and Awareness Process), 57
learning, across the organization, xix; archetypal, xix; circle, 143ff.; competencies, 72; disability, 77; organization, 72; paradigm, 113, 155; symbiotic nodes of, 7
lebh shomea, 99
left-brain-itis, 148
legends, 8
Leinberger, Paul, 33
leverage, 7, 32
Levi Strauss & Co., 87
Leviton, Richard, 40
liberation, 49
life, connected circles of, 3; quality of, 2
Lincoln, Abraham, 167
Lindeman, Eduard C., 156
linear and rational, 29
listening, xii, 151; Chinese symbol, 20

listening heart, a, 99
listlessness, 59
living treasures, 110
logic, 34
logos, 150–51
loneliness, 44
Lonergan, Bernard, 17
long-term focus, 2
looping the loops, 146
loyalty, 18, 32, 103

Madison, James, 94
magnanimity, 65
management, on bended knee, 65; intergenerational, 19; North American, 105, 110; theory, xiii, xiv
managers vs. leaders, 126
manners, social, xii
map, changing global, 3, 25; mental, xviii, 8; mind, xvii; safe myopic, xvii
Marlbork, 25, 26
Maslow, Abraham, 98
master, 104; mastery, 29, 49
materialism, 110
Mathews, David, 69
Matsushita, Konosuke, 109, 120, 136
matters, relationship, 4
maturity, xvi, 53
Mayer, John, xii
MBWA, 111
meaning, xiv, 20, 53, 54, 58, 77, 96, 104, 141, 153; quest for, 4
measurement, 1; measuring stick, 162
mediocrity, 46
meditation, 60, 157
memory, 22; corporate, 8, 20, 122
"Mending Wall," 34
mental frontier, new, 24
mental toughness, 110, 112
mental beachcombers, 5
mental baggage, 54
Mentor, 114
mentoring, xix; teams, 105
Merck Frosst, 122, 145
mergers and acquisitions strategy, 25
meritocracy, 37
Merton, Thomas, 43, 54, 58
metanoia, xvii, 55, 56, 57, 57, 68, 79, 96
Michener, James, 42
military, Greek, 115; metaphor mindset, 27
millennium, 17, 150, 168
mind, globalized, xi
mind map, xvii
minds, 12

mindset, 25, 63, 152; military metaphor, 27; rationalism, 35
Mintzberg, Henry, 48
mirror, 57, 63, 68
mission statement, 152
moats, 27
model, xvi
monks, 152
Monroe, Marilyn, 15
Montaigne, 150
Moore, Thomas, 70, 117
moral coherence, 52; crisis, 49, 52, 115; decay, 110; vision, 77
Morin, William J., 39
Morita, Akio, 66
Mormon ethics, 25
mythology, 15, 116
myths, 8

Naisbitt, John, 29
Napoleon, 28
narcissism, 117; Narcissus, 117, 138
nation-state, 143
National Center on the Educational Quality of the Workforce (EQW), 31
nations, community of, 85
Nelson, Admiral, 132
Never-Ending Story (Part I), The, 117
new clear thinking, 23, 51
New Individualists: The Generation after the Organization Man, The, 32–33
New Communities Corporation, 69
Newton, Isaac, xv, 36, 119; Newtonian world, 7
Nicodemus, 20
night sea journey, xiv
nomos, 142
NorTel, 2; Northern Telecom, 2
Nothing, the Great, 117
noun or verb, 131
Novell Inc., 25
numbers, 142

objective, corporate, 12; shared, xviii
obligations, 108; relationship, 137
obsolescence, 46
Odysseus, 34, 35, 114
Ohmae, Kenichi, xv
Olsen, Kenneth, 141
openness, 57, 64, 109, 129, 168
opportunity, 57, 62, 77; window of, 26
oral tradition, 116, 145, 165
organism, archetype of living, 95
organization, great, 123; 117; as organism, 9
Orpheus, 43

Osmen, Sarah Ann, 116
Ouchi, William, xv
oxygen, 4, 9, 20, 17, 156

Pacioli, Luca, 118
Paine, Thomas, 51
Panasonic, 19
paradigm, xvi, 6, 9; management, xviii; mental, 23; paralysis, 46; rational, xv
paradox, 29
participatory management, 117
Pascal, Blaise, 17
passion, 26, 114
path, ancient valued, xix; instinctual business, 3; mental, 23
pathos, 150–51
Peloponnesian War, 114
people, pride, profit, 2, 4, 7, 109, 114
Pericles, 94, 114
perseverance, xvii, 43
perspective, 129; explanatory, 17
Peters, Tom, 4, 48, 107
Petro-Canada, xv
philosophia, 91, 97
philosophical value lance, 79
"pig to the slaughter," 92
Pilgrim Fathers, 33
pilgrimage, 56
Pitt, William, 23
planning, discovery, 3; generational, 19; strategic, 3
Plato, 66, 165
Platt, Lewis, 18
pleasure, 164
pneuma, 20
Poland, 25
policies, 100
politics of rights, 137
population, world's, 139
Porter, Michael, xv
poverty, 64ff.
power, xii
practicality, 98
practices, modern, xvii
predictability, 113
predispositions, xiii
preparation, 57
presenteeism, 112
prestige, xii
primitivism, tough-guy, 17
principle of duty, 70
priorities, 62, 65
prism, 88
Procter & Gamble, 19
production, axis of economic, xiv
Productive Workplaces, 96

productivity, xiv, 31
profit, xiv, 13, 37, 121; profitability, 13
Prometheus, xvii
promise, xix, 18
prophet, 15, 37
prosperity, 3, 124
Protagoras, 113
protectionism, xi
Protestant work ethic, 70
Proust, Marcel, 119
public affairs, 114
Publius Syrus, 165
purpose, 121, 145, 147; common, xix, 106

quantification, 34, 152; experts, xvi; veneration, 37

radius of trust, 65
Ramphal, Sir Shridath Surendranath, 27
rational, xviii, 6, 24, 29, 60, 136; rationalization, 5
"rats feet" (T.S. Eliot), 64
reactiveness, 57
readiness, 25
receptivity, 128, 129
recession, 142
recognition, 105
Red Sea, 34, 58; cinch point, 63
reflection, 59, 61, 157
Reich, Robert, 81–82
relationship, xvii, 24; adversarial, 2; matters, 4
remembering, 114
Renaissance, 102
repentance, xvii, 55
respect, 10
responsibility, 69, 107, 143; social, 31
responsiveness, 57
results, 11
reverence, 107
rightsizing, 8
rigidity, 142
Rilke, Rainer Maria, 148
risk, 35
rite of passage, 157
rituals, 108
rocks, 159
ROI, xiii, xvii, 49, 87, 113
ROI and GM's shift to ROIR, 135
ROIR, xiii, xviii, 8, 9, 49, 66, 107, 113, 144, 129; factors, 107; success of, 87
Roman vs. Greek way, 97ff., esp. 98
Round Table, 45
Rousseau, Jean-Jacques, 140
rowing, 134
Royal Bank of Canada, 17, 69

INDEX

ruach, 20, 156
rusting smokestacks, 23, 24

Sabelli, Fabrizio, 76
sabotage, silent, 39
Sacred Places, 116
sacrifices, 8
sages, 110
Saillant, Claude, 107
Salovey, Peter, xii
Samarkand, 45
Santa Claus, 139
saunterers, 5
scientific management, 79
Scylla, 34, 37
seamless solutions, 24
self-centredness, 86; self-development, 80; self-discipline, 110; self-government, 94; self-gratification, 52; self-image, 4; self-limits, 96; self-sufficiency, xi; self-worth, xiv, xvii, 19, 24, 71
Semco S/A, 147
Semler, Ricardo, 147
sensitivity, xii
sensus fidelium, 18
Sentiments, A Theory of, 30
separation, 4
servant leadership, 154
shadow, 90, 100; organizational, 103; projection, 151
Shakespeare, 134, 165
shaman, 133
shareholder, 19
shock, 14
short-term, 19; goals, xviii; profit mentality, 121; vision, 2
sickness, 59
Siegel, Bernie, 60
significance, 16
silent sabotage, 39
silos, functional, 23
simplicity, 29
sincerity, 143
skills, interpersonal, xii; relational, xii
slavery, 7, 64, 139
Slywotzky, Adrian J., 32
Smith, Adam, 30
smoke and mirrors, 17
smokestacks, rusting, 23, 24
social conscience, 71
social contract, 31
Socrates, 60, 98, 100, 114
Socrates, 60
soft stuff, 66
sojourner, 43, 44, 160
solidarity, 69

solutions, 38; seamless, 24
Soviet Union, 46
Sparta, 114
Spartacus, 143
spirit of enterprise, 4, 10, 21, 25, 48, 72, 73, 95, 105
spirit, pioneering, 24
spirit-oxygen context, 95
spiritual imprint, 163
spirituality, 56, 156
spreadsheet, 142
spunk, 4
stability, 14, 19, 31
stages, 62
standard of living, 7
Stanford, James M., xv
Star Wars, 37
Stark, Andrew, 35
steering, 125, 134
Steinbeck, John, 146
stewardship, 77
stockholder, 154
storymaking, 8; storyteller, 8
strategic empathy, 9, 37, 39
strategy, 28, 126; mergers and acquisitions, 25; survival, 37, 63
studenthood, 92
subtlety, 76
success, xii, 26, 27, 57
suffering, 54
survival-of-the-fittest, 3
sustainable future, 19
sympathy, 31
synchronicity, 85
synergy, 70
system, family, xvi

Taco Inc., 31
talents, 123
Tamatoa, King, 42, 43
Taylor, Frederick Winslow, 79
teachers, great, 114
teams, 4
techno-elites, xiv; techno-peasants, xiv
technology, xiv, 9
Telemachus, 114
temenos, 7, 144, 147
temple, 115
temptation, 64
tempus, 123
tensions, 64
terror, 44
test, 62, 105
Teutonic Knights, 25, 26, 28
TGIF, 30
thankfulness, inner, 162

theory, management, xiii, xiv, 37
theory, management, 8
thinking, bordered, 6, 26; *both-and*, 1; bottom-line; congruent, 5; *either-or*, 2; paradoxical, 29; top-line, 6; sequential vs. synchronous, 129
Thomas, Franklin, 69
Thoreau, Henry David, 5
Thought Summit, 47
Thucydides, 94, 114
time, 58
tolerance, 143
top line, 6, 9, 61, 136
Torch Energy Advisors, Inc., 126
Total Quality management (TQM), xv
tradition, oral, 8
Tradition, The Dawns of, 29
traditions, xix, 77
training and development, xiii, 107
transformation, xiii, 27, 32, 128, 170
transition, 42, 55, 156
tribal, ancestors, 13; cultures, 133; tensions, 64
Trismegistus, Hermes, 92
trust, xvii, 32, 33, 37, 38, 42, 52, 56, 65, 69, 105, 107; betrayal of, xii; radius of, 65
Tucker, Bruce, 33

uncertainty, 29, 47, 147, 158
unconscious, 6; organizational, 38, 90
underclass, 2
unfoldment, 170
United Nations Development Program (UNDP), 24, 47
universe, mental, 1
unselfishness, 94
USX Corporation, 3

vacuum, 31, 54
validity, 5, 32
value cables, organizational, 108
value compass, 160
value code, 69, 71, 150; huddle, 39; leadership, 10
Value Migration: Strategies to Preempt the Markets of Tomorrow, 32
values, xvi, xix, 1; ancient, xvii; founding, 4
veneration, xix
verbalism, 156
vessel, 147
vicissitudes, 43
Vikings, 152
vision, xix; short-term, 2; teams, 103, 105
vision-driven companies, 8, 21

visionaries, 137
visionary economists, 159
Vistula River, 25
visualization, 111
voice, 38; collective, 20, 88
volunteerism, 122
voyage of discovery, xiv

walkabouts, 112
walling in, walling out, 34
walls, ideological, 53
wanderings, 5
Washington, George, 51
Waste Land, The, 64
Watson, Thomas, 123
wave, xvii; tsunami, 5
we versus *them,* 3
Wealth of Nations, 30
weapons, inner, 151
Weber, Eberhard E. H., 31
Weisbord, Martin R., 96
Welch, Jack, 31, 132, 142
well-being, xiv, 4, 32, 49, 84, 103
western canon, 163
White, John Hazen, 31
Whitehead, Alfred, 98
Whiz Kids, xvi
whole-start methods, 117
wholeness, 95, 56, 95, 116, 142
wickedness, 56
wilderness, 33, 42, 44, 58, 110, 156; journey, 36
wind (*ruach*), 20
window of opportunity, 86
window, open, 1
wisdom, xi, xvi, 8, 13, 34, 144; ancient, xiv
wonder, 34
Woodman, Marion, 119
work, wealth, well-being, xviii, 3, 5, 31, 105
work ethic, 33
workaholism, 94
workplace, changed, xv; more civilized, 17
World Watch Institute, 139
World Bank, The, xii, 76
worldview, 4, 76
worry, 169 worth, community, 3
worth place, 14, 34, 116

Yali, 76
Yeats, William Butler, 148
Young, Victor, 63

zeitgeist, 87
Zen wisdom, 43

THE 7 PILLARS JOURNAL
PILLAR I ♣ VISIONING

Write your reflections here about the concepts discussed in Pillar I.

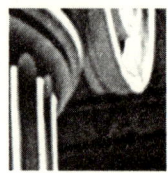

THE 7 PILLARS JOURNAL
PILLAR II ♣ MAPPING

Write your reflections here about the concepts discussed in Pillar II.

THE 7 PILLARS JOURNAL
PILLAR III ♣ JOURNEYING

Write your reflections here about the concepts discussed in Pillar III.

THE 7 PILLARS JOURNAL
PILLAR IV ♣ LEARNING

Write your reflections here about the concepts discussed in Pillar IV.

THE 7 PILLARS JOURNAL
PILLAR V ✤ MENTORING

Write your reflections here about the concepts discussed in Pillar V.

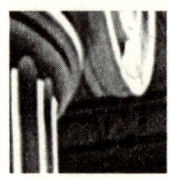

THE 7 PILLARS JOURNAL
PILLAR VI ✣ LEADING

Write your reflections here about the concepts discussed in Pillar VI.

THE 7 PILLARS JOURNAL
PILLAR VII ♣ VALUING

Write your reflections here about the concepts discussed in Pillar VII.

WHAT'S ON THE CD-ROM

The companion CD-ROM contains many of the learnware concepts discussed in the book, as well as proven personal, organizational, and community assessment, measurement, and development tools to evaluate your thinking and enhance your learning.

WINDOWS 3.1 INSTALLATION INSTRUCTIONS
1. Insert the CD-ROM into your CD-ROM drive.
2. From File Manager or Program Manager, choose Run from the File menu.
3. Type *<drive>* **SETUP** and Enter, where *<drive>* corresponds to the drive letter of your CD-ROM. For example, if your CD-ROM is drive D, type **D:SETUP** and press Enter.
4. Follow the on-screen instructions in the installation program. Unless you choose a different directory during installation, files will be installed to a directory named \LVP.

SETUP creates a Windows Program Manager group called LVP 7 Pillars. This group contains icons for exploring the CD-ROM. Once installed, click on the *7 Pillars* icon.

WINDOWS95 INSTALLATION INSTRUCTIONS
If Windows95 is installed on your computer, and you have the AutoPlay feature enabled, the *7 Pillars* CD-ROM program starts automatically when you insert the disc into your CD-ROM drive.

If you do not have the AutoPlay feature enabled, follow the installation instructions for Windows 3.1, but for Step 2, substitute the following: Click on **Start**, and choose **Run**.

HOW THE AUTHORS RECOMMEND USING THE 7 PILLARS OF VISIONARY LEADERSHIP AS AN INTERACTIVE PROGRAM

1. Read the book.
2. Read the book and make one page of point-form notes for each Pillar.
3. Read the book, take your point-form notes of each Pillar, and do the following:
   a. Devote a quiet time each day (for seven days) to journey through one Pillar of the visionary learning images on the CD-ROM. This will help you to develop the breakthrough thinking and mental structure required to sustain change.
   b. Complete your leadership value path assessment instruments (in the Appendix at the back of the book and also on the CD-ROM).
   c. Evaluate the learning required to connect and align your thinking from your personal, organizational, and global mindscape assessment results.